THE COMPLETE ROTTWEILER

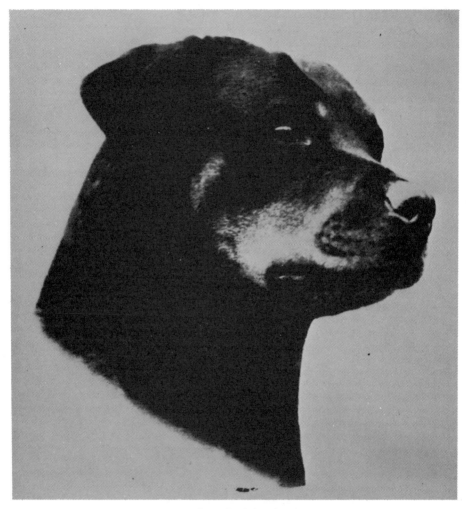

A classic bitch head.

The Complete
ROTTWEILER

by Muriel Freeman

FIRST EDITION

HOWELL
BOOK HOUSE
New York

Howell Book House
Macmillan Publishing Company
866 Third Avenue, New York, NY 10022
Collier Macmillan Canada, Inc.

Library of Congress Cataloging in Publication Data

Freeman, Muriel.
  The complete Rottweiler.

  Bibliography: p. 288
  1. Rottweiler dog.   I. Title.
SF429.R7F74   1984   636.7'3   83-22688
ISBN 0-87605-269-3

Macmillan books are available at special discounts for bulk purchases for sales promotions, premiums, fund-raising, or educational use. For details, contact:

Special Sales Director
Macmillan Publishing Company
866 Third Avenue
New York, NY 10022

20   19   18   17   16   15

Printed in the United States of America

To the memory of
BERNARD FREEMAN
upon whose insistence, despite all my
protestations, we purchased the first of these
"Ugly Dogs"—
and without whose love and guidance throughout
the vital part of my life, this writing could
not have been possible.

Trophy for Best Breed Group at Klubsieger Show, Germany—a perpetual trophy donated in honor of Bernard Freeman. Designed and executed by Martin Hillgemann.

PERSIAN PROVERB

He who knows not
> and knows not that he knows not,
>> is a fool . . . shun him.

He who knows not
> and knows that he knows not,
>> is ignorant . . . teach him.

He who knows
> and knows not that he knows,
>> is asleep . . . wake him.

He who knows
> and knows that he knows,
>> is a wise man . . . follow him.

Selected tomatoes—and selected puppies, too. Six weeks old from a von Gailingen litter, by Ch. Hintz v. Michelsberg ex Ch. Anka von Gailingen. Owner, C. M. Thompson.

Contents

Acknowledgments

IT IS well nigh impossible to put into words the appreciation I owe the many unnamed friends who have contributed to this effort with suggestions and moral support.

Those who wrote articles are properly identified at the beginning or end of their articles.

Credit is given for pictures which were so generously contributed.

Much of the material in Chapter 1 (In The Beginning) appeared in an article prepared by the author for insertion in the *The New Complete Dog Book* (16th Edition), the official publication of the American Kennel Club, and is included here with its permission, for which I express appreciation.

Much thanks is also due James Crowley and Hilde Weihermann at the AKC, for ferreting out old records. The research would have been an endless task without their able assistance.

I must also single out Ab Sidewater, the Editor. Although he held a gun to my head, instead of pulling the trigger he was ever ready to lend his expertise.

"Anyone for golf?"
— *Courtesy, Gun Sharp*

At leisure with a friend.
Muriel Freeman with Am. & Can. Ch. Groll vom Haus Schottroy, Am. & Can. CD.
— *Photo: Charles Goodman*

On A Great Friend and Teacher . . .

by Geoffrey J. Nightingale

I first met Muriel Freeman on the patio of her gracious home in Manhasset, Long Island, on a very warm afternoon in the summer of 1967. I was there with my wife and two small children to talk about Rottweilers and to determine whether or not that was to be the breed for us. What I did not realize, initially at least, was that Muriel saw that situation somewhat differently—as a formal interview which would decide my suitability to own and be owned by a Freeger Rottweiler. We passed inspection and fell in love with the breed at about the same time that a big, friendly Rottweiler bitch, a long-time resident of the Freeman household, decided the reason my infant son was fussing related more to the state of his diapers than his personality and proceeded to let my wife know about it in no uncertain terms. That infant is now a sophomore in high school, and we have had a Freeger Rottie in the house ever since.

Whenever I try to describe Muriel to someone, the one word which always comes to mind is, "dedicated." As a breeder she was the first to recognize and actively support the use of X-ray screening as a means for controlling that crippling disease, hip dysplasia, in Rottweilers. It was largely as a result of her efforts that the Orthopedic Foundation for Animals (O.F.A.) program was adopted as the official X-ray screening program—first by the Colonial Rottweiler Club and later by other Rottweiler organizations in this country—and that the first code of ethics forbidding the breeding of dysplastic animals was written and adopted by breed clubs. Her years of leadership as an officer and as president of the Colonial Rottweiler Club provided that organization and other regional

Geoffrey Nightingale has been a Director of the Colonial Rottweiler Club, and Editor of its *Newsletter*.

11

breed clubs in this country with a legacy of progress and growth that may never again be equalled.

Her personal support of educational programs for Rottweiler owners and breeders opened the door to many new ideas and concepts. She was instrumental in the formation of the American Rottweiler Club and its positioning as a parent breed club organization. It was largely because of her encouragement that the first Rottweiler registry was launched. Her direct involvement with foreign breed organizations—most notably the *Allgemeiner Deutscher Rottweiler Klub*—established the United States as a World Class participant in the breeding of Rottweilers. And in her "spare time" she established an enviable record as a breed judge of enormous stature. Most recently, her knowledge and contributions were further recognized by her appointment to serve as a Working Group judge, and her election in 1983 as president of her beloved O.F.A.

Yet, no matter how busy her schedule, Muriel always has had time to talk to owners, breeders, would-be owners and the just-plain-curious about her beloved Rottweilers. Members of royal families, construction workers, heads of major corporations, New York City cops—in fact, anyone sincerely interested in learning about Rottweilers has always been welcome in Muriel Freeman's home.

It is said you can't make an omelet without breaking some eggs. Because of her strong sense of ethics and love of the breed, Muriel has probably broken more eggs than most. Through the years, she encountered opposition—sometimes loud, sometimes tireless. But no matter how strong the criticism, Muriel never wavered from beliefs she held true. And—funny thing—while those critics are now mostly gone and forgotten, Muriel Freeman's prestige has continued to grow and today she is recognized as one of the world's most expert and influential Rottweiler specialists.

It is most fitting that this dedicated friend of the breed has been asked to write the definitive work on the Rottweiler. And, it is not surprising that despite a heavy personal schedule, she accepted the assignment and has carried it out with the same dedication, drive and attention to detail that have marked her many other accomplishments.

Benjamin Disraeli said: "*The secret of success is constancy to purpose.*" Through the years, as a breeder, a teacher and a judge, Muriel Freeman has chalked up one of the most dramatic records of success in the history of Rottweiler breeding in this country. That she has shown that all-important constancy of purpose in everything she has done goes without saying. That she has managed to do so as a warm, loving, caring human being is what sets her apart, in my mind, from other successful people I have known. But, then, isn't that what always sets the truly "great" apart from the "near great"?

Introduction

P LUTARCH, the ancient Greek historian and moralist, chronicling the life of Alcibiades (an Athenian general and politician of the 5th Century B.C.), relates the following anecdote: Alcibiades bought himself "a very handsome dog" for which he paid the "enormous price of 7,000 drachmas." Despite this outlay he decided to cut off the dog's tail. When questioned as to why he had mutilated this valuable dog, Alcibiades retorted, "that the Athenians may have this story to tell of me, and may concern themselves no further with me." A well-calculated diversionary tactic.

Man's mentality has changed little in 2,500 years. There are still those who will pay an enormous price for a dog and then, either deliberately through guile or accidentally through ignorance, proceed to pervert the nature of the animal it took so very many generations to develop and for which they paid so high a price.

This book is intended to impart, to all who read it, an appreciation of the Rottweiler's great heritage, a desire to preserve that heritage, and the knowledge necessary to be able to pass it on to future generations intact.

— Muriel Freeman

Rottweil, Germany.

1

In The Beginning

T HE ORIGIN of the Rottweiler is not a documented record. Once this is recognized, actual history, tempered by reasonable supposition, indicates the likelihood that the Rottweiler is descended from one of the drover dogs indigenous to ancient Rome. This drover dog has been described by various accredited sources to have been of the Mastiff type, with great intelligence, rugged, dependable, willing to work and with a strong guarding instinct.

The transition from Roman herding dog to the dog we know today as the Rottweiler can be attributed to the ambitions of the Roman Emperors to conquer Europe. Very large armies were required for these expeditions and the logistics of feeding that number of men became a major consideration. No means of refrigeration existed, which meant that meat for the soldiers accompanied the troops "on the hoof." Understandably, the services of a dog capable of keeping the herd intact during the long marches were needed. The above-described "Mastiff type" was admirably suited to this task, and to shoulder the additional responsibility of guarding the supply dumps at night.

Campaigns of the Roman Army varied in scope but the one concerning us took place approximately 74 A.D. Its route was across the Alps, terminating in what is now southern Germany. There is much evidence pointing to the vital role of the fearless Roman drover dog on that trek from Rome to the banks of the Neckar River.

Arae Flaviae, as the new territory was called, had natural advantages of climate, soil and central location. As a consequence, it was designated an Imperial Roman City, acquiring the attendant grandeur of all such Roman cities.

We have no reason to doubt that descendants of the original Roman drover dogs continued to guard the herds throughout the next two centuries. Circa 260 A.D., the Swabians ousted the Romans from Arae

An 1890 Rottweiler photo.

Flaviae, taking over the city. Agriculture and the trading of cattle remained their prime occupations, insuring the further need for the dog.

About 700 A.D. the local duke ordered a Christian church built on the site of the former Roman Baths. Excavations unearthed the red tiles of Roman villas. To distinguish the town from others, it was then named *das Rote Wil* (the red tile) which, of course, is recognizable as the derivation of the present name, Rottweil.

Rottweil's dominance as a cultural and trade center increased unabated, and by the mid-12th Century further fame and fortune came to it. An all new town, with elaborate fortifications, was built on the heights above the river. The security thus provided attracted yet-increased commerce in cattle. Butchers concentrated in the area and, inevitably, more dogs were needed to drive the cattle to and from the markets.

The descendants of the Roman drover dog plied their trade without interruption until the middle of the 19th Century, at which time the driving of cattle was outlawed and, in addition, the donkey and the railroad replaced the dog cart.

The Rottweiler *Metzgerhund* (butcher dog), as he came to be called, then fell on hard times. His function had been severely curtailed, and in those days dogs earned their keep or there was no reason for their existence. The number of Rottweilers declined so radically that in 1882 the dog show in Heilbronn, Germany, reported one poor example of the breed present.

The annals of cynology make no further mention of the breed until 1901, when a combined Rottweiler and Leonberger Club was formed. This club was short-lived, but is notable because the first Rottweiler standard appeared under its auspices. It is of value for us to know that the general type advocated has not changed substantially, and the character called for not at all.

In those years, 1901-1907, the Rottweiler again found favor as a police dog. Several clubs were organized: the *Deutscher Rottweiler Klub* (DRK)—January 13, 1907, and the *Internationaler Rottweiler Klub* (IRK)—April 26, 1907. Dissension was common until the clubs were united August 14, 1921 in Wurzburg and it was decided to form the *Allgemeiner Deutscher Rottweiler Klub* (ADRK). By that time 3,400 Rottweilers had been registered.

Duplications and confusion ended when the ADRK published its first stud book in 1924.

Since its inception, despite the difficulties encountered during and in the aftermath of World War II, the ADRK remained intact and through its leadership, enlightened, purposeful breeding programs have been promoted both in Germany and abroad.

Perhaps the Rottweiler has departed physically from his Roman ancestor, but assuredly the characteristics for which he was so admired in Roman times have been preserved and are the very attributes for which the Rottweiler is held in such high esteem today.

Ch. Dasso von Echterdingen, W-189828, 1-9-48—8th AKC champion.

Ch. Alma of Palos Park and Arno of Palos Park.

A nice male. (Unidentified photo, circa 1952.)

Ami of Crestwood.

Four photos (circa 1952) of Rottweilers owned by Mr. and Mrs. Eugene Schoelkopf of Palos Park, Ill. — *Photos courtesy of Dr. Beverlee Smith.*

2

The Rottweiler in America

$\mathbf{I}$N THE *Deutsche Kynologie Zeitung* of 1928, it is mentioned that three Germans migrated to the United States with Rottweilers. In 1929, the same periodical identifies them as Otto Denny, of Forest Hills, New York; Fred Kolb, of Scarsdale, New York; and August Knecht, of Lindenhurst, Long Island, New York.

Otto Denny, whose kennel name was *v.d. Landeck,* apparently was an established German breeder. He bred his first litter in 1918 and had bred eleven subsequent litters before his arrival on these shores. It was quite fitting that the first litter of which we have any record as being whelped in the United States was his "N" litter, whelped September 5, 1930. Not only is that vital information for us, but what makes it far more interesting is that this litter, conceived and born in the U.S.A. prior to AKC recognition of the Rottweiler, is nowhere recorded in our annals but does appear in the German Stud Book.

The first Rottweiler was admitted to the AKC Stud Book in 1931. She was **Stina vom Felsenmeer,** AKC number 805867, ADRK number 15965, owned by August Knecht and bred by Adolf Wagner.

On the 26th of January, 1931, Stina whelped a litter which was to become the first AKC registered Rottweiler litter, even though, as afore-mentioned, it was actually the second litter whelped in this country.

The sire of Denny's litter, as reported in the German *Stud Book,* was **Arras von der Gerbermuhle,** 13349. Arras was also the sire of Mr. Knecht's "A" Wellwood litter with the AKC number 812849. The next four numbers, 812850-812853, were assigned to **Alma, Ada, Alda** and **Asta of Wellwood.** Mr. Knecht had assumed the kennel name of Wellwood. Since

19

Mr. Denny never listed any of his other dogs with the AKC, it can safely be assumed Arras was registered at Mr. Knecht's request.

Mr. Knecht certainly was no gambler, hedging his bet as far as the AKC was concerned. He also registered the litter in the German *Stud Book,* and it's interesting to note a discrepancy. The Germans show an additional two males, Arno and Alpha. Perhaps they were repatriated at an early age and were, therefore, never AKC registered.

It is also interesting to note that, at that time, dogs of a breed were acceptable for AKC registration before the breed standard had been approved.

Mr. Knecht's "B" litter produced one dog and one bitch. The German registration shows he kept the bitch and sold the dog to a Mr. Sinclair, of Park Avenue, New York City. We can just bet that **Baron of Wellwood** created quite a sensation walking up Park Avenue in the early '30s.

The *Deutsche Kynologie Zeitung* column was reported by Fr. Bazille, the most respected early chronicler of our breed. His last coverage of the Rottweiler in America appeared in 1929, when he states that efforts are being made in North America to form a club and draft a standard.

Two aspects concerning this data are amazing. The first was that although they had migrated to the United States, these Rottweiler breeders did not divorce themselves from the German Club, but registered their litters as though they were still in Germany. The second, equally surprising, is that the authorities accepted registration despite the impossibility of being able to check on the litters. One can only hazard a guess that Otto Denny, with his experience of many years and twelve litters, may have been an early breed warden. In that event, his evaluation of the puppies and the fact that he presented them for registration would not have been contested.

It would be difficult to find a better illustration of the quality of leadership and the scope of influence of the ADRK, and the respect it engendered. Were it not for the accuracy and permanency of its records, the inception of the breed in America could never have been authenticated.

THE FORMATIVE YEARS

From these beginnings it took until August of 1939 for the first Rottweiler to be published as having earned a Companion Dog (C.D.) degree in Obedience. He was **Gero v. Rabenhorst,** A268387 (*henceforward, all numbers, unless otherwise identified, are AKC*), ADRK 22 851, bred by Alfred Nitzsche and owned and trained by Arthur Alfred Eichler. Gero was sired by **Carlo von der Leinburg,** ADRK 18 952, out of **Bärbel vom Römmerberg,** Sch H1, A268980, ADRK 19 071. Carlo was linebred on **Alfons** *(Brendle),* ADRK 12 646 PH, an outstanding progenitor of the breed. Gero achieved the first Companion Dog Excellent (C.D.X.) title in 1940, and his Utility Dog (U.D.) was also a first, in 1941. Amazingly, no Rottweiler managed the distinction of earning a U.D. for another 27 years, when **Ch. Don Juan,** WA201076, a Swedish import owned, trained and handled by Margareta McIntyre, became the second AKC U.D. Rottweiler and the first Champion U.D. Rottweiler. Shortly thereafter, **Ch. Axel v.d. Taverne** became the first U.D.T. (Utility Dog Tracking) Rottweiler, owned, trained and handled by Jim and Erna Woodard.

Gero von Rabenhorst had a distinguished career as an Obedience dog. He, and his dam, Bärbel, were equally important as breeding stock. Of interest is that Mr. Eichler imported both the dam, Bärbel, and her only surviving puppy of that breeding in Germany—Gero. It is also interesting to know that Bärbel was sired by **Bruno vom Pfalzgau,** ADRK 16 958, out of **Siegerin Elli von der Hauptwache,** SchH 3, ADRK 14 350. It is likely that Bärbel was a bit of a handful for our Obedience rings and, therefore, never achieved her C.D. Nevertheless, it will be seen that her unquestionable background of correct phenotype and correct character provided the sound breeding basis for so many of our early dogs.

On August 5, 1940, a litter was whelped by **Freid of Wellwood,** 913339. It was sired by **Prinz v. Hoheneck,** A380290, and the breeder was William Huppert, of New York City. We, of course, recognize the Wellwood kennel name of Mr. Knecht, one of the three original Germans to migrate to the U.S.A. with Rottweilers and the owner of the first AKC registered Rottweiler, Stina. Freid was descended from Stina and **Jon v.d. Steinlach,** 805868, back to Alma v. Kork and **Sieger Arco Torfwerk,** ADRK 955, also early pillars of the breed in Germany.

Six of the Prinz-Freid litter were registered, of which the most significant from a historical point of view was **Erwin,** A436652, sold to Noel P. Jones. Remember these names.

The next names with which we must deal are Martin E. and Henrietta Herrmann. They imported **Arras vom Birkenwäldchen,** A268109, ADRK 21 208, a grandson of the outstanding progenitor **Sieger Hackel vom Köhlerwald,** SchH II, ADRK 15 691, whose sire was Alfons (Brendle). Arras sired a litter out of Eichler's Bärbel, two of which made history—**Herlind v.d. Schwarzen Eiche,** CD, A325402, and **Hada v.d. Schwarzen Eiche,** C.D.X., A325403. Herlind remained with the Eichlers, but Hada went to the Herrmanns. Herlind became the first bitch to attain an AKC Obedience title. Hada became the first bitch to acquire a C.D.X.

Your attention was drawn to the name of Noel P. Jones and his dog, Erwin, inasmuch as Erwin was to be the choice of the Eichlers to sire Herlind's litter. From this mating resulted **Delga,** W7480, wh. 12/13/44. Delga went to Noel Jones. We will leave her there for the moment to grow up.

In the same era, Hada, owned by the Herrmanns, was bred to Gero v. Rabenhorst (a half-sister to half-brother breeding), producing the "A" litter of Crestwood, the kennel name the Herrmanns adopted. With this litter, the plot begins to thicken. **Asta of Crestwood,** A614754, remained with the Herrmanns, but **Alva,** A854833, went to Helen Louise Langan in co-ownership with Perrin G. Rademacher, and subsequently bred to **August Der Grosse,** W12410, produced **Alaric,** W100143, and **Astrid, W100144, of Rodsden,** wh. 3/31/47. The registered owner of Astrid was Joan G. Rademacher. This is Rottweiler history in the making; Joan became Joan R. Klem and in partnership with her brother and sister-in-law, Pat and Marthajo Rademacher, established Rodsdens' Kennels, which has consistently produced top breeding stock. More of this later.

Asta of Crestwood was also bred to Erwin, resulting in **Ami of Crestwood,** A854829, and **Bonnie of Crestwood,** A854832, both significant producers. Bonnie went to Mr. and Mrs. Herman Heid, whose Ohio kennel was most successful up until the late 1970's when, unfortunately, Mr. Heid passed away. Through the years the Heids imported some of the finest German dogs to replenish their stock. They owned, among others, **World Sieger 1956 Hektor von Burgtobel, SchH 1,** WA59399, ADRK 32 969, a model for the breed in Germany. They also imported a daughter of Hektor, namely **Diana vom Remstal, SchH 1,** ADRK 35 516. Unfortunately, she died a tragic death at an early age. She was perhaps one of the two best bitch phenotypes ever to come to this country.

Ami, the sister, went to the Midwest and became the foundation bitch of Mr. and Mrs. Eugene Schoelkopf's von Palos Park Kennels.

While we tarried in the Midwest, Delga was bred to **Kris,** W20574 (Franz v. Burgermeister, A969042 ex Beatrice, A752846), also owned by Noel P. Jones. Margaret A. Dalson was his breeder. They produced (on March 19, 1947) a litter of which two became the first AKC Rottweiler champions. **Ch. Zero,** W34126, bred, owned and handled by Jones, was listed first 1/49, and **Ch. Zola,** W34130, also listed 1/49, was second. Zola was also handled by Jones, but owned by Helen H. Pritchard. Interesting to note, this was at least the second breeding for Delga, yet she was just a little over two years old. Kris, at the time he was first bred, was under nine months of age. What is more, they were rebred at Delga's next heat and from that union the third AKC champion, Kurt, evolved.

I see no record of outstanding progeny for Zero. However, Zola produced, bred to **Domossi v. Hohenreissach,** W64326 (Tropf von Hohenreissach, ADRK 22 529 ex Bonnie of Crestwood) the fourteenth champion who was **Ch. Benedict,** W187568, owned by John T. and Erna L. Pinkerton.

A litter sister to Zola and Zero, **Zada,** W34133, owned by Mr. and Mrs. Andrew J. Cooper, was bred to Arritz v.d. Schwarzen Eiche and produced a litter of nine, wh. 7/21/48. **Ch. Zada's Zenda,** W103249, was at 2½ years old the sixth champion and the first Obedience titled AKC champion. Her litter sister, **Zada's Zeitgeist,** W103247, finished three years later. Zada was also bred to Domossi vom Hohenreissach and on 7/19/49 whelped **Heide,** W176863, and **Eric,** W181780, who were to become the tenth and eleventh AKC champions, respectively.

At this point the following names should be duly impressed upon your mind:

Mr. and Mrs. Arthur Alfred Eichler deserve much credit for their enormous contribution, through Gero v. Rabenhorst and Gero's dam, Bärbel, to the working character as well as the proper phenotype of our dogs. When it is realized that the first six Obedience titles were conferred on dogs the Eichlers owned or bred, and the next three on their "grandchildren," we can begin to appreciate the magnitude of this endowment they handed down. It will be shown that their breeding of Herlind to Erwin resulting in Delga was a milestone in American Rottweiler annals.

Noel P. Jones must be remembered as having handled the first three Rottweilers to attain championship status, but for posterity his ownership of Erwin, the breeding of Herlind to Erwin resulting in Delga, the breeding of Asta of Crestwood to Erwin resulting in Ami of Crestwood and Bonnie of Crestwood, the purchase of Kris and the subsequent repeated breedings of Kris to Delga, constitute the real contributions he made. There are those of us on both coasts and in the Midwest, who can readily trace back to these two combinations of breeding partners. Familiar kennel names owing foundation stock to this source include: von der Heid, Rodsden, von Palos Park, Giralda, T.O. Wall, von Stahl, de la Motte, Panamint, Follow Me, Freeger, Srigo, von Schauer, von Gailingen, Merrymoore—and, undoubtedly, there are others.

Our next not-to-be-forgotten pioneers are Martin E. and Henrietta Herrmann of Crestwood. From their breeding of Gero v. Rabenhorst to Hada v.d. Schwarzen Eiche descended the great majority of AKC champions until the mid '60's.

In giving thanks, we must not forget Mr. Knecht, the stalwart German who set the wheels in motion when he registered the first Rottweiler with AKC and the first litter with AKC, and finally bred Freid of Wellwood, who produced Erwin.

So much for recapitulation. Now for a few critical comments, which are necessary because with the passage of time the truth will be masked and there will be no one about to ferret out the facts.

Unfortunately, a most regrettable policy was begun by several of the prominent and most prolific breeders, a policy which still persists—that of purchasing a German dog from a recognized German breeder with a protected or patented (as they call it) kennel name and then using that kennel name on American-bred dogs from that line. To my way of thinking, this is plagiarism, pirating, or whatever name you may wish to call it. It serves only to confuse the correct heritage for generations thereafter.

In this connection, von Hohenreissach, von Hohenzollern, von Robern, von Schildgen, vom Kursaal, Sofienbusch, Kurmark, Forstwald, Hungerbühl, Kastanienbaum are kennel names which must be carefully scrutinized to correctly assess the breeder of dogs bearing these suffixes. Future students of pedigrees are now alerted.

Giralda's Alex. Bred and owned by Mrs. M. Hartley Dodge.

Ch. Rex von Stahl, CD (at 3 years) and Ch. Pomona (2 years), in a 1957 photo. Owned by Mr. and Mrs. W. C. Stahl.

Going back in the history to the point where we left off in the late '40's, we must note the entry into this country of **Dasso von Echterdingen,** W189828, ADRK 27 944 and **Seffe vom Gaisburg,** W189287, ADRK 28 485. Both were imported by Eugene Schoelkopf, located in Illinois, the fortunate owner of Ami of Crestwood. Both Dasso and Seffe attained their championships but, although Seffe came from one of the most distinguished of German breeders, Jakob Kopf, she did not make the impact on the breed in this country one might have hoped for. Bred to Dasso, one of her daughters of this union, **Aida of Palos Park,** W231207, owned by Mrs. George J. Brown, produced one champion. **Walpo's Brutus, C.D.X.,** W929440, the second C.D.X. Rottweiler champion. It must, however, be noted she had been bred to Lucius, a Domossi ex Chrys son, which somewhat overshadowed her importance. On the other hand, the breeding of Dasso ex Ami had far-reaching implications. They produced **Ch. Asto of Palos Park,** W202406, and **Ch. Alma of Palos Park,** W202409, 4/23/50, and also **Asta of Palos Park,** W202408. Asta became the foundation bitch of Fred Schaefer, who adopted the kennel name of Roberts Park. Asta of Palos Park, bred to **Krieger v. Hohenreissach,** W165626, (Domossi ex Zada) owned by Geraldine Dodge, of Morris and Essex fame, produced **Ch. Asta of Roberts Park,** W363206. The latter bred to **Joseph v. Hohenzollern of Giralda** produced **Rex von Stahl, C.D.,** W547256, wh. 7/3/54. Rex was the nineteenth AKC Rottweiler champion and the first male champion to have an Obedience title,

Shortly after Ami whelped the "A" Palos Park litter, **Chrys, C.D.X.,** W68975, (Kris ex Delga), owned by T.O. and V.B. Wall, bred to Domossi von Hohenreissach produced **Ch. Valeria,** W255605, wh. 3/14/51. It will be remembered that Domossi was also the sire of Ch. Heide and Ch. Eric out of Zada. The grandparents in both cases on the maternal side were Kris and Delga. Furthermore, **Ch. Benedict,** W187568, was also sired by Domossi, and this time the dam was Ch. Zola, also a Kris ex Delga daughter. Ch. Valeria, bred to the German import **Asso von Wittelsbach,** W401365, ADRK 32 920, bred by Anton Holzner and owned by Liljeberg, produced **Ch. Pomona,** W657115, wh. 10/12/55. Pomona was to become the foundation bitch of Mr. and Mrs. William F. Stahl (more about the Stahls is included in the chapter on the Colonial Rottweiler Club). By Ch. Rex von Stahl, Pomona produced **Ch. Gerhardt von Stahl,** W799827, wh. 4/9/57, twentieth AKC champion and the first Rottweiler owned by the author, and so responsible for all the rest of the Freeger Rottweilers. Pomona bred to **Hedeboflids Pan,** W948301, a Danish import, produced **Ch. Barhon von Stahl,** W980394, and **Ch. Missy von Stahl,** W980397, wh. 3/12/59. Missy was the foundation bitch of Felice Luburich's Srigo Kennels of countless champions and Rottweilers with working degrees.

It can now be seen how important the Kris ex Delga breeding was to the East Coast as well as the Midwest Rottweilers. Before leaving the East Coast, we must recognize Geraldine Dodge of Giralda renown. This lady, if not the most influential dog person in her time, was certainly among the most prominent. Her grounds were the venue for the most elegant benched dog show this country will ever witness. Mrs. Dodge masterminded every detail of the operation, from inviting those judges she approved, to providing what she deemed to be adequate sanitary facilities for the public. Anyone who was anyone in the dog world attended in one capacity or another. To this day, "old timers" refer to Morris and Essex with deference—there will never be another show like it.

As an early admirer of the Rottweiler, Mrs. Dodge imported stock and, using a professional handler, attempted to launch the breed in the American show ring. Despite the aura surrounding her, and all the promotion in publications, not much interest in the dog was generated. This, coupled with a possibly misdirected breeding program, resulted in that lady's loss of interest in the Rottweiler.

We proceed back to the Midwest, where we find Mr. Heid has imported **Arko v. Robern,** W265477, ADRK 26327, wh. 9/1/46. The breeder was Albert Lehn. **Frederika v. Hohenzollern** (York v. Hohenzollern ex Bonnie of Crestwood) owned by Mr. and Mrs. Wilmer F. DeVore, was bred to Arko and the resulting litter were given "G" von Robern names. Gretchen went to Mrs. Dodge and one bitch, I believe, went to Cuba. One male, **"Gunga"**, W265479, finished his championship. But **Gretel,** W265484, probably made the biggest contribution; bred to **Alf von Schildgen,** W377099, ADRK 29437, she produced a litter that was given "C" von Schildgen names after their German sire. The Devore's litter included **Claus von Schildgen,** W390291, and litter sister, **Christine,** both of which figured in the breeding programs of the mid-50's to the early 60's.

Ch. Claus was owned by Barbara Roloff, and bred to **Kezia v. Heidenmauer,** he sired **Panamint Ragnarok,** W944854, wh. 11/3/58. Barbara Roloff is better known to later Rottweiler people as Barbara Hoard Dillon. Insofar as I am able to determine from the records, Ragnarok—who attained her championship in 1961—was the first significant producer to bear the Panamint prefix, although many have followed in her footsteps. At the age of 1-1/2 on 5/21/60, she produced a litter of which three became champions. The sire was a German import, **Ch. Emir von Kohlenof,** W560081, ADRK 33545, wh. 5/21/53, bred by Ludwig Heeb and owned by John F. Lind, Jr. Bred to **Ch. El Fago Baca,** WA 227491, a son of Emir ex Darla, Ragnarok produced a litter 8/5/62 of which two became champions and one acquired his C.D. Ragnarok, bred to **Ch. Bullino v.d. Neckarstroom,** WA375014, NHSB 307200 (B/S Ch. Harras von Sofienbusch, SchH 1, WA404675, ADRK 36474 ex Recora v.d. Brantsberg, NHSB 211193) on 4/20/64, produced one future champion, and on 1/24/66 whelped two more destined to become champions. Although Panamint Kennels was located in California, the original stock and stud dogs involved were imported, owned or bred by Midwesterners, with the exception of Bullino.

Other than those already mentioned, Ludwig Werner Gessner comes

Ch. Dieter vom Konigsberg, a later import (photo, 1972) of the Panamint Kennels, owned by Barbara Hoard Dillon. By Dolf v Weiherbrunnele, SchH3, FH ex Jutta v. Rodenstein. Dieter was bred by Georg Pollitt.

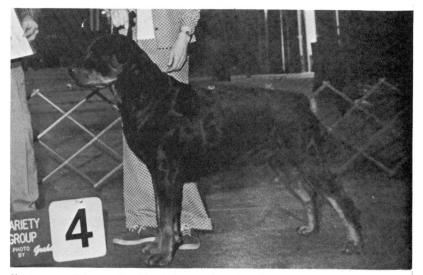

Ch. Igor von Schauer. Bred by Robert and Merle Schauer. Owned and handled by Katherine Hewitt.

Ch. Jaro vom Schleidenplatz, German import, Best of Breed at the 2nd and 3rd Colonial Rottweiler Club Specialties, 1960 and 1961. Jaro was first Rottweiler to win a Group in America. Bred by Kurt Jaekel. Owned by Charles J. McKelvey and handled by Jack Houser. — *Photo, courtesy Ed Beretta*

to mind as a moderately active Rottweiler breeder of the early 1950's. He brought back from Germany two very substantial dogs. I especially recall the male, **Alf v.d. Kugellagerstadt,** W983475, ADRK 36530. He had enormous bone and was actually quite long in body. Shown at Westminster, I cannot remember the result but I will never forget the sight of Mr. Gessner trying to get him to go up a flight of stairs. He had evidently never been exposed to stairs and Mr. Gessner was no match for Alf's complete revulsion to the whole idea. Alf completed his championship, as did Mr. Gessner's imported bitch, **Cora a.d. Lenbachstadt,** W902300, ADRK 36327, and one of their progeny, **Ch. Gessner's Burga, C.D.,** WA115360, went to Gerry Fitterer.

By the early '60's, Mrs. Fitterer had emerged as a leader in Midwest Rottweiler circles and when she transferred to the West Coast, became one of the moving forces in the early stages of the Golden State Rottweiler Club. Burga, bred to Margareta McIntyre's Ch. Don Juan, U.D. produced a litter of which four attained their championships, two a C.D. and one a C.D.X. Mrs. Fitterer is active today in Rottweilers and has the distinction of being an AKC Obedience Judge approved to judge Novice, Open and Utility since 1978.

In this time span there was an effort in northern California to establish a parent club, the Rottweiler Club of America. Due to internal friction it was not destined to succeed. However, the Colonial Rottweiler Club, in the process of formation on the East Coast at approximately the same time, did succeed and will be discussed in a future chapter.

In 1958, **Jaro von Schleidenplatz**, W877850, ADRK 35984, a German import, hit the East Coast show ring. Jaro was handled by the very competent Jack Houser to many significant wins. Jaro was the first Rottweiler to receive a Group I in America. He was the sire of **Ch. Ferdinand von Dachsweil**, WA350147, an outstandingly successful show dog in his day, who also appears in many pedigrees. Ferdinand's dam was **Follow Me's Michelle**, a daughter of **Ch. Arras v. Stadthaus**, W748536. Arras, owned by the DeVores, was certainly a dog that figured prominently in the best American pedigrees. To Betty Reinhardt must go the credit for breeding Ferdinand and to his owner, Ed Beretta, recognition for maintaining the dog in fine condition at all times. Ferdinand was an outstanding winner over a wide area. In 1968 he won the Colonial Rottweiler Specialty for the third successive year, retiring the permanent trophy donated by the Stahls, which had been in competition for ten years.

The logical progression from father to son (Jaro to Ferdinand) obviates prior mention of **Dervis von Weyershof**, WA96622, ADRK 37509, a German import owned by Swen R. Swenson and Gladys Swenson. Mr. and Mrs. Swenson and their son owned the Townview Kennels and were very active in both breeding and showing in the early '60's. The dog, Dervis, had breed type and was a worthy winner although one could have wished for a darker eye and better-knuckled front feet. He was used quite extensively and his progeny provided foundation stock for the v. Rau of

Ch. Ferdinand v. Dachsweil, son of Ch. Jaro vom Schleidenplatz, Best of Breed at Colonial Rottweiler Club Specialty Show in 1966, '67, and '68. Owner: Ed Beretta.

Wunderkinder Kennels and the Northwind Kennels of Patricia Lecuyer (Hickman), among others.

Another excellent dog, **Ch. Arno v. Kafluzu,** W745075, ADRK 35519, might never have attained his championship were it not for the discerning eye of Felice Luburich. She brought him "out of the woodwork" when he was six years old and successfully handled him through the classes to Best of Breed at the Colonial Rottweiler Club Specialty in 1962. Arno-Jaro progeny and Dervis were combined by the Raus, producing four champions in one litter. For Felice Luburich's Srigo Kennels, Arno sired the "D" litter of two champions and the outstanding "E" litter of three champions.

Ch. Follow Me's Jhan, W928583 (Arras v. Stadthaus ex Christine v. Schildgen), bred by the DeVores and **Ch. Emir v.d. Hutung,** WA251925, ADRK 37948, an import of excellent Kohlwald breeding, appear on many pedigrees and must be mentioned.

Early 1964 saw the importation by Rodsden's Rottweilers of **B/S '60, '61, '62, Int. Ch. Am. Ch. Harras vom Sofienbusch, SchH 1,** WA404675 ADRK 36474. Harras, despite his being 6-1/2 years old at the time, made his mark in this country as the top producer of his day. He himself should be remembered as one of the truly great Rottweiler phenotypes of all times. For those of us privileged to have seen him "in the flesh," it was an image of perfection we will carry with us always. Unfortunately, his exposure to the show-going public was limited. Due to mishandling in his early days, Harras was an extremely aggressive male—a characteristic deplored in this country but much admired in his day by the Germans.

Harras was used to many fine bitches, not least of which was **Ch. Quelle v.d. Solitude, C.D.,** WA16795, ADRK 38611, also owned by Rodsden's Rottweilers. She was a litter sister to **L/S'66 Quick v.d. Solitude, SchH 3 F.H.,** ADRK 38608, a dog appearing in many of our pedigrees and notable for his propensity to pass on good hips. Quelle produced good progeny out of numerous breedings and to her credit this lovely bitch retained her "girlish figure" all her days. Quelle's sire, **Droll v.d. Brotzingergasse, SchH 2,** ADRK 36212, was considered an outstanding progenitor of the breed.

Another Droll daughter having significant influence on the American Rottweiler breeding program through her progeny was **B/S '63, Schweizer Siegerin, '64 Assy vom Zipfelbach, SchH 2,** ADRK 37789. To my knowledge, the first Assy son to appear in the U.S.A. was **Ch. Yritter vom Kursaal,** WA274300, ADRK 39281. Yritter was brought to this country by Col. and Mrs. Mandel of Chicago as their housedog and was later used by the Starks of Starkrest Kennel in their breeding program. Assy, bred to **Wotan von Filstalstrand, SchH 1,** ADRK 37422, was also the dam of '66 **B/S and '66 Schweizer Siegerin, Int. Ch. Flora vom Kursaal, SchH 2,** ADRK 40526; **Ch. Falk vom Kursaal, SchH 1,** WA988601, ADRK 40523; and **Ch. Franzi vom Kursaal,** WA486076, ADRK 40527. Falk and Franzi were imported by Rodsden's Rottweilers. Interestingly, of all the Assy

German Bundessieger 1960, '61, '62—Int. & Am. Ch. Harras vom Sofienbusch, SchH1, Auf Lebenszeit Angekort—CACIB "V". Owned by Rodsden's Rottweilers, Reg. (P. G. Rademacher and R. F. Klem).

Ch. Pia vom Kursaal. Bred by Richard Schmidgall, owned by Rodsden's Rottweilers, Reg. (P. G. Rademacher and R. F. Klem.)

Bundessieger '65, World Sieger '65, Int. & Am. Ch. Erno von Wellesweiler, SchH1—RO5 (Excellent). (By Ch. Harras vom Sofienbusch, SchH1 ex Alke von Gomaringen, SchH2.) Bred by Karl Backes. Owned by Mrs. Bernard Freeman.

progeny in this country, although far from the best phenotype as will be demonstrated, the most distinguished turned out to be Franzi.

Assy's influence on the American scene was further exerted with the arrival on these shores of her two very lovely littermate daughters sired by '65 B/S, '65 W/S Int. Ch. Am. Ch. **Erno von Wellesweiler, SchH 1,** WB14926, ADRK 39499. **Am. and Can. Ch. Priska vom Kursaal,** WA669758, ADRK 41663 went to Freeger Kennels and **Ch. Pia,** WA675125, ADRK 41662, went to Rodsden's Rottweilers.

Two years later, they were followed by their eminent sire, imported by your author. Of Erno it can be said, while he was not quite the overall perfect phenotype of his sire, Harras von Sofienbusch, he was nevertheless a show stopper. His noble appearance, fine character, dignified demeanor and fantastic movement earned him a multitude of friends and admirers. Erno was the second sire considered by the Germans to be prepotent for good hips. In any case, he was brought to this country for my pleasure and fulfilled that purpose for the remainder of his eleven years.

Erno joined **Belinda of Canidom,** WA248988, **Ch. D'Artagnan of Canidom, C.D.,** WA630204 (Gerhardt ex Belinda) and Erno's daughter, Priska, to complete the Freeger complement of Rottweilers.

Through Priska RO-2 bred to D'Artagnan RO-1, my Freeger Kennels gained its reputation. They left a legacy of sound dogs of correct phenotype with outstanding character.

A few years later the importation, in co-ownership with Frances Rhodes, of **Deborah vom Kursaal** (B/S Blitz vom Schloss Westerwinkel, SchH 3, ADRK 37642, ex Flora vom Kursaal) WB109401, ADRK 43274, RO-29 and Deborah's breeding to D'Artagnan resulted in two champion OFA bitches. **Ch. Freeger's Jolly,** WB675985, RO-246, went to Mr. and Mrs. Leonard Freedman and achieved her U.D. **Ch. Freeger's Juno, C.D.,** WB675989, RO-279 made her mark in the whelping box when she produced the Freeger "N" litter of five champions. To the best of my knowledge, this set a record for a Rottweiler bitch.

The premise that holds five years to be the lifespan of most people's participation in the dog sport, certainly does not apply for Mrs. Carol Stafford. She acquired her bitch, **Ch. Una von Hohenreissach, C.D.,** WA298764, (Arras V. Stadthaus ex Numa von Hohenreissach, W897724) from Herman Heid in the early sixties. From that time forward, this friend of the Rottweiler has furthered the best interests of the breed. As a result, in a limited breeding program, multiple dogs with both championships and Obedience titles have been produced under her Rhinelander prefix.

With the importation of Harras, breeding at the Rodsden's Rottweilers kennels took on even greater momentum. He was used twice in 1964 to their Quelle. The first litter produced **Ch. Georg of Rodsden,** WA438561. The second litter resulted in two outstanding males: **Ch. Rodsden's Kurt v.d. Harque,** WA518261, OFA RO-4, owned by Mrs. Marilyn R. Putnam, and **Ch. Rodsden's Kluge v.d. Harque, C.D.,**

Am. & Can. Ch. Priska vom Kursaal, RO2. Bred by Richard Schmidgall, owned by Mrs. Bernard Freeman.

Angus of Maple Dell, wh. 1955, with owner Carola Mandel.

Ch. Yritter vom Kursaal, the first Assy vom Zipfelbach progeny in the United States (1963 photo). Bred by Richard Schmidgall, owned by Leon Mandel.

WA553102, OFA RO-50. Kurt was an outstanding show dog sweeping the West Coast competition for a considerable time. He was ably handled throughout his career by Frank Housky. Kluge, on the other hand, made his mark as a top producer.

Two other breedings to Harras bear mention. The one to **Ch. Afra von Hasenacker, CD,** WA40507, ADRK 38822, was noteworthy because Afra daughters were used extensively in Rodsden related breedings.

The breeding to Harras von Sofienbusch of Mrs. Gruenerwald's **Abington Aphrodite,** RO-36, (Ch. Arras von Stadthaus ex Ch. Dagmar von Schildgen) resulted in **Ch. Lorelei,** WA492026, from whom descended the many dogs of Mr. and Mrs. Gruenerwald's well known von Gruenerwald kennels. In three breedings of Lorelei to **Ch. Nick von Silahopp,** WA547457, ADRK 40855, RO-7, six champions resulted, of which three were OFA normal. Nick, a German import, was sired by **B/S Blitz v. Schloss-Westerwinkel, SchH 3,** ADRK 37642, out of Queen v.d. Solitude, ADRK 38610, who can be recognized as a litter sister of Quelle v.d. Solitude.

As previously stated, of all Assy's daughters in this country, Franzi was the most distinguished. Through her two breedings to Kluge resulted seven champions, three of which were OFA normal, one of which had a C.D. and another, **Ch. Rodsden's Kato v. Donnaj,** WB77486, earned his C.D.X., T.D. and OFA RO-37 certification. In addition, Kato was the first American all-breed Best in Show Rottweiler, achieving this distinction owner-handled by Jan Marshall at the Merrimack Valley Kennel Club show on May 29, 1971 under judge Raymond Beale.

The very next day his older brother, **Ch. Rodsden's Duke Du Trier,** WA873770, OFA RO-107 also went Best in Show in Peoria, Illinois under Robert Wills, a feat which Duke repeated on July 16, 1972 at Momence, Illinois and again on September 9, 1972 at Newton, Iowa. By going BIS on September 25, 1971 at Burlington, Ontario, Canada, Duke became the first all-breed Best in Show Rottweiler in Canada. He was owned by Dr. and Mrs. Nelse O. Olson of Bremerton, Washington and, to the best of my knowledge, was handled to all these wins by Richard Orseno.

Kato's litter sister, **Ch. Rodsden's Kirsten du Trier, C.D.,** WB93538, was sold to Forest M. and Dave Schneider. She had a fine show career; among other achievements was her BOB at the Golden State Rottweiler Club Specialty in 1971—a win no other bitch has thus far accomplished.

In this period Mrs. Dillon's Panamint Kennels saw the titling of Panamint dogs variously sired by Bullino and **Ch. Dingo von Kupferdach,** WA661449, ADRK 41559 (Erno von Wellesweiler ex Bonni v. Muhlberggrund, ADRK 39267).

The mid-sixties saw the advent of some new names in Rottweiler people on the West Coast, among them Mary G. Lucas. Under the von Lucas suffix, Mary bred her imported bitch, **Circe von Gertrudenhof, C.D.,** WA723452, ADRK 41201, RO-38 to Mrs. Putnam's Kurt v.d.

Ch. Rodsden's Kato v. Donnaj, CDX, TD, the first American all-breed Best in Show Rottweiler (1971), owner-handled by Jan Marshall.

Mrs. William Gruenerwald with one of her many champions.

Ch. Lyn-Mar Acres Arras v. Kinta, son of Ch. Ferdinand v. Dachsweil. Bred, owned and handled by Mrs. M. Lynwood Walton.

Harque which resulted in two champions, one with a C.D. The following year, repeating this breeding, four OFA normal champions, one attaining a C.D.X., were produced—a total of six champions in two litters.

Across the Canadian border, a significant breeding took place when Pat Lecuyer (Hickman) bred her bitch, **Can. Ch. Northwind's Tina,** Can. 612008 to Rodsden's Kluge, resulting in four champion progeny of which three were OFA normal and one achieved her C.D.

Another significant newcomer arrived on the Southeastern scene in the mid-sixties. Mrs. Shelley Moore, adopting the kennel name of Merrymoore, had her start with the Harras son, full brother from a previous breeding that later produced Kurt and Kluge. He was **Ch. Georg of Rodsden,** WA438561, and when bred to **Cora v.d. Grürmannsheide,** ADRK 42555, sired a litter of which three attained their championships; although none had working degrees, **Merrymoore's Chug-A-Lug,** WB51428, was RO-88 and **Merrymoore's Behexed,** WB51429, was RO-185.

With this start, Merrymoore Kennels has produced many champions and a great many OFA normal dogs in the ensuing years.

The emergence to prominence of the kennel names, von Schauer, Kuhlwald, von Molzberg and Lyn-Mar Acres shortly after the mid-sixties heralded the advent of some very active Rottweiler admirers. The Schauers have been successful in both conformation and Obedience and add another dimension with their daughter's competency in Junior Handling Competition.

The addition of **Ch. Cara v.d. Chaussee,** WB32901, ADRK 41460 (B/S Blitz v. Schloss-Westerwinkel, SchH 3, ADRK 37642, ex Quanda v. Hohenreissach, ADRK 38960) to the von Schauer kennel contributed significantly to the future quality of the Schauer dogs. Bred to Kluge, Cara was the dam of **Ch. Erika v. Schauer,** WB214139, RO-82. Erika was mated to Ferdinand v. Dachsweil. It will be remembered Ferdinand was a Jaro ex Follow Me's Michele, WA116576, son and was bred by Betty C. Reinhardt. This union produced **Ch. Igor v. Schauer,** WB678882, RO-235 and **Ch. Ingrid v. Schauer, C.D.,** WB678886. Igor, owned by Katherine Hewitt, had an outstandingly successful career as a stud dog in the East, producing many excellent phenotypes out of bitches of various lines—the acid test of a stud dog's quality.

In the late '60's the Lyn-Mar Acres' Kennels of Mrs. M. Lynwood Walton made its mark with a litter in which three males finished, two of which received OFA normals, **Arras v. Kinta,** WB70779, RO-121 and **Arbo v. Kinta,** WB70776, RO-125. The third was Lyn-Mar Acres' **Atlas v. Kinta,** WB70778. Two bitches also received OFA normal ratings. The sire of the litter was Ferdinand von Dachsweil and the dam was a Kluge daughter. The dog, Arras, figures prominently in the Eastern breeding stock and the dog, Atlas, was successfully used in the Midwest, siring two litters out of Hylamar's Heidi which resulted in five champions all of which had OFA numbers—quite a record. Concurrently Arras bred to Ron Gibson's Plaisance Irma in three litters produced eight champions, two of which acquired OFA numbers.

Arras bred to Srigo's Mädchen produced the Srigo "Z" litter of four champions. **Zarras,** WC820345, RO-791, **Zoom, C.D.,** WC820339, **Zinger, C.D.,** WC820340, RO-1083 and **Zeitgeist,** RO-1983.

Arras bred to a Harras v. Sofienbusch granddaughter, Shearwater Ginger Snap, produced a litter of three champions, all of which were OFA normal, and one of which, Indian Sunrise, became a foundation bitch for Lyndhausen. The male, **Cochise,** WC147402, went Best in Show at Brookhaven K.C., Middle Island, New York under judge Col. Wallace Pede in 1976, handled by Alan Levine.

This is an outstanding producing record for any dog.

The Kuhlwald Kennels of Mr. and Mrs. Paul Harris typify the previously referred to generality regarding the expected 5-year lifespan of people in dogs. The Harrises were enormously active for a short time importing at least eight Rottweilers of the finest German breeding stock. Among them, **Fetz vom Oelberg, SchH 2,** WA845097, ADRK 38416, RO-25, too sharp to be shown in this country, was one of the three German stud dogs of his day, considered to be prepotent for passing on good hips to his progeny. The Harrises also imported: **Bodo vom Stüffelkopf,** WA765753, ADRK 40499, RO-28; **Assi vom Dahl,** ADRK 41300, RO-12 (a German born daughter of Fetz); and later **Ch. Axel vom Schwanenschlag,** WB753207, ADRK 44778, RO-166 (Fürst v.d. Villa Daheim, ADRK 42204 ex Cora v. Grevingsberg, ADRK 42691).

A student of pedigrees must observe and absorb the significance of the foregoing data. Appreciating that Harras von Sofienbusch is the sire (in chronological order) of Erno, Bullino, Lorelei, Kluge and Kurt and is, therefore, either the sire or the grandsire of all these outstanding foundation Rottweilers, our dogs' heritage would have been considerably poorer without him!

In this era of the late 160's and early '70s, specific mention must be made of **Ch. Srigo's Mädchen v. Kurtz,** WB220789 (Erno von Wellesweiler ex Econnie v. Lorac). Mädchen, perfectly trained and always impeccably presented by her breeder, Felice Luburich, was an enormously successful show dog. Winner of BOB in 1973 at the Colonial Rottweiler Specialty, she was several times BOS at this function—the last time from the veteran class. Her BOB wins at lesser functions over top males were numerous. At the Maryland K.C. supported show, judged by the eminent German authority, Head Breed Warden—Friedrich Berger, Mädchen went BOB over all comers including her cousin, BIS dog Rodsden's Kato.

Your attention is again directed to the importation by Kuhlwald Kennels of Axel v. Schwanenschlag. That he sired litters with multiple dogs making their championships is what makes him important. Although he was owned by Mr. Harris, Axel spent time with Dorit Rogers of Bergluft Kennels, Reg., and it was Mrs. Rogers who showed him to his

Ch. Srigo's Madchen v. Kurtz, BOB at the 1973 Colonial Rottweiler Club Specialty. Bred by Felice Collesano Luburich and owned by Lucille and Donald Kurtz.

Ch. Merrymoore's Xorcist, by Ch. Dino von der Kurmark, CD ex Ch. Merrymoore's Behexed. Bred and owned by Mrs. Shelley Moore.

championship. She also whelped the Kuhlwald litter Axel had sired out of **Ch. Kuhlwald's Little Iodine, C.D.,** WB14432 (Bodo vom Stuffelkopf, ADRK 40499 ex Andra v.d. Vohsbeckshöhe, ADRK 407690). This was a litter of which four made their championships and three of the four passed the OFA. Perhaps the most important aspect of that breeding was the resulting **Ch. Kuhlwald's Tara of Ronlyn,** WC14432, RO-330. Tara was sold to Radio Ranch Kennels and became their foundation bitch. Their foundation sire, **Ch. Rodsden's Nomad v.d. Harque,** WB619089, RO-201 (Kluge ex Rodsden's Gypsy) was a Harras grandson on his father's side and a Harras great-grandson on his dam's side. Radio Ranch Kennels of Mr. Crump and Pamela Weller have since their inception been extremely active breeding quality Rottweilers in the Virginia area, showing them widely and successfully on the East Coast. Their **Ch. Radio Ranch's Axel v. Notara,** WC584381, RO-599 (Nomad ex Tara) is to date the most successful of their dogs.

Subsequently, Axel von Schwanenschlag sired a litter of four Bergluft champions out of Dorit Rogers **Ch. Drossel v. Molzberg,** WB113298, RO-132, and his third litter of four champions out of **Ch. Amsel von Andan, C.D.,** WB828781, RO-300, owned by Pauline Rakowski, bear the von Paulus suffix. This litter was by far his outstanding contribution with four OFA'd champions, two with working degrees and two of which, the dog **Ch. Donnaj Vt. Yankee of Paulus, CDX, TT,** WD139569, RO-964T and the bitch **Ch. Andan Indy Pendence of Paulus,** WD132678, RO-1002T, were excellent phenotypes. Yankee was a three-time winner of the Colonial Rottweiler Club Specialty Show—thus retiring the Freeger Trophy. He was the second of Jan Marshall's Rottweilers to gain an all-breed Best In Show (Ladies Dog Club, Wellesley, MA, June 2, 1979 under judge Mrs. W.P. Wear). Mrs. Tilghman's Indy was a consistent Best of Breed winner while she was being campaigned and, I might add, a very popular choice among the spectators.

In a sense, I have put the cart before the horse, as Amsel, the dam of Yankee and Indy, was bred by Mrs. Tilghman with the kennel name of Andan. Mrs. Tilghman's foundation bitch, **Ehrenwaches Andernach,** RO-111, was a Fetz v. Oelberg daughter. Amsel's sire was Rodsden's Kato and Amsel also claims a BIS brother, **Ch. Adler v. Andan,** WB828781, RO-284, bred and owned by Mrs. Tilghman. He is pictured in this book going BIS in Bermuda—a first for a Rottweiler. Both Adler and Indy were expertly handled throughout their careers by Clayton Fell.

Returning to the West Coast, note must be made of the breeding of Annie Anderson's **Dees v. Odenwald** (Ch. Balmain, **C.D.X.,** WA662999, RO-18, a Swedish import ex Quitta vom Kursaal, ADRK 41771, a German import) to Rodsden's Duke du Trier. This mating was repeated twice, producing in all five champions, one with a C.D. and four of which passed the OFA. **Ch. Duke's Derek v. Altmeister,** WC368908, RO-735, a product of the second breeding, became the first son of a Rottweiler Best in Show

Ch. Anka von Gailingen, bred, owned and handled by Catherine Thompson.

Ch. Kuhlwald's Little Iodine, CD, foundation bitch at Bergluft, Reg., owned by Dorit Rogers.

Ch. Panamint Right Bright, CD, owned and handled by Thelma Wade (De Riemer Kennels).

Exemplifying true greatness in phenotype and genotype. Ch. Dux v. Hungerbühl, SchH1, RO-0234, CACIB "V"-Angekort, top producer of all time, as of October 1980. Best of Breed at Westminster, 1973, and winner of the 1973 Golden State Specialty, and the 1st independent Specialty of the Medallion Rottweiler Club. Sire of the 1978 Bundessieger, and sire of the 7-times Best in Show Ch. Rodsden's Bruin v. Hungerbühl, CDX, TD. Owned by Elizabeth Eken, M.D. and P. G. Rademacher, Rodsden's Rottweilers, Reg.

dog to himself achieve that honor. Duke's Derek's win was at Anderson K.C. in Anderson, IN on 8/17/75.

Two weeks previously, on the East Coast, a German import, **Ch. Erno von Ingenhof,** WC604512, ADRK 46332, RO-477, owned by Charles Hill and handled by Kim Knoblauch, distinguished himself by going Best in Show at Perkiomen Valley K.C. on 8/3/75 under judge Donald Sandberg. Erno's sire was Dux vom Stüffelkopf, ADRK 44461. His dam was Dedda vom Kursaal, ADRK 43275. As a point of interest, three of his grandparents and two of his great-grandparents had been German Bundessiegers or Bundessiegerins. For whatever reason, Erno never reproduced his quality.

In the era of the early 1970s new names appeared on the roster of Rottweiler breeders. Thelma Wade on the West Coast adopting the DeRiemer prefix bred her **Ch. Panamint Right Bright, C.D.,** WA964259, RO-16 to **Ch. Panamint Seneca Chief,** WB313967, RO-115. Four of the litter finished.

Mr. and Mrs. William Carroll, using the kennel name Morgen Carroll, also got their start in this time period and remain in the ranks of the most successful breeders and exhibitors. In 1975, the third generation of their breeding resulted in a litter of which four made their championships.

Judith and William Johnson were involved with Rottweilers for some time before their Graudstark Kennels embarked on a breeding program in the early '70's. They have subsequently bred many champions including **Ch. Titan Sujon,** WC32407. He was owned by the Mammanos, impeccably presented by Ross Petruzzo and was twice Best of Breed at the Colonial Rottweiler Club Specialty.

Dorothy Wade owned and showed several Rottweilers before acquiring **Dago v.d. Ammerquelle,** WB208031, ADRK 43606, RO-68. Thus in 1970, when she handled Dago from the classes to Best of Breed over a large array of professionally handled champions, no one was too surprised. Doroh Reg. is her kennel name and she is actively engaged in breeding, handling and training her dogs for the conformation and the Obedience rings. Her interest furthermore extends to promoting Junior Showmanship as an activity for the children of Rottweiler owners. Doroh Kennels is located in Maryland.

We must interrupt the roll call of breeders to recognize the entry into this country of another great producing Rottweiler, **Ch. Dux vom Hungerbühl, SchH 1,** WC18804, ADRK 43753, RO-234, whelped 3/28/68. Dux (Kuno von Butzensee, SchH 3, ADRK 40415 ex Britta von Schlossberg, ADRK 39075) was a full brother to **B/S, K/S, Int. Ch. Bulli von Hungerbühl, SchH 2,** ADRK42465. Bulli dominated both the show scene and the stud scene in Germany for many years, producing dogs of excellent phenotype with a wide spectrum of bitches. Dux's performance in the American show ring was moderately successful but his real impact was made as a producer of top quality Rottweilers bred to a wide range of bitches. As a phenotype he was of medium size, possessed of a masculine head, fantastic color of markings and as good movement as has ever been seen in the Rottweiler ring. Dux was imported by Rodsden and co-owned by them with Dr. Elizabeth Eken.

Continuing with the breeders of the early '70's, Catherine Thompson, eventually to adopt the suffix v. Gailingen, also began what was to remain an active involvement with the Rottweilers in the early '70's. Her **Ch. Natascha v. Hohenreissach, C.D.,** WB416168, wh. 4/1/69, was purchased from Herman Heid in the Midwest. Natasha bred to the Rodsden import, Dux von Hungerbühl, produced the "A" v. Gailingen litter. **Anka,** WC341715, RO-522, retained by her breeder, finished her championship and was bred to Ch. Hintz v. Michelsberg (Lyn-Mar Acres Atlas son) producing three champions, of which two passed the OFA. Anka's second breeding to Igor v. Schauer produced three champions all passing the OFA. Gailingen's "D" litter was Anka bred to Ch. Srigo's Zarras v. Kurtz, WC820345, RO-791 (Lyn-Mar Acres Arras ex Srigo's Mädchen) producing champion, tracking and Obedience-titled progeny. This breeding was repeated. Cathy Thompson remains interested in the breeding and training of Rottweilers.

Way back in this history, note was made of the first Ch. U.D. Rottweiler being owned and trained by Margareta McIntyre. This lady's involvement with all phases of the Rottweiler started in her native land, Sweden, and has never diminished. Unfortunately, her breeding program in the 1960's was plagued, as were the programs of so many breeders, with dysplastic dogs. She decided, in 1969, to make a new start. She acquired **Freeger's Ingela,** WB457457, in co-ownership and promptly earned the bitch's championship, training her also to a C.D.X. Bred to **Ch. Blitz von Lucas,** WB90335, RO-51 (Rodsden's Kurt ex Circe v. Gertrudenhof, C.D., WA723452, ADRK 41201) two champion OFA progeny resulted, **Ch. Freeger's Lisa Gatstuberget,** WC393320, RO-523, owned by Dr. Daniel Siegel, and **Ch. Freeger's Leif Gatstuberget,** WC405125, RO-520, owned by Josephine Lipp. The latter also achieved his C.D.X., as did **Freeger's Lotta Gatstuberget,** owned and trained by Charles Wood.

Ingela's next breeding was to Dux vom Hungerbühl. The co-ownership had been dissolved, so the resulting all-champion litter was given the Gatstuberget prefix. **Ch. Eskil Jarl, C.D.,** WC658272, RO-645 was a successful show dog and companion dog to Michael Grossman (Wencrest), **Ch. Esbjorn Jarl, C.D.** remained with the McIntyres, **Ch. Elegant Essi,** owned by Janna Morgan, achieved her U.D.T. and **Ch. Erika, C.D.,** WC733368, RO-646 joined her half-sister Lotta in the Wood household to become their foundation bitch. Presently Mrs. McIntyre is carrying on her breeding program with an Ingela daughter line bred on Erno von Wellesweiler.

MODERN TIMES

From this point forward records are being assiduously compiled on AKC computers. Thus statistical information is readily available to anyone desiring these facts.

Some names which come to mind as being active in Rottweiler circles are mentioned, alphabetically, with comments. The last word has not been written on any of the following. The absence of a person or kennel rightfully belonging on this list, but not appearing, should be construed as a fault of omission rather than commission, and for that I apologize.

Baerenhof—Gerri Crawford: relative newcomer successfully active in breeding, showing and obedience. Competent editor of Club Newsletter.

Bethel Farms. A new kennel. The foundation bitch was of Graudstark breeding—a granddaughter of Harras. In their first litter Richard and Lavinia Bolden bred five champions. Thus Graudstark's Irma La Deuce became the second Rottweiler bitch to produce a litter with five champions resulting.

Big Oaks: Cat Klass, another newcomer fortunate to have started with

Ch. Adler von Andan, CD, Best in Show all-breeds at Bermuda, 1975. Several USA Group placements. Whelped 3/18/71, by Am. & Can. Ch. Rodsden's Kato v. Donnaj, CDX, TD ex Ehrenwaches Andernach. Breeder-Owner: Mrs. Benjamin C. Tilghman. Handler: Clayton Fell.

Ch. Amsel von Andan, CD, dam of 9 champions. Bred by Anna Tilghman. Owned by Pauline Rakowski.

a lovely bitch. She exhibits regularly in her area, is interested in proper breeding principles, all facets of club work and may well go on to make a name.

Birch Hill: Jane Weidel, an outstanding, all-around Rottweiler person. She bred her first litters with Rodsden. Adopted Birch Hill prefix when she struck out on her own. Has bred some top notch dogs in a short time, is an excellent trainer of all phases of Obedience—now approved to judge tracking (*see Chapter 9 for her article on Obedience Training*).

Bratiana: Jonathan Bratt residing in the San Francisco area, a breeder with a long-time involvement in Rottweilers—a charter member of the ARC. A litter registered by Mr. Bratt appeared in the AKC Stud Book in 1957.

Centurion: Leslie Fulcher, breeder of some very good Rottweilers in the mid 1970's, most outstanding of which was Ch. Centurion's Che v.d. Barr, WC815176, RO-757, a multi-Group and Specialty Show winner in the Midwest, owned by Josef and Donna Hedl and ably handled by Josef and by Richard Orseno.

Chutzpah: Margaret Teague's principal activity has been in the field of Obedience–Tracking—Schutzhund.

Donnaj: Donald and Jan Marshall, a name known to all interested in the exhibition of Rottweilers. Donnaj dominated the show ring in the early '70's with Kato, and again in the late '70's with Yankee. To her credit, Jan owner-handled both dogs and trained them to C.D.X. degrees. More on them in future chapters.

Ebenehaus: Earl, Jr. and Gwen Chaney, Medallion Rottweiler Club members with a family involvement. Interested in conformation, Obedience, breeding and promoting Junior Showmanship. (*See Article on Carting*).

Ebonstern: Cheryl Wheeler—breeder distinguished for the proportion of OFA normal dogs she was able to produce in every litter.

Elessar: Judy Goodrich. Her foundation bitch was Am. & Can. Ch. Rodsden's Beorn, C.D., WC518427, RO-584T, an Erno von Wellesweiler, Fetz von Oelberg, Quick von der Solitude great-granddaughter. Breeding in conjunction with Ebonstern, several champions were produced. Colonial Rottweiler Club is fortunate to have so diligent a member to supervise its Rescue League.

Frolic-n Kennels: Stephen and Charlotte Johnson and Linda Schuman—people with interest in the total dog. They have imported some excellent dogs, have acquired stock from Panamint and are now breeding. As trainers, they must be second to none—having taken an aggressive German dog and "tamed" him to work with one of their males so successfully that this pair went Best Brace in Show in Canada in January, 1976, and again at the Seattle Kennel Club all-breed show in February, 1976. This achievement was topped when their team of four went Best in Show at the prestigious Golden Gate Kennel Club show, February 1, 1981. (*See article on Carting.*)

Georgian Court: Andrea Vrana—active in the mid '70's, and produced a raft of champions in two or three litters.

Ch. Centurion's Che von der Barr. Wh. 1/24/74, by Am. & Can. Ch. Northwind's Barras ex Ch. Rodsden's Ericka Diedre Dahl. Bred by Leslie Fulcher, and owned by Josef and Donna Hedl. Shown as a Special 160 times, Che had 130 BOBs and 26 Group placings including 5 Firsts. Pictured winning the Medallion Rottweiler Club Independent 1977 Specialty.

Ch. Imor von Stolzenfels, RO-2150 (Ch. Centurion Che v.d. Barr, RO-757 ex Ch. Cosi vom Steigsträssle, RO-495). Bred by Jack P. Ellman, and co-owned by him with David Eaton.   — Courtesy, J. Hedl

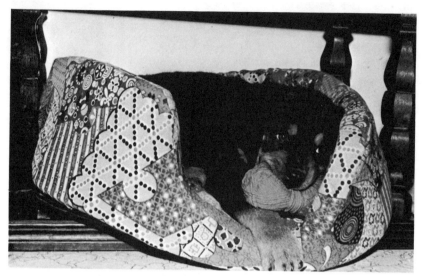

Learning to knit. Puppy of the Frolic'n Kennels.

Glyn Mar's: Guidry—located in Texas and doing some nice breeding.

Golden West: Fred McNabb—training, breeding and active in club work for Golden State Rottweiler Club. Very successful in the show ring with his imports and his own breeding stock.

Green Mountain: Anthony Attalla, owner of Ch. Donnaj Green Mountain Boy, a top winning dog. Mr. Attalla has done some breeding and has been most successful in exhibiting his stock.

Haserway: Joan Griffin—Midwest kennel breeding litters containing multiple champions.

Haus Kalbas: Robert and May Kalbas. Robert is a competent trainer. They have been interested in the Rottweiler for a very long time, and bred several champions in their "B" litter, with C.D.'s and OFA's.

Ironwood Farms: George and Sandy Chamberlin have been Rottweiler owners for over ten years, with Rodsden and imported Rottweilers. George's main impact thus far has been as a club worker for Colonial Rottweiler Club and American Rottweiler Club, having served as President for both organizations, and in several other capacities for Colonial Rottweiler Club.

Jessnic Rottweilers: Jessica Nichols' original stock was from Northwind Kennels. Fine record in the ring was established with her male, Kaiser. Is presently starting a breeding program.

Kertzenlicht: Jeffrey and Geraldine Kittner, owners of the strongest winning Rottweiler show dog to date, Ch. Rodsden's Bruin v. Hungerbuhl, C.D.X., WD375753. Now breeding and exhibiting, and working in Obedience. (*See chapter on Dogs of Distinction.*)

Lauffeuer: Debbie Gallegos—In a limited breeding program has produced well. Interested in all phases of the Rottweiler and a diligent club worker. Foundation bitch was a daughter of BIS Ch. Rodsden's Duke du Trier.

Limehouse: Harry Isaacs—perhaps the Rottweiler person with the longest involvement in dogs. He is an AKC judge of Bulldogs, Kerry Blues and French Bulldogs. His affinity for Rottweilers is more recent. Imported Ch. Caro vom Zimmerplatz, WB784427, ADRK 45323, RO-287, in the early '70's; followed by Ch. Liane von Schloss-Stauffenberg, WB867003, ADRK 45026, RO-288, a Bulli vom Hungerbühl daughter; and Erno von Ingenhof, an eventual BIS dog. Von Meadow foundation stock is Limehouse.

Mondberg: Ruth Parker—started with an Andan bitch and has produced well. Distinguished for breeding the first O.T.Ch. Rottweiler, Mondberg's Donnamira v. Beier, U.D., owned by George Beck.

Noblehaus: Mark and Pat Schwartz are relatively new in Rottweilers. They own a nice dog—Ch. Graudstark's Luger, WD815105, (Radio Ranch's Axel ex Shearwater Pyewacket). He is producing well. They are embarking on a breeding program using Northwind lines in combination with their dogs.

Odenwald: Margot Schmidt—knowledgeable German-born breeder who imports and breeds some very good dogs. Handles and trains her dogs herself.

Pandemonium: Valerie Cade—another successful newcomer with numerous males of good phenotype, embarking on a breeding program. Proficient handler, trains and shows her own dogs.

Powderhorn: Clara Hurley—long involvement with the breed, importer of several Dutch and German dogs in partnership with Michael Grossman (*Wencrest*). Two v.h. Brabantpark brothers, Oscar and Quanto, distinguished themselves in the ring. Mrs. Hurley is an active club member and is the keeper of the Biodex (*see Chapter 13 on Hip Dysplasia, and Chapter 8, Distinction in the Show Ring*).

Rawlings, Surely: A newcomer to the Rottweiler ranks. An ardent exhibitor having enormous success in the show ring with her first bitch, Ch. Erdelied Astraea, C.D., "Star", perhaps the most perfectly trained Rottweiler in the ring today and no wonder, as her owner first had experience with porpoises and other sea-going animals. The moral is, "If you can train a porpoise, a Rottweiler shouldn't be a problem!"

Riegele: Henry and Ellen Walls are ardent Rottweiler admirers and breeders. Ellen is very active in club work and a regular competitor in the conformation ring. Bred Ch. Riegele's Agreta Maid, the foundation bitch of Robert Timmerman's Kennel.

Shearwater: Connie Schwartzberg—active in Rottweilers on and off since 1965. Breeder of BIS Ch. Shearwater Cochise and several other Shearwater champions, among them a foundation bitch for Lyndhausen Kennels.

Skoghult: Chuck and Peggy Wood have been active since 1973 when they bought their first Rottweiler of Freeger-Gatstuberget breeding. Lotta was trained to a C.D.X. by Chuck. Both Peggy and Chuck are ardent supporters of the best for our dogs, reliable club workers and interested in the breeding, showing and training of their dogs.

Southwood: Linda Howard—occasional breeder; some nice dogs carry this kennel name.

Starkrest Kennels: William and Mildred Stark. As Mildred said, in her own words, "Though we were small breeders, we did contribute something good to the breed"—a very accurate statement. Perhaps their most successful Rottweiler was Ch. Starkrest's Polo-R, the sire of approximately twenty champions, incorporated in the breeding programs of several outstanding kennels producing champions for Haus Kalbas, Graudstark, Gruenerwald, Haserway, Radio Ranch and others.

Stolzenfels: Jack and Evelyn Ellman, owners of Rottweilers since the '60's, used German imports for their foundation stock. Some excellent phenotypes were produced and shown successfully in the Midwest.

Sunnyside: Marcia Tucker—a very successful newcomer located in Florida. In her first litter produced Ch. Phaedra's Amax of Sunnyside, WD112171, RO-975T (Ch. Igor v. Schauer ex Ch. Rodsden's Windsong Phaedra, C.D., RO-450) and two other champions. In 1978 Amax was #1 in the ARC rating. Marcia is also a prominent Miniature Pinscher breeder, an all around dog person and a diligent club worker—a valuable commodity these days.

Tegelhagen: Marie Ekman—limited breeding program. Produced "A" litter of three champions, two OFA. Has bred several subsequent champions.

Trollegen: Maureen Wilkinson—a knowledgeable, competent breeder and handler. Her "F" litter of two excellent males and two lovely bitches excelled in the show ring and produced successfully. There are more good ones on the way.

Von Arktos: Judith Hassed, interested in showing, breeding and training of Rottweilers in the Colorado Springs area. Started with a Panamint bitch bred to Nick von Silahopp.

Von Isarstrand: Marcus, Meyer and Ida. Another couple with a longtime involvement. They are ardent admirers of the correct German dog and can always be counted upon to support what is best for our breed. Their first bitch, Naomi von Rau of Wunderkinder, was acquired in 1962. Subsequently, they have imported some very fine German dogs. First and foremost was Adda von Dahl, SchH 3, WB510553, ADRK 41299 (Fetz von Oelberg, ADRK 38416, SchH 2 ex Assy von Borsigplatz 39372). To have seen Adda in her prime was a lesson in Rottweiler feminine pulchritude. Only the roundness of eye shape marred an otherwise ideal specimen (*see photograph*). Their last import, Ch. Hella vom Märchenwald, WC853502, ADRK 48755 (Elko von Kastanienbaum, SchH 3, ADRK 46340 ex Cora von Reichenbachle, ADRK 44738) distinguished herself by winning the Colonial Rottweiler Club Specialty under Peggy Adamson in 1978.

Von Kruse: Alan and Karen Kruse, Midwest Rottweiler fanciers doing some breeding and showing; recently have acquired co-ownership of

Adda von Dahl, SchH3—V1, Bundessieger Show, 1968; VI, Bundessieger Show, 1969. Owner, Meyer Marcus.

Ch. Starkrest's Polo-R, sire of 20 champions out of limited breedings.

Everything's coming up roses for this puppy of the Von Meadow Kennels.

a German import. Active in ARC club work.

Von Meadow: Donna Wormser is also a horse person, definitely an advantage in breeding dogs. Donna is an enthusiastic Rottweiler breeder and exhibitor with a sincere desire to produce outstanding dogs and the ability to accomplish her aims.

Von Ross: Murray and Kelly Ross are newcomers with some excellent German and Dutch imports. It is a family involvement which includes conformation titles and Obedience degrees acquired by their daughters.

Von Ursa: Rebecca Chriscoe—newcomer with some very lovely Rottweilers bearing her kennel name.

Von Weissenburg: Marvin and Beverlee Smith. They are zealous in their desire to breed the best and uphold the highest standards, and building on Gruenerwald and Rodsden lines, have bred some very successful dogs. They have bred Ch. Weissenburg's Don't-U Dare, WE376304, RO-2934, BOS at the Medallion Rottweiler Club Specialty under breeder judge Margareta McIntyre in 1981.

Waxel: Dr. Richard and Vee Wayburn acquired their first Rottweiler from Merrymoore. "Franchi," C.D.X. will always occupy a special spot and will be remembered as "the climbing Rottweiler." She was followed by Ch. Wakefields Donka, C.D., Ch. Rodsdens Adam v. Brabant and an import, Ch. Luna v. Stüffelkopf. The Wayburns have a vital interest in the good of the breed and do more than their part to reinforce this aim.

Welkerhaus: Rita Welker, owner of Ch. Welkerhaus Rommel, U.D., owner-handled to his championship and his U.D. Rommel completed his C.D., C.D.X., and U.D. within a twelve month period—quite a feat for handler and dog. Rita is currently breeding, showing and training.

Woodward, James and Erna—Another couple devoted to the best for the Rottweiler. They are longtime members of Medallion Rottweiler Club and have for many years actively participated in that Club's many activities. Mentioned earlier in the history as the owners-trainers of Ch. Axel v.d. Taverne, they also owned and showed Am,. & Can. Ch. Panamint Banner v. Hohenwald, Am. & Can. C.D.

53

Ch. Radio Ranch's Merry v. Notara, Best of Winners at Medallion Rottweiler Club Specialty 1978. Breeders, F. and E. Pogue. Owner, Tom Roberts.

Canine "Olympic swimmer" and diver, Ch. Luna vom Stuffelkopf. Owners, Dr. and Mrs. R. Wayburn.

54

This headstudy is of Ch. Birch Hill's Hasso Manteuffel, CDX, TD—multi Specialty winner owned by Vicki Wassenhove. For more on Hasso and his wins, see page 108. Below he is pictured in various stages of his development.

Hasso at 8 weeks.

At 12 weeks.

At 6½ months.

As an adult.

3

Guidance for a
Potential Owner

THERE IS MUCH to know about our breed. It is not possible in these few pages to satisfactorily answer the many questions that will arise and to which you should have answers before seriously considering the purchase of a Rottweiler. Our aim here is to give you some insight of a general nature and to whet your appetite for further investigation.

It is important that you read the opening chapter on the history of the Rottweiler, as it establishes the fact that, since the days of the Roman Army, the Rottweiler has done service for man in one capacity or another. Ours is a working dog. As such, it has been bred for characteristics which by now are deeply instilled. These characteristics must be recognized and understood if they are to be assets for the potential owner.

Although the Rottweiler's earliest recorded job was to herd cattle and sheep for the Roman Army, in his career the Rottweiler has also been a cart dog, a guide dog for the blind, a police dog, a guard dog, a retriever, tracker and, most important, a companion dog.

All of these functions he is still able to perform, but not without training. It is most important that potential owners understand the value of early and proper training of their Rottweiler puppy. An obedient Rottweiler is a pleasure. An undisciplined one can grow to be a menace. "A leopard cannot change its spots," nor does a Rottweiler belie its heritage. So, as wise President Truman once said, "If you can't take the heat, stay out of the kitchen!"

A Rottweiler is not a toy. The demands put upon dogs in our society

Observe the handler-dog eye contact in this picture of Vicki Wassenhove and Ch. Birch Hill's Hasso Manteuffel, CDX, TD. She has his attention, and he obviously wants to please her.

Ch. Rodsden's Quelle v.d. Harque, UD, Sch H2, a very tough bitch and a great favorite of mine, typifying the many facets of Rottweiler good character—always under control because the master-dog relationship was established. Owner-trainer: Charles Goodman.

are a far cry from those of their original habitat. The owner has the responsibility to fill this gap and to channel the dog's actions along a constructive path. If you do not have the time nor the inclination, a Rottweiler is not your breed!

Now, to answer a few questions in very general terms—questions which are natural for people who have had little or no exposure to this breed of dog:

Yes, they are extremely intelligent, though their intelligence is sometimes masked by the fact that they are also extremely stubborn and willful. Here again their background requiring them to think on their own, to make decisions and to implement those decisions, is manifest. You as an owner must be intelligent, consistent and fair, thereby earning the status of "master." Once this relationship is established, the dog's goal is to please you. Your problems are over and you then have not only a fast achiever on your hands, but also one with a memory bank worthy of an I.B.M. computer.

Both males and females make excellent house dogs. Which one is more suitable depends upon the family. The male's looks are more impressive. He is usually more difficult to train in the beginning and more to handle in every way. The bitch is generally easier to live with. However, if she is not spayed, you face the problem of her seasons. Mature males run 95 to 140 pounds and bitches somewhere between 75 and 100 pounds. However, it should be kept in mind that weight should be a concern only when the dog appears too fat, or too lean. What "looks right" most often *is* right.

As growing puppies, Rottweilers eat anywhere from 1½ pounds of meat and 7 or 8 cups of kibble per day for a very large, active male in the most rapidly growing stage, to as little as ½ pound of meat and 1 cup of kibble for a mature female who is a "good keeper." In addition, puppies should be given supplements and whatever extras—cottage cheese, occasional raw eggs, milk, etc.—the breeder recommends. (See Chapter 11.)

They do shed twice a year. The amount varies with the climate and the individual dog.

They do need regular and organized exercise. The amount depends upon the age, sex, temperament and, to some extent, the aspirations of the owner. If one intends to show a dog, then it must be properly conditioned for the ring.

They do suffer from extreme heat and the male, especially, must be catered to in this respect.

Yes, they can be trusted with children, but here again training is of the essence, for otherwise their protective instinct would never allow strange children to play rough with "their" children, and, of course, their type of interference could be most serious.

The only Rottweilers I have ever known not to adore riding in a car are

58

Getting along like cats and dogs.
— Courtesy, Frolic'n Kennels

Cats prefer a Rottweiler's back to lying on cold bricks.
Ch. Gerhardt von Stahl and "Muffin."

those who are taken in them infrequently, and then to the vet. Most are so addicted that C-A-R has to be spelled out in conversation to avoid the inevitable wild enthusiasm.

Yes, they can be expected to get along with cats if raised with them.

No, it is not wise to have two dogs of the same sex as your housepets. It should work out in the case of two females, if intelligently handled, but in the case of two males, it is always a potentially dangerous situation.

No, the Rottweiler should *never* be chained, but should, during the day, especially as a young dog, be put outside in an enclosed area in which shelter is provided from heat, cold, and dampness. At night, a Rottweiler should be inside sharing your home and protecting it.

Yes, you do have to anticipate veterinary expenses for vaccinations, puppy wormings, rabies shots and heartworm medication in most areas. However, if you purchase good stock, and feed and care for your puppy properly, veterinary bills should be minimal.

No, no one can guarantee that a seven or eight-week-old puppy will be a champion. Your best indication of what the future portends for a puppy is to judge by the parents.

Yes, our dogs are candidates for hip dysplasia, as are all dogs that mature over forty pounds. You should inform yourself by reading on the subject. You should also be aware that guarantees may be in order, although it is not possible at this writing for a breeder to discern at seven or eight weeks whether a puppy will or will not be dysplastic at maturity. However, by breeding dogs with normal hips, we are opting for 25 percent more puppies with normal hips and, therefore, responsible breeders adhere to the policy of breeding only O.F.A. certified stock. (*See Chapter 13 for discussion of hip dysplasia.*)

No, the term, "AKC Registered," is NOT a guarantee of quality. It means only that both the sire and dam of the puppy, or dog, are purebred Rottweilers, whose respective sire and dam are purebred, etc.

No, a puppy sold without AKC registration, that is, without "papers," is NOT AKC registrable, cannot be shown in conformation at an AKC event, and should not be bred. This does not mean the puppy has something seriously wrong with it; it simply means that in the opinion of the breeder, the puppy has faults which indicate that it should not be shown and should not be bred. Temperamentally, it may be a very charming puppy.

Exception to this rule can be made in the case of Obedience. The breeder or owner can apply for an ILP number which, when assigned, entitles the dog to be entered at any and all Obedience events.

Yes, unfortunately, there are some Rottweilers whose temperaments could be a bit less sharp (i.e., less aggressive). The breeder from whom you buy should be willing to discuss with you the temperament of his breeding stock. You, as the buyer, should satisfy yourself that the puppy has a temperament with which you can "get along."

"Echo Sleeping." This painting is one of four enormous murals ("The Echo Series") in the New York City house-studio of famous artist Lowell Nesbitt, depicting his Rottweiler as studio companion. Mr. Nesbitt is one of the foremost living painters of flowers, and his works include the famous stamp series commissioned by the United States government. The bond between Lowell Nesbitt and "Echo" is easily understood. A Rottweiler has the special sensitivity that a man of such talents would look for in a companion dog.

Having read the history of the Rottweiler and this chapter describing the basic character and characteristics of the dog, some of my readers will have determined a Rottweiler is the dog for them. Once that is decided, the question arises as to how to locate a puppy.

By writing to the American Kennel Club, 51 Madison Avenue, New York, New York 10010, the names and addresses of current Rottweiler Club secretaries can be obtained. The choice of which local club to contact is generally made in accordance with the section of the country in which the prospective buyer is located. The American Rottweiler Club serves all. (See Chapter 7 for additional information on Clubs.)

Most clubs have an information booklet and a Breeder's List available for the asking. Breeders in the vicinity should be contacted and an appointment made to see the dogs. The appointment should be kept promptly and the entourage restricted to members of the family who will be living with the dog. Visiting a kennel is not an alternative to taking the neighbors' children to the zoo.

At this point, the prospective buyer who has studied the Rottweiler Standard is able to ask intelligent questions of the breeder when he sees the dogs. He is also better equipped to evaluate the integrity and knowledge of the breeder. Certainly, if he is conversant with the Standard, when he sees the live dog he will have some idea of where it resembles and where it departs from the description of the ideal dog.

After visiting several kennels, attending a dog show would also be helpful. Dogs from different kennels can be compared and individual preferences will surface. This is an excellent way to sharpen the eye.

When sufficient time has been spent on searching out a puppy, the prospective buyer must decide on the breeder of his choice. He must approach this breeder stating his desires honestly. Most breeders will represent their dogs in one of two categories, as "show quality" or "pet quality." Pet quality puppies are sold at much reduced figures and, quite correctly, AKC papers are withheld.

Some additional DO's and DON'Ts:

1. Do not even consider the purchase of a Rottweiler from other than a responsible breeder.

2. Do not think AKC or any of the breed clubs are your umbrella. Make your own investigations and choose your breeder with care. His or her integrity and knowledge are what you are dealing with.

3. Reconsider many times the responsibility you will have incurred in buying a puppy, and don't make the commitment lightly. The Rottweiler will be pledged for life. You must be equally committed.

4. Read, and be sure you fully understand, any contract you are asked to sign.

5. Don't be intimidated or turned off by the preceding admonitions; just profit by them and your decision to live with a Rottweiler will be one of the wisest moves you will ever make!

The following books are recommended to enhance your basic knowledge:

Der Rottweiler, Hans Korn, translation from German. (Available through the Colonial Rottweiler Club.)

The Complete Dog Book, official publication of The American Kennel Club. (Available from the AKC or Howell Book House.)

American Rottweiler Club Pictorial, 1975-76, 1978 and 1983. (Available through the American Rottweiler Club.)

"I love you." They can be trusted with children.
— Courtesy, Joseph Prizzi

Checking the new arrival.
Ch. Von Gailingen's Dassie Did It, UDT. Breeder-owner: C. M. Thompson.

4

A Member
of the Family

"My son's dog, Azor, rules my son; he rules his mother; she rules me; I rule Athens; and Athens rules the world; therefore, the dog, Azor, rules the world."
    —Pericles, Ruler of Athens when it was at its highest material and intellectual state.

T HE SOURCE does not reveal the historical event which occasioned this amusing syllogism, but evidently for some reason Pericles wanted the dog's importance to his family known.

This chapter is dedicated to all Rottweilers sharing the family life. Some belong to the rich, some to the moderately well-to-do, and others to those making a sacrifice to feed them. Some belong to families with children, others live with just one person. They may be large Rottweilers or small ones, males, females or neutered dogs. Their owners may be urban, suburban or farm dwellers. It doesn't matter, the common denominator being that they are housedogs.

The pictures selected to illustrate this subject were all given with great love as each family believes its relationship with its dog is unique, and so it is. They wanted you, my reader, to share the pleasure of this relationship.

In this chapter I am going to indulge in some story telling. This book has been an arduous task, requiring discipline in excess of what I was prepared to muster. I have very honestly made every attempt to inject as little of myself as was commensurate with attaining the proper objective. The exception to this statement is the discussion of hip dysplasia.

However, it is my great love for these dogs, my appreciation of them in the capacity of devoted nursemaid and playmate for children, companion to the wife, and protector of all that belongs to the master, which prompted me to give up more than two years of my life to write this book. As a result, I feel entitled to self expression in this chapter.

"We're ready!" L. to r.: Maxie, Katie and Truna.

Truna's son, "Maxie," Ch. D'Artagnan of Canidom, CD.
Canidom Kennels and Mrs. Bernard Freeman.

THE STORY OF TRUNA

At eight weeks of age she was wished on me, despite my protestation that Gerhardt was enough Rottweiler for one house. Here's how it happened. I went to visit and the elderly German co-owner informed me he had set her aside for me. He said she was special, "a little angel, who never did nothing wrong", as he put it. For six months I never saw that side of her. Instead, we bore scars from sneak nips and our clothes were tattered and torn from her indefatigable herding instinct. She was independent, yet affectionate, easily housetrained, and a voracious eater. When she was nowhere to be found, a search of the bathrooms would find her, sound asleep in one of the tubs—evidently the coolest spot in the house. How she got in or out we weren't able to discover as she never performed this feat in public.

After two months, I took her back to the elderly German for a visit. He took one look at her and said, "You're de von who dug up my rose bushes." I never again took Mr. Kapp's word for Gospel, but I was also eternally grateful for the harmless deception which had resulted in our having Truna.

When Truna was about six months old my husband and I embarked on a trip around the world. I bid Gerhardt, her father, a tearful farewell knowing he and I would miss one another terribly. I gave Truna an off-handed pat and departed thinking she would not miss me at all. She had her father and my sons and others to keep her company.

This proved to be the most erroneous judgment I ever made with any of my dogs. When I walked into the house two months later, she virtually screamed and from that day forward never voluntarily let me out of her sight. To this day I am confounded by that reaction. How in my absence had a six-month old difficult puppy metamorphised into a most devoted companion? I have never been able to explain it as, in my experience, devotion of the kind she instantaneously displayed for the very first time upon my return, is never as a result of separation. It is always the result of constant contact which fosters interdependence. Nevertheless, this phenomenon did occur.

When she was 15 months old the second crisis in Truna's life took place. My husband decided he was tired of commuting 12 months out of the year. We were to live in a hotel/apartment in New York City from November through March and go to Manhasset for weekends. Brave and brazen as I was in those days, I could see no way to take two Rottweilers into this situation. Naturally, Gerhardt went and Truna stayed in Manhasset.

Every weekend the greeting I got was wilder and every Sunday night the scene at the door as we departed was more upsetting. We took to putting her out of sight. She screamed and carried on as she had never done. She, who had been the most dependable of eaters, refused food. She was inconsolable until we reappeared.

Sandra Stranckmeyer and her mother (Mrs. Frances Stranckmeyer) with Sandra's dog, Rodsden's Tara v. Ludwig, CD—#5 Ken-L Ration Dog Hero of 1972 and member of the Medallion Rottweiler Club Hall of Fame. In a nasty fall at their home, Mrs. Stranckmeyer had struck her head and lay bleeding profusely. Tara continued barking until Sandra, asleep in another bedroom of the house, was awakened. She found her mother, administered first aid and called the ambulance.

A family portrait. Northwind's Amie (7 years); Doroh's Jaegerin v. Noblehaus (10 months); Ch. Graustark's Luger (5 years); and Ch. Noblehaus Ain't Misbehavin' (2 years). Owners, M. and P. Schwarz.

By the end of that winter, I thought it best to place her in another home where she would have a family all to herself and would not be subjected to our coming and going. I screened many and finally a young couple with children came who were acceptable. I shall not forget the day they returned to take her. Although I thought I was doing the best for her, it was my turn to be inconsolable. I spoke to her people every day for weeks, then it got to be weekly. Finally, by the time six months had elapsed and she was obviously adjusted, I agreed to pay a visit.

I rang the bell. She was at the door as it was opened, ready to take on any challenger. When she realized who was there, it was as if we had never been separated. I ended up on the couch with her on top of me. I volunteered to take her for a short walk before I left. She quickly performed all the necessities, thinking we were going in the car. When I brought her back and left her at the door, I exited with the same screaming we had suffered in Manhasset. I vowed never to put myself and her through that again.

Fate intervened and due to a strange set of circumstances I was able a year later to offer her owners twice what they had paid for her, plus a puppy to get her back. They refused my offer. Three days later I got a call and these were the exact words, "OK, you can have her. I somehow always knew I had Muriel's dog." I picked her up. Although the better part of two years had passed since she had been in Manhasset, it was as though she had never left. When I let her out of the car, she ran across the property to the fenceline and there I saw her digging for all she was worth. A minute later she came up with a large knuckle bone she had evidently buried two years previously. They talk about the memory of an elephant!

As the years passed, we bred her and she produced dogs of impeccable character, unusual stamina and great intelligence. We kept one of her sons, Ch. D'Artagnan of Canidom, CD, "Maxie." She always loved him dearly. As time went on I imported a puppy bitch with an eye to breeding her to Maxie. Truna hated her. Poor Katie! She came smelling bad and Truna never let her forget it. Every female has a "bitchy" side and Katie surely evoked Truna's.

The next four-legged addition to the family was a five year old German import, *Bundessieger* '65, *World Sieger* '65, Int. Champion Erno von Wellesweiler, SchH1. At the appropriate time I took Truna from the house over to meet him. She was not impressed and proceeded to wander about far away from the area in which he was enclosed.

I called her over and said, "Truna, he is lonely. He has come a long way to strange people, strange dogs, all strange surroundings. Be nice to him." She looked at me and walked over to the fence and pressed her rear end right up against the wire as much as to say, "This is what he could like best about me." You know what, she was right. Erno always loved Truna, and as time passed, she returned the affection. In fact, one time on the 27th day of her season, I found them in a love embrace. Strange she never allowed Maxie the privilege of even sniffing her as much as she loved to play with

Rottweilers can be taught to retrieve on land or in water. This is Am. & Can. Ch. Birch Hill's Juno, CD, TD, bred and owned by Jane Wiedel.

A Rottweiler can be taught to do any thing—even climb trees! This is Franchi Owned by Dr. and Mrs. R. Wayburn.

him. He was her son and owed her respect. With Erno it was correct in her book.

She had definite opinions about so very many people and had a way of sharing them with me. In fact, I thought I would never be able to select my puppy buyers once Truna was not around to tell me what was what. In that vein, one day prospective puppy owners arrived with a little girl about three years of age and an infant in arms. I was involved in telling them about the breed. They were all ears. The baby started whimpering, but no one paid much attention. After about five minutes of that, Truna got up, walked over to the baby, sniffed its diapers, and in her loudest voice gave one sharp bark right in the mother's face. "Stop the talk and clean up your child!", was Truna's message.

My husband called her "the Enforcer." Her ideas of propriety were always correct. She had infallible judgment and although she never bit anyone in her life and never got into a dog fight, she always managed to get her way on important issues. No man or beast ever challenged her. As an example, it was my habit to pick up my dog meat in Connecticut, about an hour's drive from Manhasset. On one occasion Truna and I took a friend along for company. This lady was one of Truna's great favorites. When we arrived at the supplier, the parking lot was full, necessitating my standing the car behind a truck. I went in to inform them I was there to receive the order. While I was waiting at the counter the truckman came in and asked me to move the car as he was pressed for time. I thought it rather silly of my friend not to have obliged him, but when I got to the car I had the answer. She had tried to move over to my seat. Truna had come from the back of the wagon and given her one sharp bark while pressing on the left side of her face. The message was clear, "Get out of that seat. It's my mother's and not yours." As she moved over, my friend got a fast kiss—"You're a good person and a fast learner," was Truna's thought, and she knew how to express it.

Truna lived to be 11 years old and the day I had to put her to sleep will forever be one of my most tragic hours. Her picture hangs in my house in a silver frame. Although no championship precedes her name, she will always be my favorite.

5

The Standard

$\mathbf{W}$EBSTER defines the word *standard* as: "that which is established by authority, custom or general consent as a model or example."

The need for a standard in each breed is obvious. Were it not for the recognized standard, there would be no correct breed type. As it is, those breeds which are fortunate enough to have a well-written, explicit standard as a guideline are the breeds in which breeders can properly select their stock and judges have a workable criterion by which to evaluate the dogs.

We must never lose sight of this. Dog shows are not held to satisfy the egos of the winning owners, to feather the nests of professional handlers, or to give judges a sphere of action in which to ply their trade. Dog shows exist in order to provide breeders with an arena in which to compare their stock. Were it not for dog shows, most breeders would have no measure of their success or failure. Given sufficient exposure, it becomes rather obvious who is "on the right track."

So, a good standard is one which describes "perfection" and furthermore evaluates the deviation from this ideal. A discussion on the subject is an eye-opener to the novice. A standard must tell the story correctly, concisely and with some appeal. It cannot be a tome which, by virtue of its lengthiness, fails—dragged down by its own weight. On the other hand, it must sufficiently describe the dog to allow no gross misunderstanding, adequately painting the picture for judges and novices to correctly evaluate all salient points and, at the very least, alluding to what is correct where absolute definition is not feasible.

The first Rottweiler standard was approved by the American Kennel Club in April of 1935. Some forty years later, when the breed had gained

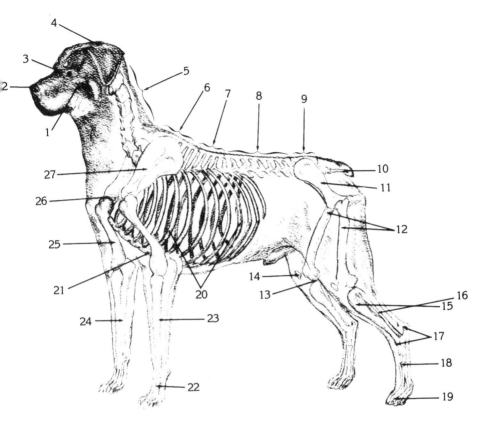

(This drawing is not anatomically correct, but is designed solely to identify the parts of the dog.)

1. Cheek
2. Nose
3. Stop
4. Occiput
5. 7 Cervical Vertebrae—(Neck)
6. 8 Dorsal Vertebrae—(Withers)
7. 5 Dorsal Vertebrae—(Back)
8. 7 Lumbar Vertebrae—(Loin)
9. 3 Sacral Vertebrae—(Croup)
10. Tail—3 to 26 Vertebrae
11. Pelvic Bone Hip
12. Femur or Upper Thigh
13. Stifle or Knee Joint
14. Patella or Knee Cap

15. Tibia ⎱ Gaskin or Lower Thigh
16. Fibula ⎰
17. Hock Joint or Heel
18. Hock or Metatarsals
19. Toes or Phalanges
20. Ribs (13 pairs)
21. Sternum or Breastbone
22. Pastern or Metacarpals
23. Ulna ⎱ Lower Foreleg
24. Radius ⎰
25. Humerus—Upper Foreleg
26. Shoulder Joint
27. Scapula or Shoulder Blade

enormously in numbers and Rottweiler entries at dog shows were sizeable, it was realized that a revision was indicated.

The 1935 AKC Standard for the Rottweiler
(Approved April 9, 1935—no longer effective)

General Appearance and Character: The Rottweiler is a good-sized, strongly built, active dog. He is affectionate, intelligent, easily trained to work, naturally obedient and extremely faithful. While not quarrelsome, he possesses great courage and makes a splendid guard. His demeanor is dignified and he is not excitable.

Head: Is of medium length, the skull broad between the ears. Stop well pronounced as is also the occiput. Muzzle is not very long. It should not be longer than the distance from the stop to the occiput. Nose is well developed, with relatively large nostrils and is always black. Flews which should not be too pronounced are also black. Jaws should be strong and muscular; teeth strong—incisors of lower jaw must touch the inner surface of the upper incisors. Eyes are of medium size, dark brown in color and should express faithfulness, good humor and confidence. The ears are comparatively small, set high and wide and hang over about on a level with top of head. The skin on head should not be loose. The neck should be of fair length, strong, round and very muscular, slightly arched and free from throatiness.

Forequarters: Shoulders should be well placed, long and sloping, elbows well let down, but not loose. Legs muscular and with plenty of bone and substance, pasterns straight and strong. Feet strong, round and close, with toes well arched. Soles very hard, toe nails dark, short and strong.

Body: The chest is roomy, broad and deep. Ribs well sprung. Back straight, strong and rather short. Loins strong and deep, and flanks should not be tucked up. Croup short, broad, but not sloping.

Hindquarters: Upper thigh is short, broad and very muscular. Lower thigh very muscular at top and strong and sinewy at the bottom. Stifles fairly well bent, hocks strong. The hind feet are somewhat longer than the front ones, but should be close and strong with toes well arched. There should be no dewclaws. Tail should be short, placed high (on level with back) and carried horizontally. Dogs are frequently born with a short stump tail, and when tail is too long it must be docked close to body.

Coat: Hair should be short, coarse and flat. The undercoat which is absolutely required on neck and thighs should not show through outer coat. The hair should be a little longer on the back of front and hind legs and on tail.

Color: Black, with clearly defined markings on cheeks, muzzle, chest and legs, as well as over both eyes. Color of markings: tan to mahogany brown. A small spot of white on chest and belly is permissible but not desirable.

Height: Shoulder height for males is 23-3/4 inches to 27 inches, for females, 21-3/4 to 25-3/4 inches, but height should always be considered in realtion to the general appearance and conformation of the dog.

Faults: Too lightly built or too heavily built, sway-back, roach back, too long body, lack of spring of ribs. Head too long and narrow or too short and plump. Lack of occiput, snipy muzzle, cheekiness, top line of muzzle not straight, light or flesh-colored nose, hanging flews, overshot or undershot, loose skin on head, ears set too low, or ears too heavy, long or narrow or rose ear, or ears uneven in size. Light, small or slanting eyes, or lack of expression, neck too long, thin or weak, or very noticeable throatiness. Lack of bone and muscle, short or straight shoulders, front legs too close together or not straight, weak pasterns, splay feet, light nails, weak toes. Flat ribs, sloping croup. Too heavy or plump body. Flanks drawn up. Flat thighs, cowhocks or weak hocks, dewclaws. Tail set too high or too low or that is too long or too thin. Soft, too short, too long or too open coat, wavy coat or lack of undercoat. White markings on toes, legs or other parts of body, markings not too well defined or smudgy. The one-color tan Rottweiler with either black or light mask or with black streak on back as well as other colors, such as brown or blue, are not recognized and are believed to be cross-bred, as is also a longhaired Rottweiler. Timid or stupid-appearing animals are to be positively rejected.

Under the auspices of the newly formed American Rottweiler Club, a Standard Revision Committee was appointed. This committee suffered several metamorphoses, but eventually emerged with Barbara Hoard Dillon as Chairperson, and Gerry Fitterer, Felice Luburich, Margareta McIntyre, Carol Stafford, William C. Stark, Peggy Walton and Muriel Freeman serving. Mrs. Dillon, Mrs. McIntyre and I were AKC recognized Specialist judges at the time, so it was appropriate that we participate in this important function. Several revisions were submitted to the membership of the American Rottweiler Club. The final revision was accepted and approved by the American Kennel Club on September 11, 1979. Copies of the 1935 standard and the 1979 standard are included in this chapter.

Notable changes and illuminating clarifications follow:

Size: Height changed in males from 23¾"-27" to 24"-27". Height changed in bitches from 21¾"-25¾" to 22"-25".

Correct body proportion is stated as 10 is to 9, with depth of chest 50% of height at the withers. Correct head characteristics are also defined, especially in the case of mouth faults, where three of the six disqualifications occur. The remaining three disqualifications refer to coat quality and/or color, only one of which, lack of any markings, was not mentioned in the previous Standard.

There is no questioning that the 1979 Standard is a vast improvement over the 1935 version. However, it falls somewhat short of the German Standard in its call for rigid adherence to the ideal.

The Current
OFFICIAL AKC STANDARD FOR THE ROTTWEILER
(Approved September 11, 1979)

General Appearance:
The ideal Rottweiler is a large, robust and powerful dog, black with clearly defined rust markings. His compact build denotes great strength, agility and endurance. Males are characteristically larger, heavier boned and more masculine in appearance.

A fabulous specimen. Note overall balance, head, proportion, bone, depth of body, and carriage

Size:
Males — 24" to 27", Females — 22" to 25".
Proportion should always be considered rather than height alone. The length of the body, from the breast bone (*Sternum*) to the rear edge of the pelvis (*Ischium*) is slightly longer than the height of the dog at the withers; the most desirable proportion being as 10 to 9. Depth of chest should be fifty percent of the height.
Serious Faults: Lack of proportion, undersize, oversize.

Head:
Of medium length, broad between the ears, forehead line seen in profile is moderately arched. Cheekbones and stop well developed; length of muzzle should not exceed distance between stop and occiput. Skull is preferred dry; however, some wrinkling may occur when dog is alert.

Muzzle: Bridge is straight, broad at base with slight tapering towards tip. Nose is broad rather than round, with black nostrils.

Lips: Always black; corners tightly closed. Inner mouth pigment is dark. A pink mouth is to be penalized.

Teeth: 42 in number (20 upper and 22 lower); strong, correctly placed, meeting in a scissors bite—lower incisors touching inside of upper incisors.
Serious Faults: Any missing teeth, level bite.
Disqualifications: Undershot, overshot, four or more missing teeth.

Eyes: Of medium size, moderately deep set, almond shaped with well-fitting lids. Iris of uniform color, from medium to dark brown, the darker shade always preferred.
Serious Faults: Yellow (bird of prey) eyes; eyes not of same color; eyes unequal in size or shape. Hairless lid.

Ears: Pendant, proportionately small, triangular in shape; set well apart and placed on skull so as to make it appear broader when the dog is alert. Ear terminates at approximate mid-cheek level. Correctly held, the inner edge will lie tightly against cheek.

Neck:
Powerful, well muscled, moderately long with slight arch and without loose skin.

Body:
Topline is firm and level, extending in straight line from withers to croup.

Brisket: Deep, reaching to elbow.

Chest: Roomy, broad with well pronounced forechest.

Ribs: Well-sprung.

Loin: Short, deep and well muscled.

Croup: Broad, medium length, slightly sloping.

Tail:
Normally carried in horizontal position — giving impression of an elongation of top line. Carried slightly above horizontal when dog is excited. Some dogs are born without a tail, or a very short stub. Tail is normally docked short close to the body. The set of the tail is more important than length.

Forequarters:
Shoulder blade — long, well laid back at 45-degree angle. Elbows tight, well under body. Distance from withers to elbow and elbow to ground is equal.

Legs:
Strongly developed with straight heavy bone. Not set closely together.

Pasterns: Strong, springy and almost perpendicular to ground.

Feet: Round, compact, well arched toes, turning neither in nor out. Pads thick and hard; nails short, strong and black. Dewclaws may be removed.

Hindquarters:
Angulation of hindquarters balances that of forequarters.

Upper Thigh: Fairly long, broad and well muscled.

Stifle Joint: Moderately angulated.

Lower Thigh: Long, powerful, extensively muscled leading into a strong hock joint; metatarsus nearly perpendicular to ground. Viewed from rear, hind legs are straight and wide enough apart to fit in with a properly built body.

Feet:
Somewhat longer than front feet, well arched toes turning neither in nor out. Dewclaws must be removed if present.

Coat:
Outer coat is straight, coarse, dense, medium length, lying flat. Undercoat must be present on neck and thighs, but should not show through the outer coat. The Rottweiler should be exhibited in a natural condition without trimming, except to remove whiskers, if desired.
Fault: Wavy coat.
Serious Faults: Excessively short coat, curly or open coat; lack of undercoat.
Disqualification: Long coat.

Color:
Always black with rust to mahogany markings. The borderline between black and rust should be clearly defined. The markings should be located as follows: a spot over each eye; on cheeks, as a strip around each side of the muzzle, but not on the bridge of nose; on throat; triangular mark on either side of breastbone; on forelegs from carpus downward to toes; on inside of rear legs showing down the front of stifle and broadening out to front of rear legs from hock to toes; but not completely eliminating black from back of legs; under tail. Black penciling markings on toes. The undercoat is gray or black.

Quantity and location of rust markings is important and should not exceed ten percent of body color. Insufficient or excessive markings should be penalized.
Serious Faults: Excessive markings; white markings any place on dog (a few white hairs do not constitute a marking), light color markings.
Disqualification: Any base color other than black; total absence of markings.

Gait:
The Rottweiler is a trotter. The motion is harmonious, sure, powerful, and unhindered, with a strong fore-reach and a powerful rear drive. Front and rear legs are thrown neither in nor out, as the imprint of hind feet should touch that of forefeet. In a trot, the forequarters and hindquarters are mutually co-ordinated while the back remains firm; as speed is increased, legs will converge under body towards a center line.

"Movement"—reach and drive, and a level back!

Character:
The Rottweiler should possess a fearless expression with a self assured aloofness that does not lend itself to immediate and indiscriminate friendships. He has an inherent desire to protect home and family, and is an intelligent dog of extreme hardness and adaptability with a strong willingness to work.

A judge shall dismiss from the ring any shy or vicious Rottweiler.

Shyness:
A dog shall be judged fundamentally shy if, refusing to stand for examination it shrinks away from the judge; if it fears an approach from the rear; if it shies at sudden or unusual noises to a marked degree.

Viciousness:
A dog that attacks or attempts to attack either the judge or its handler is definitely vicious. An aggressive or belligerent attitude towards other dogs shall not be deemed viciousness.

Faults:
The foregoing is a description of the ideal Rottweiler. Any structural fault that detracts from the above described working dog must be penalized to the extent of the deviation.

Disqualifications:
Undershot, overshot, four or more missing teeth.
Long coat.
Any base color other than black; total absence of markings.

AN OVERVIEW OF THE STANDARD

In order to correctly judge our breed and evaluate breeding stock, credence must be given to the fact of German origin; the significance of this statement can be readily appreciated when one reads the chapter on Germany. Knowledgeable Americans seek to breed a dog which in every detail resembles the phenotype as described in the German standard. Your author, the first American recognized as a German specialist judge, has always subscribed to this policy.

In 1979, an American Rottweiler Club committee presented a revised standard. Despite having a voice on the committee, some sections of the document I feel lack clarity of definition and some serious omissions exist.

Only those parts of our standard which seem to be at odds with the German version, or those which need further clarification will be singled out for discussion.

General Appearance:

The Rottweiler is a medium-large working dog. Therefore an ideal example of the breed must be strong and vigorous, well-muscled, yet extremely agile. Only dogs in optimum condition, carrying no excess weight are capable of the endurance required to perform the tasks for which the dog was bred.

Secondary sex characteristics should be obvious, with the male more massive throughout, and the bitch reduced in size exhibiting a distinctly feminine head with softer expression.

Size:

The German standard in defining correct proportion says length from breastbone to ischium is 15% greater than the height at the withers; this allows for more length of body than the 10 to 9 proportion called for in our standard. It also states that the depth of chest should not be more than 50% of the height at the withers but not much less.

The range as permitted in our standard is about 1/3 inch, on average,

An excellent, balanced mature male.

Ideal forequarters. Dog is stretched too much, spoiling topline
and rear angulation.

larger than that called for in the German standard. Caution must be used not to exceed or diminish size by any appreciable amount. We are breeding a dog in the medium-large to large category—not a giant breed and not a medium size one. The most balanced individual within the defined limits should always be recognized.

Head:

The head of the Rottweiler, as in many breeds, is highly indicative of breed type. In describing the head, the occiput and the zygomatic arch (bony structure which outlines the cheek and forms a receptacle for the eye) must be well developed. The German standard defines the correct proportion of back-skull (measurement from inner corner of eye to occiput) to muzzle (measurement from inner corner of eye to tip of nose) is as 3 is to 2, making certain the underjaw is neither weak nor too prominent.

Lips: It is felt a pink mouth may be the forerunner to general loss of pigment. The call for dark mouth pigment is in an effort to prevent this eventuality.

Teeth: Recalling the purpose for which the Rottweiler is bred, it can be readily understood why three disqualifications occur as mouth faults. Actually mis-aligned jaws (wry mouth or open bite) are equally deficient and should be included among the disqualifications. It must be noted that *any missing* teeth and/or a *level bite* are a serious fault. Dogs with faulty mouths are receiving too many high placements. These are breeding faults, and will lead to problems in future generations.

Eyes: A serious omission occurs in this section. Entropion, a condition where the eyelids are inverted should be a disqualification. It is a severe disorder of hereditary nature. Therefore, if it occurs, the breeding which produced the affected individual should not be repeated. The individual itself should never be bred and both the parents and the siblings of the affected individual are suspect as breeding partners. Ectropion (eyelids roll outward) and extremely light eyes must be so severely penalized as to effectively eliminate the dog from competition.

Surgery is usually indicated to relieve these problems, but it goes without saying that such dogs are ineligible to enter the show ring. Eye infections of a temporary nature, i.e., insect bites, allergies or conjunctivitis, must be cured before the dog is exhibited.

Body:

The AKC standard calls for a "*straight line from withers to croup.*" However, a slight indentation may be found behind the withers on many of the best specimens. This is where the spinous processes of the vertebrae change direction, causing this perceptible, natural depression. With age and optimum exercise it will often disappear in the prime years, only to return in the declining years. The underline is distinct in that there is only a

Headstudy demonstrates desired straight line of muzzle, correct truncated finish, proper depth. Flews ideally could be tighter, but allowance is made for slight "wetness" in a male.

Flews are too open. Much too throaty. Coat incorrect.

Flying ears and round eyes spoil the expression.

Desired type. Could use a bit more depth of body and better feet.

"Fearless expression . . . intelligent dog of extreme hardness . . . strong willingness to work." Somewhat over-angulated in rear.

Excellent phenotype.
Mature male—head in proportion, good top and underline, posed correctly.

A "typey" dog of incorrect proportion. Legs are a couple of inches too short.
Angle of picture distorts head size.

suggestion of tuck-up in the mature Rottweiler. A Greyhound-like build or a paunchy look is equally incorrect. When viewing a Rottweiler from above, the width at the shoulders, spring of rib and breadth across the hips are of similar dimension.

Forequarters:

If the depth of chest as stated previously must not exceed 50% of the height at the withers, and the chest should reach to the elbow, it follows that elbow to ground must be at least one half the height of the dog. Too many short-legged Rottweilers, especially bitches, are seen in the conformation ring today.

A minor point, but in Germany, front dewclaws are not removed.

Hindquarters:

Muscling on both the inside and outside of the thigh should be apparent. Note that the standard states "*metatarsus nearly perpendicular to ground.*" In posing a dog, too many handlers stretch the dogs excessively, thereby straightening the stifle and causing the illusion of incorrect balance.

Coat:

The call for "*undercoat must be present*" is unrealistic. In some climates, there is absolutely no need for such protection and nature reacts appropriately by not supplying an undercoat.

Please note carefully the recommendations on trimming. To the educated eye, an excessively trimmed and sculptured Rottweiler is unacceptable. "Black penciling" on the toes called for in our standard is not mentioned in the German version.

Character:

Again, it cannot be stressed sufficiently, the Rottweiler has been bred for hundreds of years as a guard dog. It has not been bred to conform to AKC rules of deportment in a Show Ring. No exhibitor with a sense of responsibility should ever enter a dog with known vicious or questionable temperament. On the other hand, judges or any stranger (if only for reasons of self-preservation) should not put their faces on a level with the dog's. As it is not a coated breed, the Rottweiler can be properly assessed with a minimum of handling.

Faults:

The Rottweiler is a working dog, and as such, faults which would in any way impede the working ability of the animal are to be most heavily penalized, while those of cosmetic nature must be evaluated in those terms.

A longhaired Rottweiler—of course, incorrect.

This otherwise nice bitch is lacking in markings—a condition called
melanism. Her head could be a bit more in ideal proportion.

At 3 months, he would be very hard to beat. Breeder: Doroh, Reg. Owner: C. L. Rawlings.

This 5-months-old bitch will never grow into those ears, nor will the eyes darken sufficiently. (She stuck her nose into something white.)

A promising 11-month-old male. Forelegs set too far forward.

Not the desired head type, nor topline.

6

Preparing to Show
A Worthy Puppy

O NE of the more frequent requests I receive is to evaluate a puppy in terms of potential show material. This is not an easy task as in order to perform with any degree of accuracy, one must really be acquainted with the growth pattern of the puppy's line. As a general statement I would say people are much too impatient. Rottweilers are large dogs and it is a fact that the larger breeds mature much more slowly. Furthermore it is generally believed those dogs which mature at a slower rate, last longer. I am of that school of thought. All too often, the young dog that has it together at a year is overdone at three and way over the hill by the time it is four. So we should not be in a hurry.

Elsewhere in this book the importance of early socialization of puppies has been stressed. Anyone intending to show a dog should be aware that this lays the groundwork for a better show dog. Puppies that have ridden in cars and that don't get carsick on the way to the show, that have been in crowds and are not intimidated by it, that learn to go on the leash away from home, that have walked up and down steps, or have ridden in an elevator, etc., are not disoriented when confronted with these conditions at a show. From the word go, they are out in front. Many excellent phenotypes never make show dogs simply because their puppyhood was devoid of proper socialization. No amount of effort later on will ever totally overcome the time lost.

So, the first observation I make regarding any puppy's potential is its attitude. The more bravura it exudes, the better I think its chances for success.

In considering correctness of a 6-8 month old, I first form a general impression—just as I do with an older dog. From then on there is a difference. When judging a puppy one must look first for those qualities which should be set by 6-8 months, such as full and proper dentition, proper eye color and ear carriage, adequate bone, length of neck and proper pigment. Then one looks for those things which may be in a developmental stage. They include depth of brisket, spring of rib, firmness of topline, natural positioning of fore and hind feet, slightly ascending or descending croup, etc. All these can improve—and yes they can further deteriorate also.

If in my opinion the temperament and/or attitude are satisfactory and the overall phenotype is superior, which of course implies sound movement, I would then advise the novice owner to enroll in a handling class. Such classes are often conducted by experienced exhibitors or professional handlers and the neophyte will be given instruction as to how best to present the dog. Not every such instructor will be sufficiently acquainted with Rottweilers to be aware of the virtues and faults of a given specimen but they should, at least, be able to teach proper management of the lead and the "to be expected" procedure a judge will follow.

The fortunate pupil is the one who finds an instructor who knows the breed. Such a person can help a handler minimize faults and show to advantage the virtues. It is always the judge's job to recognize a faulty dog well-handled, as well as a good dog poorly handled. Nevertheless, from years of observation, I believe more faulty dogs, cleverly handled, prevail over good dogs, badly handled, than vice versa.

In any event, we are dealing with good dogs and they might as well be correctly handled. There's less margin for error that way.

During the course of training it is well for the novice to enter some matches for practice. Matches are informal shows, most often judged by aspiring judges. No points are awarded, but generally some memento commemorates a significant win. The ribbons for placements are of a different color than those in point shows. The entry fee is much lower and the atmosphere should be relaxed and conducive to encouraging beginners.

However, I recommend attendance at Match Shows only after a puppy is six months old and fully innoculated. The practice of taking very young puppies is, in my view, an exceedingly risky proposition and not at all wise. Whereas instructors in training classes can and should require certificates of vaccination for Parvo and DHL of all their participants, it is not feasible at a Match Show. As a result many puppies are known to have contracted infection at such gatherings.

The availability of matches varies from location to location. In certain areas bulletins are published well in advance announcing dates, show sites and judges. In others, it is a word-of-mouth affair. Information is usually available at a training class, feed store or oftentimes the veterinarian will be advised by the committee or his clients of an upcoming event.

At many of the Matches or organized Training Classes necessary paraphernalia for showing a dog is available for purchase. Basic is a collar

Ch. Wiessenburg's Blau Max exemplifies a balanced, nice topline.

A promising young dog, under 2 years of age, lacking as yet in body. Head, front and rear angulation, bone, and coat are excellent. Eye is too large. The fading marking on back of rear leg will darken.

and lead. The collar should preferably differ from the one used in Obedience Training and the lead should be lighter weight but always sufficiently strong to assure control of the dog. Another common purchase is one of many products sold to add lustre to the coat. Such concoctions do little more than cleanse the dust from the outer coat. A dull, out of condition coat remains just that, but it's worth a try.

For those dogs who insist on lying on bare, rough surfaces and as a result have worn the hair off their elbows, a tiny bit of vaseline rubbed into the callous will darken those unsightly areas.

Most puppies will not exhibit build-up of tartar on the teeth but should one be showing an older dog, be certain the teeth are clean. Many judges take it as a personal insult when presented a dog with a filthy mouth. It is, at the least, a sign of carelessness and at worst can be interpreted as neglect.

Perhaps I should call attention to the disqualification in our Standard for undershot or overshot jaws and 4 or more missing teeth. Thus a judge is required to minutely observe the mouth for any of these conditions. Proper understanding of how to open the dog's mouth and training of the dog to cooperate are greatly appreciated by every judge. It saves unnecessary waste of time and as it is a requirement, dogs should be trained to submit gracefully. In addition, when the judge approaches the head a handler has the right to ask permission to show his own dog's mouth. If he is able to do it correctly, he has eliminated the hazard of his dog being passed infection from another exhibit.

The matter of trimming is well covered in our Standard and I suggest that anyone exhibiting a Rottweiler read that section carefully. Breeder judges especially resent being shown a "clippered" dog. It is distinctly against the rules and a judge is within his or her rights under the AKC rule covering alteration of appearance to dismiss such a dog from the ring. At this time it would be well for me to recommend *The Rules Applying to Registration and Dog Shows* to every potential exhibitor. This booklet is obtainable for the asking from the American Kennel Club. Not only are the rules clearly defined (and one should always know the rules of a game before participating) but the format for Dog Shows is outlined, making it far easier for the novice to follow what is going on.

Books on the subject I would recommend for those who are not able to get to a training class, as well as for those who are: *The Forsythe Guide to Successful Dog Showing,* by Robert and Jane Forsythe, Howell Book House; *Preparation and Presentation of the Show Dog: The Complete Guide* by Jeff and Betty Brucker, Brucker Enterprises, 5071 Peachtree Dunwoody Rd., N.E. Atlanta, Ga. 30342 and a little booklet entitled *Showing to Win* by Vern and Norma Price available through the Goldcoast Kennel Club in Chicago.

Any one or all three of these guidebooks will be helpful.

One last thought—the showing of dogs for all but professional

A bitch of quality, Ch. RC's Magnum Force von Ursa. Bred, owned and handled by Rebecca L. Chriscoe.

A bitch of quality. Am. & Can. Ch. Trollegens Kyra v. Sonnenhaus, WE 303612, wh. 4/11/79. (Ch. Wotan vom Kastanienbaum ex Ch. Trollegens Fantasy.) Breeder, M. Wilkinson. Owner, Hildegard Mikoleit.

This dog exemplifies the strong, tight back called for in the standard, but so seldom found. Ch. Chaka vom Steinkopf, Sch H2, WF 91300, ADRK 51343, wh. 7/14/76 (Benno v. Amselhof ex Cora v. Leingarten). Breeder, Reinhold Salzmann. Owners: Alan P. Kruse, Benson Ford, Pam Weller.

handlers should be a sport. The word sport is defined in Webster as "that which devotes, and makes mirth; pastime, diversion." Unfortunately, the true meaning of the word is little understood and sadly misused in present day society. This certainly is not confined to dog show circles; it's even more flagrant in the world of horse races, or on the tennis courts, the golf courses, the basketball courts, or the baseball diamonds. The importance of the almighty dollar has replaced the importance of a pastime.

Although there is little chance a dog show can be counted on to provide "mirth" I should like to think I can influence those who read these pages to put the experience into proper perspective. An exhibitor should always bear in mind he is in fact attending a sporting event; he is not engaged in a life and death struggle. He must never forget that of his own free will he entered his dog for a particular judge's opinion. Should he be dissatisfied with that judge's decisions, it is his privilege never to show under that judge again. It is his privilege to write to the AKC with any bona-fide complaint to which he is willing to sign his name. It goes without saying, anonymous letters are given no credence. It is also his privilege, in privacy, to dissuade his friends from giving that judge a future entry. But it is not his privilege to mouth off at ringside. Such behavior detracts from the sport in general and the Rottweiler in particular.

Ch. Rodsden's Ansel v. Brabant, dominant breed winner in the Southeast over a period of five years, with 150 Bests of Breed, 4 Group Firsts and many placements. BOB at Westminster, 1982. Wh. 4/18)76, by Ch. Falco v.h. Brabantpark ex Ch. Rodsden's Gay Lady. Breeders: Jane Wiedel and Joan Klem. Owners: Harold and Ruth O'Brien.

Ch. Phaedra's Amax of Sunnyside, ARC top rated dog 1978. Multi Bests of Breed, dominating the South when being shown. Whelped 6/17/75, by Ch. Igor v. Schauer ex Ch. Rodsden's Windsong Phaedra. Bred and owned by Mrs. B. Murray Tucker, Jr.

Ch. Jaheriss Drummer Boy, pictured scoring BOW at the 1974 Golden State Rottweiler Club Specialty at Santa Barbara. Drummer Boy was bred by Patie and Jerry McCormack, and is owned by Howard and Maureen Wilkinson.

Am. & Can. Ch. Freeger's Nike, Am. & Can. CD. One of 5 champions in litter by Ch. Caro vom Zimmerplatz ex Ch. Freeger's Juno, CD. Bred by Mrs. Bernard Freeman and Joan Laskey. Owned by Robert and Margaret Waters, and owner-handled to all her titles.

7

AKC and the Rottweiler Clubs

IN FUTURE CHAPTERS, International Cynological hierarchy is described. In the United States the American Kennel Club, located at 51 Madison Avenue, New York, NY 10010, is the official governing body.

Membership in the AKC is by Club, not by individual. Clubs qualify for membership and when they do, they select a delegate to represent them. The delegates meet quarterly and in these meetings policy is set. The Board of Directors is elected from among the ranks of the delegates and with few exceptions these persons serve without remuneration.

The American Kennel Club is to the dog society what the U.S. Government is to the American people. It is just about as remote, just about as sympathetic to the problems and proportionately just about as widely respected. Its constituency supports it through taxation in the same manner as the U.S. Government is funded.

AKC has a multitude of functions, principal of which is the registration of purebred dogs, from which incidentally is derived the main source of its income.

The registration of a purebred dog with the American Kennel Club is a very simple matter if and provided the sire and dam of the dog are AKC registered and the breeder has kept accurate records.

The litter must first be registered with AKC. Forms are provided which require that both the breeder (owner of the dam) and the owner of the stud dog testify to the mating of the two dogs which, of course, are of the same breed. The litter form requires that the breeder enumerate the number of puppies of each sex which resulted. For each puppy the AKC

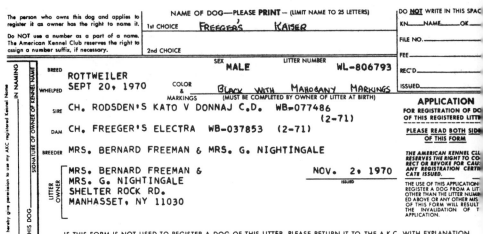

The person who owns this dog and applies to register it as owner has the right to name it.

Do NOT use a number as a part of a name. The American Kennel Club reserves the right to assign a number suffix, if necessary.

NAME OF DOG—PLEASE PRINT — (LIMIT NAME TO 25 LETTERS)

1st CHOICE — FREEGER'S KAISER

2nd CHOICE

DO NOT WRITE IN THIS SPAC

KN_____NAME_____OK_

FILE NO._____

FEE_____

IN NAMING

SIGNATURE OF OWNER OF KENNEL NAME

I hereby give permission to use my AKC registered Kennel Name

THIS DOG.

BREED — ROTTWEILER

WHELPED — SEPT 20, 1970

SIRE — CH. RODSDEN'S KATO V DONNAJ C.D. WB-077486 (2-71)

DAM — CH. FREEGER'S ELECTRA WB-037853 (2-71)

BREEDER — MRS. BERNARD FREEMAN & MRS. G. NIGHTINGALE

LITTER OWNER — MRS. BERNARD FREEMAN & MRS. G. NIGHTINGALE SHELTER ROCK RD. MANHASSET, NY 11030

SEX — MALE

LITTER NUMBER — WL-806793

COLOR & MARKINGS — BLACK WITH MAHOGANY MARKINGS (MUST BE COMPLETED BY OWNER OF LITTER AT BIRTH)

NOV. 2, 1970 — ISSUED

REC'D_____

ISSUED_____

APPLICATION FOR REGISTRATION OF DO OF THIS REGISTERED LITTE

PLEASE READ BOTH SIDE OF THIS FORM

THE AMERICAN KENNEL CLU RESERVES THE RIGHT TO CO-RECT OR REVOKE FOR CAU ANY REGISTRATION CERTII CATE ISSUED.

THE USE OF THIS APPLICATION REGISTER A DOG FROM A LIT OTHER THAN THE LITTER NUMB ED ABOVE OR ANY OTHER MIS OF THIS FORM WILL RESULT THE INVALIDATION OF T APPLICATION.

IF THIS FORM IS NOT USED TO REGISTER A DOG OF THIS LITTER, PLEASE RETURN IT TO THE A.K.C. WITH EXPLANATION.

This is the AKC blue slip. One is provided for each puppy in a litter at the time of litter registration and sent to the breeder. In turn, the breeder must either register the puppy individually or turn over this slip to the purchaser, or he must return it to the AKC. In the case shown here, the slip was retained as the puppy was sold as a pet with provisions made in a contract signed by the breeder and the purchaser that if certain conditions corrected, the AKC registration was obtainable.

provides a blue slip (a sample of which is reproduced above). This blue slip entitles the owner to apply for registration of the dog. Some breeders register all puppies individually themselves. Others give this blue slip to the new owner at the time of purchase and the new owner then sends it in at his leisure. Either practice is acceptable.

In the case of a foreign-born dog, the process is a bit more complicated. A special form is provided upon request and the dog must first be individually registered in the country of origin. A foreign registry five-generation pedigree for AKC files and photographs of the dog from the front and the side must accompany the application. Most important is the fact that AKC does not recognize every foreign registry. They discriminate against any whose records have not proven to be accurate, or of which they have no knowledge.

The elapsed time for processing an application after it has been filed is in the vicinity of three weeks.

AKC registration of a dog does not allege anything other than that both parents are AKC registered and of the same breed. It does not imply the resulting puppy has merit as a representative of the breed, notwithstanding that some novices are fooled into thinking it does.

AKC will celebrate its centennial in 1984. One way to measure the growth of the sport is to realize it took 51 years (until 1935) for the millionth dog to be registered. In 1956, 21 years later, five million was the tally and in 1966 AKC had realized its ten millionth dog registered.

Much more astounding are the registration figures relating to the Rottweiler. Here they are by decade year.

1940 — 11
1950 — 67
1960 — 77
1970 — 428
1980 — 4,701
1982 — over 9,000 were registered

and the figure is still rising. Rottweilers are 31st in registration and 15th in the number of dogs shown in the regular classes.

In addition to the registration of 1,037,149 dogs of 125 different breeds in 1982, AKC supervised over 9,200 events in that year. This figure included All-Breed Shows, Specialty Shows, Obedience Trials, Beagle, Retriever and Pointer Trials and Tracking Tests. AKC does not recognize Schutzhund (SchH) work as a sport and as a consequence, maintains a very hands-off policy on this score.

AKC also monitors Match Shows. A Match Show serves a very definite purpose in the scheme of things. It provides the arena for an aspiring judge to try out his talents, as well as for novice owners and handlers to expose their young dogs. Match Shows are also the testing grounds for new clubs seeking recognition. To attain recognition, new clubs must demonstrate to the satisfaction of the AKC a sufficiency of dog

Litter of 5-week-old puppies, sired by Ch. Centurion's Che v.d. Barr ex Starkrest's Brenna.
— Courtesy, Mildred Stark

show wise people on their membership rolls to successfully put on a minimum of three B Matches and two A Matches. The difference between an A and a B Match is a matter of formality, i.e. premium list distribution, the processing of entries and the preparing of a judging schedule and publication of a catalogue. An A Match is the finished product, as it must be run in the same manner as a Specialty Show.

To date, five Rottweiler Clubs have satisfied this requirement. One, the Rottweiler Club of America, is defunct. The other four clubs are, in chronological order of their recognition: the Colonial Rottweiler Club, based in Philadelphia; the Medallion Rottweiler Club in Chicago; the Golden State Rottweiler Club in Los Angeles; and the parent club, the American Rottweiler Club.

Colonial, Medallion and Golden State are "local" Specialty clubs with the majority of their members residing in the area. The three clubs are autonomous, but this is not to say cooperation among them does not exist, because it does. Occasionally they share in the expense of a foreign judge. They regularly contribute trophies to one another's Specialties. They cooperate in the funding of Rottweiler projects for the good of the breed.

All three Clubs have in common mandatory signing of a Code of Ethics as a prerequisite for membership. These codes vary only slightly and one (the Colonial's) is reproduced in the Appendix for your study. Each Club publishes a Newsletter—monthly or bi-monthly. Each holds a yearly Specialty Show, and in the case of the Colonial Rottweiler Club regularly supports the entry with trophies at several widespread All-Breed shows from Massachusetts to Georgia. This is in an effort to afford the entire membership personal contact with other Rottweiler owners and members

Judge C. Ross Hamilton placed his Open dogs at the 2nd Colonial Rottweiler Club Specialty, 1960, in this order: Gerhardt von Stahl (Freeman); Wilhelm of Townview (Swenson); Hedeboflids Pan (Stahl); and Leopold von Kafluzu (Bowen).

of the Board of Directors, as well as to provide competition in as widespread an area as possible.

The Medallion Rottweiler Club, it seems, has been the most active in promoting Tracking work. Members of both Medallion and Golden State are more frequent participants in Sch H work, although one member of the Colonial Rottweiler Club accomplished a Sch H2 degree with a bitch in an official trial held in Canada under German rules. I believe that bitch is the first Rottweiler whelped in America to be so honored. Unfortunately, the picture of Sch H training of dogs in this country is not always so pure. Many of the so-called trainers are no more than overzealous maniacs, inciting dogs to attack, with no knowledge of, or even desire to know how to control them. This is one of the very real hazards facing our breed today as these self-same maniacs are among those who also (as a sideline) breed Rottweilers with absolutely no knowledge of bloodlines and less motivation to properly place their castoffs. We have entered an era of commercialism in dogs in our country and, unfortunately, that, accompanied by the age of world-wide violence, makes the sturdy Rottweiler most attractive for some very questionable reasons. The devastation caused by war, pestilence and drought can be withstood because the better specimens survive those ordeals. However, inevitably, the destruction of a breed is accomplished when unknowledgeable people persist in contaminating the gene pool with unsuitable matings. Rottweilers in America are a somewhat endangered species. Generally speaking and without going into detail, exploitation is the most serious problem facing our breed and it follows that if the leadership in our clubs is dedicated, this is the problem to which it will address itself.

In order to accomplish unity and gain representation with AKC, recognized breeds form a parent club. A parent club, as the name implies, is the "guardian" of the breed and, customarily, the local clubs look to the parent club for leadership. Unfortunately, the situation in Rottweilers has been somewhat reversed. It is, therefore, the hope of most serious Rottweiler people that the American Rottweiler Club will recognize the need for discipline and provide the quality of leadership necessary to promote the welfare of our breed.

An important contribution to breed advancement made by the American Rottweiler Club has been its sponsorship of the Rottweiler Pictorials. Prepared under the dedicated aegis of Dorothea Gruenerwald and Ann O. Maurer, and issued periodically, the splendid Pictorials include photographs, short pedigrees, and the conformation and obedience records of current dogs—an invaluable guide for fanciers.

To conclude the discussion on Clubs, Western Rottweiler Owners is an unrecognized club of long standing in Northern California. Several new local clubs have been formed, with more in the process of being organized, and we may surmise that in a matter of years others will be needed as a result of the increase in popularity of our breed.

Note: The information on the Rottweiler clubs that follows has been compiled from official AKC records.

ROTTWEILER CLUB OF AMERICA
(*now defunct*)

First Sanctioned Match: 7/19/48—Plan C (Burlingame, CA)
First Sanctioned Match: 5/15/49—Plan C (Redwood City, CA)
First Specialty: 3/4-5/50—with Oakland Kennel Club
First President: Ian Mill
January, 1966—defunct

COLONIAL ROTTWEILER CLUB

Initial inquiry: 12/21/55—letter from William Stahl
Club organized: 1/06/56
Letter approving "B" Matches—waived
Letter approving "A" Matches—4/25/56
Letter approving Licensed events: 1/22/59
First Specialty Show: 5/3/59

Club presidents, with years in office:

William C. Stahl	1/06/56 - 5/62
Samuel Zinnanti	5/62 - 5/66
Edward H. Beretta	5/66 - 5/70
Mrs. Bernard Freeman	5/70 - 5/21/73
Bert Daikeler	Acting President - May 1974
Mrs. Bernard Freeman	5/74 - 5/76
Arthur Twiss	5/76 - 5/78
Alfred J. McNerney	5/78 - 5/79
Mrs. Henry R. Walls, Jr.	5/79 - 5/80
Mrs. John Wehrle	5/80 - 10/81
Ruth Twiss	Acting President 10/81 - 5/82
George Chamberlin	5/82 -

Newsletter Editors: Charles E. Tuttle, Geoffrey Nightingale, Dorothy Wade, Mr. & Mrs. James L. Harwood, Meyer Marcus, Anna Tilghman, Art and Ruth Twiss, Mary and Dorothy Stringer, Geraldine Crawford.

Colonial Rottweiler Club Specialty Winners

1959   Ch. Reidstandt's Rudiger
1960   Ch. Jaro vom Schleidenplatz
1961   Ch. Jaro vom Schleidenplatz
1962   Arno vom Kafluzu
1963   Dervis vom Weyershof
1964   Ch. Schon of Townview
1965   Ch. Rodsden's Felicia
1966   Ch. Ferdinand von Dachsweil
1967   Ch. Ferdinand von Dachsweil
1968   Ch. Ferdinand von Dachsweil

Ch. Dago von der Ammerquelle, RO-68, going Best of Breed (from Open Class) over 60 Rottweilers at Colonial Rottweiler Club Specialty, 1970, under judge Peter Knoop. Owner-handler: Dorothy Wade.

Ch. Srigo's Garret v. Zaghin, BOB (from Veteran Class) at the Colonial Rottweiler Club Specialty, 1972. Pictured here 3½ years earlier in win at Westchester. Breeder: Mrs. Felice (Conover) Luburich. Owner: James E. Ryder.

Ch. Hella vom Marchenwald, RO-729 (wh. 3/15/74, by Elko vom Kastanienbaum ex Cora vom Reichenbachle), BOB at Colonial Rottweiler Club Specialty, 1978. Breeder: Artur Gallas. Owners: Ida and Meyer Marcus.

1969 Rodsden's Panzer von der Hardt
1970 Dago von der Ammerquelle
1971 Ch. Rodsden's Duke du Trier
1972 Ch. Srigo's Garret v. Zaghin
1973 Ch. Srigo's Mädchen v. Kurtz
1974 Ch. Titan Sujon
1975 Ch. Srigo's Viking Spirit
1976 Ch. Titan Sujon
1977 Ch. Donnaj VT Yankee of Paulus
1978 Ch. Hella vom Märchenwald
1979 Ch. Donnaj VT Yankee of Paulus, CDX
1980 Ch. Donnaj VT Yankee of Paulus, CDX
1981 Ch. Rodsden's Kane v. Forstwald, CD
1982 Ch. Northwind's Kaiser of Mallam

MEDALLION ROTTWEILER CLUB

Initial inquiry: 12/1/59—letter from Nancy L. Levine
Club organized: 7/11/59
Letter approving "B" Matches—12/24/60
Letter approving "A" Matches—8/17/67
Letter approving License—12/11/68
First Specialty Show: 7/5/69

Ch. Srigo's Viking Spirit (WC355451), BOB at the Colonial Rottweiler Club Specialty 1975, BOB at Westminster, and at Maryland under eminent breed authority Friedrich Berger. Numerous other BOBs and Group placements. Wh. 6/20/72, by Ch. Panamint Seneca Chief ex Srigo's Honeybun. Bred by Felice Luburich and owned by Joyce V. Reid.

Am. & Can. Ch. Panamint Banner v Hohenwald, CD & Can. CD, a multi BOB and Specialty winner. Pictured going BOB at Golden State Rottweiler Club Specialty, 1974. (Wh. 3/6/70, by Ch. Falk v. Kursaal ex Ch. Panamint Torkeln vd Eichen.) Bred by Barbara Hoard. Owned by James H. and Erna H. Woodward.

Club presidents, with years in office:

Nancy Levine	7/59
Gerry Fitterer	1/60
Perrin G. Rademacher	5/61
Richard F. Klem	6/62
Otto Mueller	10/63
John F. Millet	7/64
Kirk Englund	6/66
Jim Woodard	7/68
Judith Hassed	7/74
Jane Wiedel	7/76
Joan Klem	7/78

Newsletter Editors: Marthajo Rademacher, Doris and John Millet, Sandy Stranckmeyer Gilbert, Bonnie Kuhlman.

Medallion Rottweiler Club was the first Rottweiler Club to hold an Independent Specialty 8/4-5/73, the first to hold a Futurity (in connection with their 1979 Specialty), the first to hold a Tracking Dog test (9/27/80), and also the first to hold a Tracking Dog Excellent test (12/8/81).

Medallion Rottweiler Club Specialty Winners

1969   Ch. Dago v Kallenberg, CD
       Judge, Albert Van Court
1970   Ch. Axel v d Taverne, UDT, Can. CD
       Judge, Mrs. Mary Macphail (England)
1971   Am. & Can. Ch. Rodsden's Duke du Trier
       Judge, Mrs. Muriel Freeman
1972   Am. & Can. Ch. Rodsden's Duke du Trier
       Judge, Richard Renihan
1973   Ch. Dux vom Hungerbuhl
       Judge, Heinz Eberz (Germany)
1974   Am. & Can. Ch. Panamint Banner v Hohenwald, CD, TD, Can. CD
       Judge, Peter Knoop
1975   Am. & Can. Ch. Panamint Banner v. Hohenwald, CD, TD, Can. CD
       Judge, Mrs. Margareta McIntyre
1976   Am. & Can. Ch. Alck v d Spechte
       Judge, Mrs. Gerd Hyden (Sweden)
1977   Ch. Centurion's Che v d Barr
       Judge, Glen Sommers
1978   Am. & Can. Ch. Rodsden's Zarras v Brabant, Am. & Can. CD
       Judge, Robert Moore
1979   Ch. Rodsden's Kane v Forstwald, CD
       Judge, Heinz Eberz (Germany)
1980   Am. & Can. Ch. Erno v d Gaarn, CD
       Judge, H.M. Cresap
1981   Ch. Birch Hill's Hasso Manteuffel, CDX, TD
       Judge, Mrs. Margareta McIntyre
1982   Am. & Can. Ch. Birch Hill's Governor, Am. & Can. CD
       Judge, Roy Ayers

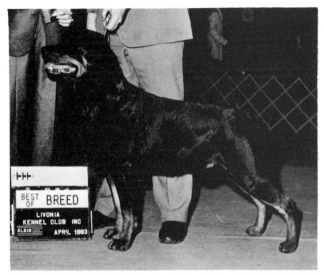

Am. & Can. Ch. Birch Hill's Governor, Am. & Can. CD, TD, RO-2643. Best of Breed, Medallion Rottweiler Club Specialty, 1982. Breeder: Jane F. Wiedel. Owners: Debbie and Mike Conradt.

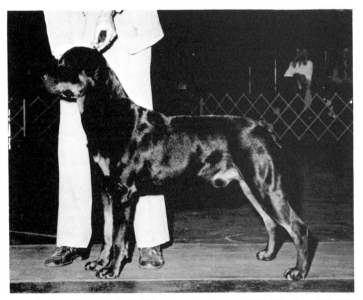

Am. & Can. Ch. Rodsden's Elko Kastanienbaum, CDX, TD, Can. CD, RO-1448 (pictured at 15 months). Winners Dog, Medallion Rottweiler Club Specialty 1978. Breeder: R. F. Klem. Owner: Gary S. Klem.

GOLDEN STATE ROTTWEILER CLUB

Initial inquiry: 5/23/62 letter from John McIntyre
Club organized: 6/23/62
Letter approving "B" Matches—3/31/66
Letter approving "A" Matches—3/12/68
Letter approving License—4/10/69
First Specialty Show: 7/27/69

Club presidents, with years in office:

Huburtus von Rettburg	1963
Gerry Fitterer	1966
Margareta McIntyre	1967
Robert D. Bonsteel	1968
Marvin Goodfarb	1969
Robert D. Bonsteel	1970
Robert Kinkead	1971
Eileen Goodfarb	1972
Margareta McIntyre	1973
Nita Amoroso	1974
Dennis McFadden	1975
Frederic McNabb	1976
Eileen Goodfarb	1977
Michael S. Grossman	1978
Thomas Cushna	1979
Betsy Laties	1980
James Adams	1981
Clara Hurley	1982

Newsletter Editors: Leanne Camarillo, Mrs. Robert Leone, Dorothy Lynch, Winifred Maclean, Clara Hurley, Tony Lukin, Dany Canino, Eileen Goodfarb, Dawn Marshall, Jeanne Schuster, Marvin Goodfarb.

Golden State Rottweiler Club Specialty Winners

1969   Ch. Rodsden's Kurt von der Harque
Owner: Marilyn R. Putnam. Judge: Mrs. Marie A. Moore
1970   Ch. Blitz von Lucas
Owner: Mary G. Lucas. Judge: Mrs. Mary Macphail
1971   Ch. Rodsden's Kirsten du Trier, CD
Owner: Forest M. and Dave Schneider. Judge: Mrs. Bob Adamson
1972   Ch. Rodsden's Duke du Trier
Owner: Dr. and Mrs. Nelse O. Olson. Judge: Mrs. Winifred L. Heckmann
1973   Ch. Dux vom Hungerbuhl
Owner: Elizabeth Eken, M.D. and P.G. Rademacher. Judge: Mr. Heinz Eberz
1974   Ch. Panamint Banner von Hohenwald, CD
Owner: James and Erna Woodard. Judge: Mrs. Bernard Freeman
1975   Sussis Jens
Owner: Frederic M. McNabb. Judge: Mr. Samuel K. Lothrop, Jr.
1976   Edelhunde Aga
Owner: David Bernard. Judge: Mrs. Gerd Hyden
1977   Ch. Rodsden's Rough Diamond
Owner: Coleen Bailey and Samuel Rivkin. Judge: Mr. Robert H. Ward

Ch. Blitz von Lucas, RO-51. Best of Breed, Golden State Rottweiler Club Specialty, 1970, under judge Mrs. Mary Macphail (England). Breeder-owner: Mary G. Lucas.

Ch. Donar vd Hoeve Cor Unum (wh. 9/12/79, by Simba vh Brabantpark ex Ambra Hoeve Cor Unum), Best of Breed at Golden State Rottweiler Club Specialty, 1981. Owners: Clara Hurley and Michael S. Grossman.

1978   Ch. Arlo Jens von Golden West
       Owner: Dr. Melvin Cohen. Judge: Mr. Tom Stevenson
1979   Ch. Oscar v h Brabantpark
       Owner: Clara Hurley and Michael S. Grossman. Judge: Mrs. Eleanor E.
       Evers
1980* Ch. Quanto v h Brabantpark
       Owner: Clara Hurley and Michael S. Grossman. Judge: Mrs. Bernard
       Freeman
1981   Ch. Donar v d Hoeve Cor Unum
       Owner: Clara Hurley and Michael S. Grossman. Judge: Mr. Louis H. Harris
1982   Ch. Birch Hill's Hasso Manteuffel, CDX, TD
       Owner: Vicki Wassenhove. Judge: Margareta McIntyre

*Not recognized by AKC as a Specialty show.

AMERICAN ROTTWEILER CLUB

Initial inquiry: 8/12/70
Club organized: 6/13/71
Letter approving "B" Matches—10/30/74
Letter approving "A" Matches—4/23/79
Letter approving License—8/4/80
First Specialty Show: 5/29/81

Club Presidents, with years in office:
Delegate President: Mrs. Bernard Freeman		1972
William C. Stahl		1974
Elected President: Dorothea Gruenerwald		1975
George Chamberlin		1977
Jim Harwood		1978
Bob Thatcher		1979
Norma Harwood		1981

Newsletter Editors: John and Doris Millet, Norma and Jim Harwood, Sharon
Conrow, Dorothea Gruenerwald.

American Rottweiler Club Specialty Winners

1981   Ch. Donnaj VT Yankee of Paulus, CDX, TD
       Judge, J. Council Parker
1982   Ch. Birch Hill's Hasso Manteuffel, CDX, TD
       Judge, Willi Faussner

Am. & Can. Ch. Donnaj VT Yankee of Paulus, CDX, RO-964T. BOB at Colonial Rottweiler Club Specialty, 1977, '79 and '80. BOB at the 1st National Specialty of the American Rottweiler Club, 1981. Breeder: Pauline Rakowski. Owner: Jan Marshall.

Ch. Birch Hill's Hasso Manteuffel, CDX, TD, RO-2678. (Wh. 5/1/79, by Ch. Rodsden's Bruin v. Hungerbuhl, CDX—RO1189 ex A/C Ch. Rodsden's Birch Hill Hanna, CDX, TD—RO1543) going BOB at the American Rottweiler Club Independent Specialty, 1982, under judge Willi Faussner (Germany). Bred by Jane Wiedel and handled in this win by his owner-trainer, Vicki Wassenhove. Hasso was also BOB at the Medallion Specialty, 1981, under judge Margareta McIntyre.

8

Distinction in the American Show Ring

NO breed book would be complete without giving recognition to those dogs achieving the ultimate award of Best in Show (BIS).

Where it has been possible, the photograph commemorating the win is used. We must bear in mind a dog's merit should not be decided on a photograph because, unfortunately, despite the time-worn adage "one picture is worth a thousand words" not every picture does our winner justice.

Along with the Best in Show and other winners pictured in this chapter, many other worthy winners—including Specialty and Obedience stars—are pictured throughout the book. All have done their part wherever exhibited to educate the bystanders as to correct Rottweiler type and temperament.

AM. & CAN. CH. RODSDEN'S KATO v. DONNAJ, CDX, TD—WB77486, RO-37

Wh. 1/24/68. By Ch. Rodsden's Kluge v.d. Harque, CD
ex Ch. Franzi vom Kursaal.
Breeder: Laura Coonley. Owner-Handler: Jan Marshall.

Pictured winning first Best in Show for a Rottweiler in the United States—at Merrimack Valley KC, May 29, 1971 under judge Raymond Beale. Kato was in the Top 3 of the breed in the U.S. for five straight years, and was the first Rottweiler to win a Group in Canada. He scored 64 Bests of Breed and 19 Group placings including 4 Firsts.

AM. & CAN. CH. RODSDEN'S DUKE DU TRIER—WA 873770, RO-107

Wh. 1/22/67. By Ch. Rodsden's Kluge v.d. Harque, CD
ex Ch. Franzi vom Kursaal.
Breeder: Laura Coonley. Owners: Dr. and Mrs. Nelse O. Olsen.

Pictured winning second Best in Show for a Rottweiler in the U.S.—at Illinois Valley KC
under judge Robert Wills on May 30, 1971, the day after Kato's win. Duke also had U.S.
BIS wins at Kankakee (Ill.) KC, 7/16/72, under Kenneth O. Peterson, and at Central Iowa
KC, 9/9/72, under Robert H. Ward. Also BIS at Burlington (Ontario) Canada, 9/25/71.
Winner of 25 Group Firsts and 58 other Group placements, and 231 BOBs including
Westminster 1970, '71, and '72, Colonial Rottweiler Club Specialty 1971, Medallion
Rottweiler Club Specialty 1972, '73, and Golden State Rottweiler Club Specialty, 1972.
Handler, Richard Orseno.

CH. ERNO von INGENHOF, WC-604512, ADRK-46332, RO-477.
Wh. 8/4/71. By Dux von Stuffelkopf ex Dedda vom Kursaal.
Breeder: Dieter Strehlow. Owner: Charles Hill.

Best in Show at Perkiomen Valley (Pa.) KC, 8/3/75, under judge Donald Sandberg. Handler, Kim Knoblauch.   *Photo: courtesy, Harry Isaacs*

CH. DUKE'S DEREK v. ALTMEISTER, WC-368908, RO-735
(Photo unavailable.)
Wh. 12/24/72. By Ch. Rodsden's Duke du Trier ex Dees v. Odenwald.
Breeders: Annie D. Anderson and Jean A. Wilson. Owner: I Ruder.

Best in Show at Anderson (Ind.) KC, 8/17/75 under judge K. W. Mueller, Sr. Handler, Richard Orseno.

CH. SHEARWATER COCHISE, WC-147402, RO-447
Wh. 5/9/72. By Ch. Lyn-Mar Acres Arras v. Kinta
ex Shearwater Ginger Snap.
Breeder-Owner: C. Schwartzberg.

Best in Show at Brookhaven KC (NY), 9/24/76, under judge Lt. Col. Wallace Pede.
Handler: Alan Levine.

CH. DONNAJ VT YANKEE OF PAULUS, CD, WD-139569, RO-964T

Wh. 7/4/75. By Ch. Axel vom Schwanenschlag ex Ch. Amsel von Andan, CD
Breeder: Pauline Rakowski. Owner: Jan Marshall.

Best in Show at Ladies Dog Club (MA), 6/2/79 under judge Mrs. Doris Wear. Handled in most of his wins by his owner, he was handled here by Mel Goldman. A multi-Group winner, Yankee was BOB at the Colonial Rottweiler Club Specialty in 1977, '79, and '80 and BOB at the first American Rottweiler Club Specialty, 1981.

AM., DUTCH & BELGIAN CH. OSCAR van het BRABANTPARK, WE-110402, RO-1428
Wh. 10/2/73. By Gerlach v.h. Brabantpart ex Ch. Onsbessy v.d. Brantsberg
Breeder: A. Huijskens (Holland). Owners: Mrs. Clara Hurley and Michael S. Grossman.
Best in Show at Orange Empire Dog Club (CA), 7/15/79 under judge Peter B. Thomson.
Top ARC Best of Breed 1979. Handled to BIS by Sharon Zagar. Oscar had 54 BOBs, 4
Group Firsts, and 12 other Group placements. Top ARC Best of Breed winner for 1979.

CH. RODSDEN'S BRUIN v. HUNGERBUHL, CDX, WD-375753, RO-1189

Wh. 3/18/76. By Ch. Dux vom Hungerbuhl, SchH1
ex Ch. Rodsden's Frolich Burga, CD, TD.
Breeder-Owners: Jeffrey and Geraldine Kittner.

Bruin is the top Best in Show and Group winning Rottweiler to date. He has 7 Bests in Show—7/22/79, Sedalia KC, judge Langdon Skarda; 7/28/79, Kettle Moraine KC, John Cramer; 9/9/79, Livonia KC, Mrs. Eleanor Evers; 6/14/80, Rapid City KC, Haworth Hoch; 8/31/80 - (pictured) - Marquette KC, Mrs. Kay Radcliffe; 4/25/81, Packerland KC, Heywood Hartley; 5/2/81; Janesville KC, Mrs. James Edward Clark. He has won 194 Bests of Breed, and has gone on to 36 Group Firsts, 25 GR2, 17 GR3, and 17 GR4. Bruin is handled by Brian Meyer.

AM. & CAN. CH. VAN TIELEMAN'S CISCO, CD—WE 682253, RO-2713

Wh. 4/25/79. By Ch. Trollegens Frodo, CD ex Jaheriss Gunda.
Breeder: F. McWhinnie
Owners at time of Best in Show: Maureen and Howard Wilkinson
Subsequent owners: Jane F. Wiedel and Frank Brader

Best in Show from the classes at Ephrata-Moses Lake Kennel Club (Wash.), September 13, 1980. Judge for the breed and Group wins, Wm. L. Kendrick; judge for Best in Show, Mrs. Sue A. Kauffman. Handler, Bonnie Van Dervoont.

CH. RHOMARKS AXEL v. LERCHENFELD, WE-283248, RO-2744

Wh. 5/16/79. By Ch. Elexi von der Gaarn ex Ch. Chelsea De Michaela, CD
Breeders: Walter C. and Ingrid Rhodes.
Owners: Merrill K. and Hildegard M. Griffin.

Best in Show at Two Cities KC show (CA), 6/20/82, under judge James T. Bennett.
Handler, Robert Hanley. Axel's other awards in 1982 include: 32 Bests of Breed, 9 Group
Firsts, 4 GR2, 2 GR3, and a GR4.

CH. AZURO v. ROWEHAUS, WE-302853

Wh. 2/14/79. By Ch. Georgian Court Bruin ex Ch. Fuller's Roxy von Hause Hagele
Breeder: Milan Rowe, Jr. Owner: Richard D. Efird

Best in Show at Durham KC, 10/23/82, under judge Louis H. Harris. Handler, Burt Halsey.
Other wins include Best of Breed at Westminster, 1983.

AM. & CAN. CH. DONNAJ GREEN MOUNTAIN BOY—WD 731620, RO 2004

Wh. 12/18/77. By Ch. Donnaj VT Yankee of Paulus, CDX
ex Ch. Northwind's Helga.
Breeders: R. Powell Montegue and Janet Marshall. Owner: Anthony Attalla.
Handler-Agents: Carol and Ross Petruzzo.

Mountain Boy holds the record for most BOBs and most Group placements (including third in Group at Westminster 1984) by a Rottweiler, and has won over more dogs of the breed than any competitor. The third Best in Show winner in four generations beginning with Ch. Rodsden's Kato v. Donnaj, CDX, TT, he has won 3 all-breed BIS: Tri-State KC, 11/9/82 under J. C. Parker; Lumberton KC, 3/28/83 under L. Huggins (pictured); and Oklahoma City KC, 11/14/83 under N. Calicura. He is the sire of multiple champions.

122

Am. Dutch & Luxembourg Ch. Quanto van het Brabantpark (RO-1935T-Excellent), Best of Breed at Golden State Rottweiler Club Specialty 1980. Multi BOB and Group placement winner. Whelped 10/11/74 by Gerlach v.h. Brabantpark ex Ch. Onsbessy v.d. Brantsberg. Breeder: A. Huyskens (Holland). Owners: Mrs. Clara Hurley and Michael S. Grossman. Handled by Corky Vroom.

Am. Bda. Mex. & Can. Ch. Jack vom Emstal, Am. & Can. CD, Mex. P.C., SchH1, WD214351 (ADRK 47186) RO-861. Whelped 4/6/72 by Ferro v.d. Lowenau ex Dolli v. Schloss-Ickern. Member of Best in Show brace and BIS team. Owned by Frolic'n Kennels, and handled by Linda Schuman.

Am. & Bda. Ch. Andan Indy Pendance v. Paulus, RO-1002T, multi BOB and BOS winner. One of a litter of 4 champions, all OFA normal. Wh. 7/4/75, by Ch. Axel v. Schwanenschlag (ADRK 44778) ex Ch. Amsel v. Andan, CD. Breeder: Pauline Rakowski. Owner: Anna Tilghman.

Ch. Reza Birs vom Hause Schumann. A multi Best of Breed winning bitch. By B/S Benno vom Allgauer-Tor, SchH3 (ADRK 46856) ex Pasja vom Meltas (NHSB 622601). Wh. 9/28/76. Breeder: A. Kipperman. Owner: Mrs. B. Murray Tucker, Jr.

Am. & Can. Ch. Northwind's Kaiser of Mallam.
Multi Best of Breed and Group placement wins.
Best of Breed, Colonial Rottweiler Club Spe-
cialty 1982. Wh. 3/24/77, by Ch. Igor v.
Schauer ex Am. & Can. Ch. Northwind's Danka,
Am. & Can. CD. Breeder: Mrs. P. Hickman.
Owners: Jessica Nichols and Joyce deVries.

Ch. Radio Ranch's Christmas Spirit, multi BOB
and BOS winner. A favorite of judges and spec-
tators alike. Wh. 12/20/76, by Ch. Radio
Ranch's Axel v. Notara ex Schon Madchen von
Anderson. Breeders: Frank and Ethel Pogue.
Owner-handler: Tom Sallen.

Ch. Erdelied Astraea, CD. Multi BOB and
Group placement winning bitch. Wh.
9/13/78, by Ch. Donnaj Vt. Yankee of
Paulus, CDX, TD, ex Doroh's Erinys von
Eberle, CD, TD. Always owner-handled
to perfection by C. L. Rawlings.

9

The Working Rottweiler

THIS subject deserves special attention as many disturbing influences have come to bear on our breed in the last decade. However, the one positive trend is the increased interest in all facets of the working ability of our Rottweilers. Today, percentagewise, many more Rottweilers are competing and achieving distinction in working trials than was true years ago. We must encourage this activity in order to preserve the capability we so desire in our Rottweilers.

In many foreign countries dogs do not receive the championship status without a working degree. In other countries they are not even eligible to compete for top awards without first having completed a working degree. We have no such regulations, which means the responsibility of breeding for correct working temperament—as well as correct phenotype—must be self-imposed.

For those without knowledge of what is meant by a Working Degree, the following basics apply in the United States. In other countries other regulations apply. Achievement is measured in ascending levels—the first being the simplest routine and the last the most difficult. What is entailed in order to achieve each degree is contained in a booklet entitled *Obedience Regulations,* published by the American Kennel Club (AKC) and available without charge upon request. The address of the AKC is 51 Madison Avenue, New York, New York 10010.

The novice dog and handler will work towards a Companion Dog degree. When the dog has three times passed the test (qualified), at three separate AKC recognized trials, under three different judges and with a minimum of six dogs in competition, it will be entitled to have the initials,

C.D., affixed to its name after the AKC sends a certificate confirming the results. Each individual trial completed with a passing score is referred to as having "gotten a leg."

Once the C.D. is official a dog can at any time compete for the intermediate degree, Companion Dog Excellent, (C.D.X.). Though the routine to be executed is different, the format for achieving the degree is the same. A dog must have achieved a passing score upon three occasions, under three different judges, and, as in the case of C.D., there must be a minimum of six dogs competing.

The most advanced of the Obedience degrees, Utility Dog, is open to dogs with a C.D.X. A dog successfully completing Utility work is entitled to have the letter U.D. after its name.

Further competition in Obedience is offered in the form of Tracking tests and an Advanced Tracking test. A U.D. dog completing the Tracking test is entitled to add the "T" to the U.D., making it a U.D.T. suffix.

Finally there is the Obedience Title Championship, O.T.CH., open only to dogs who have earned their U.D. The O.T.CH. title when used precedes the dog's name.

As to how and where to obtain training information and advice, there are two avenues open. The first is to attend an Obedience class. The second is to purchase the book of a recognized authority and follow it. By far the more orthodox method is to seek out the best Obedience class within a reasonable driving distance. Perhaps the dog's breeder can be of assistance. I keep a list of instructors doing a good job. A neighbor with a well-mannered Doberman Pinscher is likely to be helpful, or call the local Kennel Club. Someone connected will have this information. Just be certain that the instructors teach with an eye to their pupils achieving C.D. degrees. Should an AKC-recognized Obedience judge be on the staff, you can be more than reasonably assured of proper instruction.

Although in no way am I an authority on Obedience training, I know the make-up of the dogs and should like to pass on a word of advice to the novice handler working with the novice dog. Rottweilers are intelligent dogs. Their heritage makes them independent thinkers. By nature they love a challenge and are more easily bored than dogs of many other breeds. The routine for a C.D. degree is not tailor-made to fit the Rottweiler's make-up. It is a lack-lustre activity as compared to training for all the other degrees.

Therefore, I would like to suggest that the handler learn the routine thoroughly, practice reasonably with the dog and try to get the degree without seeking perfection. Too many good dogs and potentially good trainers are lost to the sport in the effort to achieve high scores. The tedium engendered by constant repetition as a result of too much attention to details in an unchallenging routine, leads to boredom for the dog and frustration for the handler. Have fun and be less perfect. As a result, you will not run out of steam and in the end will go much further. Always remember, success in the Obedience ring is a team effort, clearly reflecting the relationship between dog and handler. Don't tarnish that relationship with nit-picking. Build it up and in the final analysis the dog will enjoy working to please you.

Following are articles of accomplished Obedience and Tracking Rottweiler trainers.

OBEDIENCE AND TRACKING

by Jane F. Wiedel

You've brought home your cute, cuddly eight-week-old bear, and from now on what he becomes and how he behaves is to a large extent up to you. It is never too early to begin training your Rottweiler. Rottweilers are extremely intelligent and it behooves the puppy owner to set limits and have clearly defined behavioral objectives from the very beginning. Since they grow into a medium to large size dog, some behavior which may be acceptable for a 20 pound puppy will become unpleasant or even dangerous for an 85 to 120 pound adult.

Formal training with a puppy can begin with Puppy Kindergarten classes which some dog clubs have. Formal Obedience classes are probably best started at around five to six months of age. Before that time, informal training sessions can be held at home to teach the pup basic Obedience—sit, down, come, stay, etc. These sessions should be short and filled with much praise and encouragement. Discipline should be firm and consistent. Rottweiler dispositions vary from calm and easygoing to energetic and strong-willed. Some Rottweilers need only to be shown what you want and encouraged with praise and enthusiasm when they are successful. Others need patience in training and firmness in correction, followed by much enthusiastic praise when they are successful.

Your new Rottweiler puppy needs play time, although it shouldn't be too strenuous or exhausting. He also needs quiet time. Just remember your pup is always learning. Make sure he is learning what you want him to.

You communicate with your puppy through the various tones of your voice and also through the leash and collar. Rottweilers grow fairly rapidly so you will find you will have to check for proper fit of the collar quite often. Because of their rapid growth and the possible danger involved with a chain choke collar, I prefer to use leather or nylon buckle collars with young puppies. Chain or nylon choke collars will be necessary for Obedience training.

Rottweiler puppies seem to enjoy decorating the house with their teeth marks and unless you want your house decor done in "early puppy tooth," it would be wise to invest in a crate. While a crate may not add much to your decorating scheme, it will save much wear and tear on your nerves. Some crying and displeasure might occur when the pup is first placed in the crate.

However if the puppy is rewarded when placed in the crate, either with praise or food, he will soon associate the crate with pleasant experiences. It is a good idea to feed the puppy in the crate and to place him there for his naps. Soon you will find that he will regard the crate as his home and refuge and will go into it voluntarily.

When your Rottweiler puppy is about five to six months old you should enroll him in an Obedience class.

The beginner Obedience classes teach basic behavior, i.e. sit, down, stand, stay, come and heel. Rottweilers are very intelligent and eager to please so you may want to continue training in order to earn a C.D., or Companion Dog degree. The C.D. is awarded by the American Kennel Club after the dog has earned a qualifying score of between 170 and 200 points at three obedience trials in the Novice obedience class. The dog must heel on and off leash, stand for examination, come on command, sit and stay for one minute and down and stay for three minutes. Although frequently Rottweilers can be seen doing these exercises in a rather nonchalant, relaxed manner barely eking out a passing score, they are capable of energetic, accurate performances. It is up to the trainer. As I said before, Rottweilers are extremely intelligent. If you are willing to accept sloppy execution of the exercises, then that is what you are likely to see. If, however, you want a happy, energetic performance, then you, as the trainer, must be energetic in your handling, profuse in your praise and firm in your corrections—never settling for less than you really want. Because, like it or not, you will get the type of performance you train for.

The next level of Obedience training is the C.D.X., or Companion Dog Excellent degree. This degree is awarded by the American Kennel Club after the dog has earned a qualifying score (between 170 and 200 points) in three obedience trials in the Open Obedience class. The exercises in this more advanced level consist of heeling off leash, dropping on recall, retrieving a dumbbell on the flat and over a high jump (34" - 36") and jumping the broad jump (68" - 72"), the sit-stay for three minutes with the handler out of sight and the down-stay for five minutes with the handler out of sight. Rottweilers can excel at this level also. There are various methods of teaching the retrieve. It would be wise to choose one that you are comfortable with and one that works for the dog also. Rottweilers with sound hips and shoulders are well able to jump the required height (usually 36"). Even Rottweilers with mild hip dysplasia can perform the jumping exercises. During training the jumping exercises do not always have to be performed at the full height. Obviously, occasionally they do have to practice over the full height. However, too much jumping by a dog as heavy as the Rottweiler is not recommended. The jumping phase of Open (C.D.X.) work should not be done before your Rottweiler is one to one and one-half years old. Jumping should not be done by a dog whose bones are still growing and developing.

The most advanced of the American Kennel Club Obedience degrees

Rottweilers have a fabulous nose. Grunberg Brummel v.d. Adel, Am.-Can. TD, passed 15 consecutive Tracking trials. Owned and handled by Arthur L. Twiss.

"At end of the track." Am. & Can. Ch. Tracydan's Brinka v. Arba, Am. & Can. CD, TD. Breeder: Judith Edelhertz. Owner-trainer: Ruth Twiss.

is the U.D. or Utility Dog degree. Again dogs must obtain three qualifying scores (between 170 and 200 points) in the Utility class at an American Kennel Club obedience trial. The exercises consist of the signal exercise, two scent discrimination exercises, directed retrieve, directed jumping and the group examination. In the signal exercise, the heeling, stand, down, sit and recall are done by hand signals only. In the scent discrimination exercise two articles, one leather and one metal, are handled by the owner (handler) and put into a group of similar articles. The dog is to pick up and bring to the handler the article with the handler's scent on it. In the directed retrieve three gloves are placed at one end of the ring; one at either corner and one in the middle. The handler (standing in the center of the ring) points to the one the dog is to retrieve and then the dog is to go to and retrieve the correct glove. The directed jumping consists of the dog being sent away from the handler down the center of the ring to the opposite end and turning and sitting on command. Jumps are placed midway in the ring at right angles to the sides of the ring and 18-20 feet apart. A bar jump is on one side and the high jump is on the other. After the judge has designated to the handler which jump is to be taken, the handler (who is at the opposite end of the ring from the dog) points to the jump and commands the dog to jump. The dog jumps and returns to the handler. The handler then directs the dog to again go to the opposite end of the ring, turn and sit. The dog is then directed to jump the remaining jump and return to the handler. The group exercise consists of a stand stay while the judge examines each dog in turn.

As is evident from a description of the exercises the Utility dog is one that is truly well trained. Rottweilers have often attained this high level of training.

In tracking, specifically American Kennel Club tracking, a dog is trained to follow the path a stranger has taken at least thirty minutes and up to two hours before. The track is to have more than two right angle turns and at least two of the right angle turns should be well out in the open where there are no fences or other boundaries to guide the dog or handler. The dog wears a harness and is connected to the handler via a 20-40 foot lead. At the end of the track is an inconspicuous article such as a glove or wallet which the dog must indicate and the handler must pick up.

The American Kennel Club recently added the T.D.X. (Tracking Dog Excellent) test which is a more difficult test of a dog's tracking ability. The track is 800-1000 yards long (versus 450-500 yards for a T.D.) and between three and four hours old. There are two cross tracks (none on a T.D. track) and there are three articles to be found by the dog on the track. Instead of the two starting stakes of a T.D. track (to indicate direction) there is one stake and an additional article (to be used to refresh the dog's scent memory, if needed). The T.D.X. track can cross anything and go anywhere—truly a test of the dog's scenting ability, and dog and handler stamina and teamwork. Many Rottweilers have attained the T.D. degree and several have already passed the challenging T.D.X. test.

Rottweilers make excellent tracking dogs. They are robust, eager to please, with a strong interest in using their noses. It seems to be best to start a puppy between three and five months old. A good indication of the best time to begin training occurs when the puppy starts putting his nose to the ground and following various scent trails. However it is never too late to train, and older Rottweilers (up to nine years old) have earned tracking degrees.

Fortunately a book has been written that helps immensely with the planning and problem solving involved in tracking training. The book is called *Tracking Dog—Theory and Methods* by Glen R. Johnson and is published by Arner Publications, Inc., 8140 Coronado Lane, Rome, New York 13440.

The training methods proposed by Mr. Johnson are rigorous (six days a week) and time consuming (one to one and one-half hours per day). However Mr. Johnson guarantees anyone who follows his regimen will be able to earn a T.D. at the end of eight weeks.

In training puppies it might be best to modify Johnson's program somewhat. The consistency and repetition of training six days a week are beneficial. However in deference to a puppy's age and size, fewer tracks each day and shorter tracks have proven successful. However, Johnson's basic plan and schedule can be followed unless progress, or lack of it, force a delay.

One of the things that is intriguing about tracking is that the dog is using an ability that man does not even fully understand. There are many theories about scent and scenting, but no one knows for sure what the dog is actually following. No one, that is, but the dog. The dog does this all because you asked him. You cannot force a dog to track. He does it because he wants to; because you made it a pleasant, rewarding experience for him.

Dog and handler teamwork is a necessity. The handler must be able to read his dog's actions and signals and must totally rely on the dog's ability to follow the track. It is a true partnership unlike any in conformation or obedience and is really based on respect and trust.

Above all, remember that working with your Rottweiler is useful and fun. Each dog is different and you have to adjust your training to both your and the dog's personality and temperament. But all dogs respond to patience, consistency, love and praise.

Ch. Don Juan, UD—the first champion UD Rottweiler (1968), with owner-trainer Margareta McIntyre.

The first Obedience Trial Champion of the breed—O.T.Ch. Mondberg's Donnamira v. Beier ("Favor"), owned and trained by George L. Beck.

THE ROTTWEILER IN ADVANCED OBEDIENCE

by George L. Beck

As our history tells us, the Rottweiler is a very old breed with a long working heritage. As with most breeds who have survived a long and successful relationship with man, adaptability is the secret to success, and while many of the Rottweiler's past jobs are now non-existent, there are still many ways to put his inherent intelligence and ability to use. One of these ways is in the sport of advanced Obedience. Those who choose this path will find it a challenging endeavor which can accentuate the strengths and weaknesses of both handler and dog. While advanced Obedience is "just a sport," most advanced handlers will agree that it definitely involves work!

The challenge, of course is to get the very best from your individual dog. In order to meet this challenge, one must build a thorough training program which must contain certain key elements. Perhaps the most important of these elements is **consistency.** The dog that is consistently rewarded for proper responses and consistently corrected for improper responses has to progress faster and be more reliable than the dog who receives inconsistent or inappropriate praise or correction from his handler for the same behavior.

Hand-in-hand with consistency goes **timing.** The Rottweiler is a large dog, and most handlers automatically assume brute strength is required to train him; but this is a negative approach. The truth is that timing is more important than strength, especially when applied to reward and correction. If too much time is allowed to elapse between the dog's action and your reaction, the training effect will be nil. Reward and/or correction should be instantaneous for maximum effect.

Briskness and enthusiasm are indispensable elements in a successful advanced Obedience training program that function not only to motivate the dog but also to retain his attention, and a slow, plodding pace is to be avoided. The Rottweiler working at a brisk pace in an alert posture is a beautiful sight to see.

Enjoyment of the work is of primary importance. Love of the work is partly an inherited trait which will vary with the individual dog, but in large part, the handler holds the key to this factor. A good handler will do everything possible to see that the dog is motivated in a positive manner and rewarded each and every time a correct response is made. Dogs in general seem to be a very pragmatic lot and the Rottweiler in particular exemplifies this, sometimes to the extreme. They tend to do what brings them pleasure and avoid what brings them displeasure. However, a good handler will recognize that this trait can be made an asset rather than a

Ch. Welkerhaus' Rommel, UD, #1 Rottweiler in Obedience for 1976 and 1977 (ARC). Much credit is due Rommel and his owner-trainer, Rita Welker. They accomplished his CD, CDX, and UD within a 12-month period.

A truly magnificent example of the benefits of Obedience training in the hands of an expert. Rottweilers of the Frolic'n Kennels winning Best Team in Show at Golden Gate KC show, 1981, under judge R. F. Hernandez. Handler: Stephen L. Johnston. L. to r.: Am. Can. & Mex. Ch. Panamint Rani v.d. Sandhaufen, CD; Am. Bda. Can. & Mex. Ch. Jack vom Emstal, Am. & Can. CD, Mex. PC; Frolic'n Grand Moff Tarkin; and Frolic'n Darth Vader.

liability, for the Rottweiler's reticence to do what bores him is surpassed only by his boundless enthusiasm for doing what he enjoys. It is therefore of utmost importance to maintain a positive and enthusiastic attitude in training in order to get the most out of your future partner.

Another element important in the advanced training program is **persistence.** The handler must not presume that the first few correct responses mean that the dog has "learned" the exercise. Most training is a conditioning process and, while the Rottweiler has above-average retention once he is conditioned, those first few correct responses are but the beginning; much more conditioning must take place in many different situations and over a long period of time before the response is ingrained to the point of permanent "memory."

The advanced Obedience classes as sanctioned by the AKC are the Open and Utility classes. Currently, these classes combined contain a total of thirteen exercises. The number of exercises, however, can be misleading. When broken down into basic components, these exercises show up as a composite of 90 to 95 bits and pieces. Approximately half of these bits are principal features which, if not done properly, will cost a zero on the entire exercise. The balance of the bits and pieces are not principal features and "only" cost points if done poorly. Upon further study, some of the apparently less significant parts take on overwhelming importance by virtue of the number of times they are repeated. For instance, the concept of "Heel" is tested in about forty ways, not including finishes. The dog must "Front" ten times as well as "Finish" ten times. The dog must retrieve five times, and clear an obstacle four times.

The point to all these statistics is that in order to be successful, the advanced dog must be well schooled in the basics, and furthermore, he must have the mental capacity to retain and produce these bits and pieces at the appropriate time—no mean feat, even with an intelligent, well-trained dog and an experienced handler!

In advanced Obedience, the handler should recognize that he is in for a long-term relationship with his Rottweiler. Every effort should be made to learn to read the dog in order to know when it's time to teach, time to praise, time to ignore, time to correct or encourage, especially if he expects to retain the confidence and respect of his Rottweiler.

Given the complexity of the exercises and the skills required by both handler and dog in the advanced classes, it's clear to see that a lot of work is involved. The work is not without its rewards, however, and the reward can come in a variety of ways. While some derive pleasure from the backyard training sessions, others enjoy getting legs and degrees or the excitement of going for championship points. Many love to give demonstrations in the park for underprivileged kids or anyone who cares to watch. Regardless of the means by which your pleasure comes, it's hard to beat that magic feeling when you bring out the working ability inherent in the Rottweiler and see it in action.

Ch. Rodsden's Goro v. Sofienbusch, UDT, SchH1, RO-76, (WB7129). Surely the most titled Rottweiler to date, Goro was an Intl. Champion, Am. Can. & Mex. Ch., Am. Can. & Mex. UDT, Can. UDTX and a SchH1 with V rating. Whelped 8/10/67 he was by Ch. Bengo vom Westfalenpark ex Frolich v. Rau of Wunderkinder. Breeders: J. Sullivan and R. F. Klem. Owner-trainer-handler: James H. Fowler. Goro and Jim Fowler exemplified the ultimate in master-dog relationship. (Pictured going BOB at the V Intl. Dog Show Circuit in Mexico City, 1972.)

Ch. Axel v.d. Taverne, UDT, first Champion UDT male Rottweiler. A Rodsden import. Owned, trained and handled by Jim and Erna Woodard.

Ch. Rodsden's Helsa von Eberle, UD. ARC Top Obedience award winner, 1974. With an overall average score of 195 (3 scores 199), Helsa had 6 High in Trial wins, 2 High Combined. Owned, trained and handled by John M. Epperly.

DISTINCTION IN OBEDIENCE

As HAS BEEN STATED in Chapter 2, the first Rottweiler to achieve a C.D., C.D.X. and U.D. was Gero v. Rabenhorst (A268387) owned by Arthur Alfred and Elsa A. Eichler of Milwaukee, Wisconsin.

Of interest, and a little known fact, is that in order to achieve a U.D. before 1947, a dog had to pass a Tracking Test. Thus all dogs with U.D. titles before 1947 were qualified trackers. After 1947, tracking became a separate degree and the T.D. designation was adopted.

The first Rottweiler T.D. was Russell's Herzchen (WA983108), owned by Barbara Hoard and Russell B. Post of San Rafael, California. Herzchen acquired the title on October 26, 1969, 22 years after the T.D. was first recognized.

In June of 1981 the first Obedience Title Championship for a Rottweiler was conferred on Mondberg's Donnamira v. Beier, (Favor) U.D., (WD589610) owned by George L. Beck (bred by Ruth Parker). Of course, this is the ultimate accomplishment for both handler and dog, and in the article on Page 133, Mr. Beck generously shares some of the secrets of his success with those who would follow in his footsteps.

The first AKC T.D.X. Rottweiler was Stechpalme's Attila the Hun (WD882582), owned by Janet Egolf. He earned the title on November 8, 1981.

Other outstanding Obedience dogs must be mentioned. Axel v.d. Taverne (WA72127), owned by James and Erna Woodard and trained by Jim, was the third U.D. Rottweiler, the second Champion U.D. and in January 1971 his T.D. was announced, making him the first U.D.T. Rottweiler.

An interesting sideline to note: Axel's sire, Bob vom Hause Hader, ADRK 36185, SchH3 was German Rottweiler Working Dog Sieger in 1960. "Like father, like son."

That same time, January 1971, Grundberg Brummel v.d. Adel (WA822306) also received his Am. T.D. Subsequently he also earned the Canadian T.D. It is notable that this dog—owned, trained and handled by Arthur Twiss (a pioneer among Rottweiler owners actively tracking)— passed 15 successive Tracking Tests despite the handicap of being severely dysplastic. Brummel's happiest moments were spent in harness with Art at the other end of the lead. The Twisses, Art and Ruth, have subsequently achieved American and Canadian Tracking Degrees with Am./Can. Ch. Tracydan's Brinka v. Arba, Am./Can. C.D., T.D. (WC356153) and Riegele's Berenger v. Arba, Am./Can. C.D., T.D. (WD24386). These two outstanding Rottweiler owners have significantly contributed to the advancement of interest in Obedience and Tracking on the East Coast. Ruth Twiss chaired every qualifying match and trial sponsored by the Colonial Rottweiler Club in its quest for recognition to conduct an Obedience Trial. The Colonial Rottweiler Club was the first Rottweiler Specialty Club licensed to conduct an Obedience Trial, thanks mostly to her efforts and that of her co-workers.

Am., Mex. and Can. Ch. Rodsden's Goro v. Sofienbusch, wh. August 10, 1967 (WB7129) will be mentioned in the chapter relating to conformation wins but this great performer, whose achievements may never be equalled, has a foremost spot in the annals of Obedience records. Owned, trained and handled by James R. Fowler, Goro was an American U.D.T., a Mexican U.D.T., a Canadian U.D.TX., a SchH1 and on the 3rd of December 1975, at the age of 8½ years, in Mexico, he passed the Obedience requirements for an International Championship. Thus Goro became the first American-bred Rottweiler to attain this much coveted FCI title.

I quote from Jim Fowler's letter — "Credit for any of our accomplishments must go primarily to the excellence, trainability and adaptability of Goro. He lived all his life on the 13th floor of a Chicago apartment building along the shore of Lake Michigan. He rode the elevator every day, walked the neighborhood and never had an unpleasant experience. He loved everyone, especially the children, and everyone loved him. Today I am known in the neighborhood because of Goro."

These are the words of a very modest man, as even the most ignorant of us understand the hours which were required to train a dog in those many phases of Obedience, the amount of time spent in conditioning him and the time and effort required to get to these trials in far away places. Goro is pictured on Page 136.

The first Ch. U.D.T. Rottweiler bitch was Rodsden's Willa v.d. Harque (WB854722), Can. C.D.X., owned, trained and handled by Jane F. Wiedel. Willa was an outstanding Obedience dog. In my correspondence with Jane she said friends called her "'practically perfect Willa' but they were wrong. She was *absolutely* perfect Willa."

Rodsden's Wotan v.d. Harque, C.D.X., T.D. (WB854733), litter brother to Willa and also owned and trained by Jane Wiedel, was the first Rottweiler to be used for search and rescue work in this country.

Although there are no more firsts to report for Jane, under the Birch Hill prefix she has bred, trained and handled several additional dogs to their conformation championships and various Obedience degrees. In addition she has just been approved by AKC to judge Tracking Trials. I am most appreciative to be able to offer my readers advice on Obedience and Tracking by so knowledgeable an all-around Rottweiler person.

Ch. Rodsden's Willa v.d. Harque, UDT, Can. CDX—the first champion UDT Rottweiler bitch. Owned, trained and handled by Jane F. Wiedel.

Willa's litter brother, Rodsden's Wotan v.d. Harque, CDX, TD—the first Rottweiler to be used for search and rescue work in the United States. Owned and trained by Jane Wiedel.

No discussion of successful Obedience dogs would be complete without reference to Ch. Rodsden's Helsa von Eberle, U.D. (WC199211). Helsa, owned, trained and shown by John M. Epperly, received the Dog World Canine of Distinction Award for achieving all three Obedience degrees in less than nine months. This was accomplished before the age of two with an average score of 194. She received the American Rottweiler Club Top Obedience Award in 1974 and also placed among the top ten Obedience dogs in the Working Group. In the course of her quest for honors, Helsa was six times High in Trial and achieved a score of 199 on three occasions. Of his experience working with Helsa, John Epperly says: "Working with Helsa was one of my most satisfying experiences. I feel that all large dogs should have the training equivalent to that required for a C.D. To be consistently 'in the ribbons' requires a great deal of time, patience and a lot of love. My experience with Rottweilers is that they respond more to kind, but firm, instruction than to the more harsh methods sometimes used in dog training. In Helsa's case a little baiting did wonders in many instances. My advice to beginners is to not start alone, but find a good club or recreational class to train with. Socialization is a must for a young dog. If you start with the idea of having a well-behaved pet, you may just end up with a real winner."

Our next first is Ch. Rodsden's Quelle v.d. Harque, U.D. (WB743561), owned and trained by Charles Goodman. Quelle was the first American-bred Rottweiler bitch to acquire a SchH1 and also the first with the SchH2 title, qualifying under German judge Dr. Schellenberg, author of our article on Schutzhund Training.

Quelle defies anyone who says "you can't teach an old dog new tricks." She was acquired by Charles as an older, somewhat of a problem dog. Chuck lives in an apartment in Queens, N.Y. and Quelle had to first learn to be mannerly. Shortly thereafter she accomplished her C.D.X., the U.D. and the two SchH degrees. She is pictured in these pages as a loving companion to Charles' grandmother and also "at work." Remember the two are anything but mutually exclusive.

Undoubtedly there are other Rottweilers with significant records in Obedience. Unfortunately, despite my efforts, their owners or breeders have not supplied me with the necessary facts and I am, therefore, unable to laud their efforts which in no way detracts from their accomplishments.

In reading this section on outstanding Obedience dogs, one cannot fail to notice that almost all of them carry the Rodsden Kennel prefix. In addition, Axel v.d. Taverne was imported by Rodsden and Goro v. Sofienbusch was bred out of Rodsden stock. Great credit must go to this kennel for their active promotion of all phases of the working Rottweiler as well as the correct phenotype. The two go hand in glove because an unsound dog, except in tracking or carting, is very limited in the work it can perform.

Patrolling the area. — *Courtesy, Jos. Hedl*

James Harris with his racing team of Harras vom Kursaal (Rottweiler), Terrimar's Navarre Blue (Siberian Husky), and Sam MacGee (Border Collie). Covering 5 miles in 24 minutes and 8 seconds, the team finished 24th out of 30 competing teams in a 1973 race.

Ch. Rodsden's Quelle v.d. Harque, UD, SchH2—the archtype Rottweiler. Affectionate companion to owner-trainer Charles Goodman and his family, willing worker and fierce protector. Shown above with Charles' grandmother, and below in training with Len Sana acting the culprit. — *Photos by Charles Goodman.*

SCHUTZHUND TRAINING

Dr. Dietmar Schellenberg has been directly involved in the training of over 3,000 dog/handler teams in such varied fields as: Obedience, agility, companion dog instruction, tracking, scent and search work, protection, guard and police dog training, demonstration team competition, show and Schutzhund work, specialized training and dog behavior problem solving, as well as in some Seeing Eye Dog training.

He has certified a large number of potential and actual service dogs, having been the first internationally licensed FCI/VDH Police Dog Judge for North America.

Yet, still more people know him as consultant, as author, as lecturer and as editor of a dog training magazine. I am grateful for his help in preparing this article.

When acquiring a dog of the Working breeds, every owner also accepts the moral obligation to train his canine. Small dogs do not require extended involvement but a powerful animal like a Rottweiler benefits both mentally and physically if his owner provides the correct outlets for his energy and talent. The type of training preferred by the owner is certainly his choice. Schutzhund training, which combines Tracking, Obedience and Protection work (Schutzhund means *protection dog* in German), deserves a top position on the list.

The Schutzhund concept evolved some eighty years ago in Europe. Concerned dog fanciers embarked on a training and testing program for privately-owned canines of the Working Group. The intention was to give the dogs a chance to develop and to demonstrate their full capabilities. In return, the handlers gained an immediate benefit from the utilization of the many talents Working Dogs have. They also received valuable clues for selecting the best breeding specimen. Besides, this training provided enjoyment and satisfaction for both members of the team, and it led to a better understanding of the man/dog relationship.

Schutzhund training is open to dogs of all breeds, even to mixed breeds, if they can do the work. Traditionally, however, German Shepherd Dogs, Doberman Pinschers, Rottweilers, Boxers, Airedale Terriers, Giant Schnauzers and Bouviers Des Flandres are the breeds most frequently used, with German Shepherd Dogs outnumbering all others.

Early training programs were highly individualistic. Exchange of ideas and competitive spirit, however, soon required that standards be established.

For the responsible Working Dog owner, this sport has much to offer. Training is versatile, challenging and most enjoyable when man and dog work as a team. What is more, it can be accomplished in small groups. The time requirements are reasonable. The satisfaction to be derived for the average dog owner of knowing his dog is under control and will behave correctly in critical situations is obvious.

The ideal Schutzhund Dog is a well-behaved, happy, friendly, yet alert, controllable family dog—an asset to society rather than a nuisance. HE IS NOT AN ATTACK DOG.

Sporadic attempts to start a Schutzhund movement in this country during the 1950's and 1960's failed. At that time two- or three-man groups practiced the Schutzhund training individually, independently and often unnoticed by the rest of the world. Their efforts were not wasted though, as today there are three firmly established national organizations in the United States.

The North American Schutzhund Association (NASA), as the older organization, utilized German judges in the beginning. It was at one of their early trials (June, 1975, with Heinz Heise of Germany as Judge) that Champion Rodsden's Quelle v.d. Harque, U.D., owned, trained and shown by Charles M. Goodman of New York, was awarded the SchH I title, the first of her breed in the United States. Quelle went on to earn her SchH II the following day, another first. Quelle is an exemplary Rottweiler, combining beauty (Champion), intelligence and trainability (UD) and usefulness (SchH II). Since then other Rottweilers have participated in Schutzhund competitions and have also earned their titles. NASA has, however, lost its role as the leader in the Schutzhund sport by compromising the trial rules in an effort to gain AKC approval.

Working Dogs of America, Inc. (WDA) was formally established on April 2, 1975 through efforts of Dr. Dietmar Schellenberg, the first licensed, FCI-accredited German Schutzhund judge to reside in North America. His following consisted of, and remain, purists who sought to abide by FCI regulations, thereby assuring international recognition of their titles. WDA is incorporated in the State of New York as a not-for-profit organization, and obtained recognition from the U.S. Government as an educational institution with tax-exempt status. WDA judges are licensed through the DHV in Germany, and as such they can award internationally recognized, FCI sanctioned Schutzhund titles.

United Schutzhund Clubs of America (USA) is the youngest and also the largest group of the three. It conducts Schutzhund trials and breed surveys for German Shepherd Dogs. Other breeds are permitted to participate in trials, but they are banned from top international competitions. USA operates an internal judges program and a title registry, and a loose arrangement exists with the Shepherd Dog Club of Germany (SV) for mutual title recognition. The USA is not affiliated with any other national or international organization.

NASA and WDA are both all-breed Schutzhund Clubs.

To date the true meaning of the sport of Schutzhund training is not understood by the average American dog owner due to the following:

Unfavorable publicity and distorted press reports have branded the Schutzhund as a killer dog.

Clever but unqualified "attack-dog trainers," through their sensational advertising, contributed to the molding of such a false image.

A limited number of properly trained instructors is available.

Pending or enacted legislation in many states classifies the Schutzhund as an attack dog.

Some breeders of working dogs resist the rigors of this type of test fearing perhaps they have lost the true "working dog" character in their quest for conformation titles.

Although AKC officials have shown attempts to familiarize themselves with the Schutzhund concept, the sanctioning of the sport by the AKC is, in the opinion of this writer, a very remote possibility. It has to be recognized that tremendous problems would have to be overcome to make any program feasible and in the long run the fact that AKC is not affiliated with the FCI virtually rules out international recognition and competition (a basic precept).

V.D.H. TRIAL RULES

Scoring System

SchH A	SchH I, II, III	FH	Rating
0- 72 pts.	0-109 pts.	0- 35 pts.	Unsatisfactory
73-149	110-219	36- 69	Insufficient
150-159	220-239	70- 79	Satisfactory
160-179	240-269	80- 89	Good
180-190	270-285	90- 95	Very Good
191-200	286-300	96-100	Excellent

Max. points: Tracking 100, Obedience 100, Protection 100, FH 100
Pass. score: Tracking 70, Obedience 70, Protection 80, FH 70

Schutzhund A

This pre-Schutzhund degree is identical to SchH I, but there is no tracking.

Schutzhund I

For this first SchH degree the dog must be at least 14 months old and it must pass a temperament test. There are three sections: Tracking (A), Obedience (B) and Protection (C).

In *Tracking* the dog must follow an unmarked track of at least 400 paces while on a 30' lead. The track is laid by his own handler and it must age at least 20 minutes. There are two turns, and two articles are dropped which must be located by the dog.

In *Obedience,* heeling is done on and off lead at normal, fast and slow paces, including walking through a group of people. A gun will be fired when the dog is off leash. If the dog should shy, he would fail the trial. There are two exercises in which the dog sits and downs while heeling and the handler continues walking. On the sit, the handler will return to the dog, and on the down the dog will be called to the handler. There is a retrieve over a 39½" jump for an article and a retrieve on the flat. The dog must also upon command leave the handler going at least 25 paces away and drop on command. The handler will pick up the dog. The last exercise is the long down with the handler some distance away with his back to the dog. The dog remains while another dog goes through his paces.

In *Protection,* the dog must first locate the agitator hiding in the field and just bark, not bite. In the next exercise, the dog heeling off-lead must attack the agitator who will come out of hiding and attack the handler. The dog will be hit with a stick and must not show fear. He must stop his attack on command. The agitator will then run, acting in a belligerent manner, and the handler will send the dog after the man to attack and hold. After the command to release, there is a side transport to the judge.

Schutzhund II

This is the second degree for a protection trained dog, again including Tracking (A), Obedience (B) and Protection (C). The dog must have already obtained the SchH I title.

In *Tracking,* the dog must find two lost articles over a strange trail, approximately 600 paces long, at least thirty minutes old, while on a 10 yard lead. The strange trail includes two right angles, to the right or to the left.

Obedience includes heeling on and off lead at normal, fast and slow paces, including walking through a group of people. A gun will be fired when the dog is off leash after the crowd exercise. If the dog should run away from his handler when the gun is shot, he would fail the test and be excused. There are two exercises in which the dog sits and downs while heeling, the handler continuing. On the sit, the handler will return to the dog, and on the down, the dog will be called to the handler. There are three exercises requiring the dog to retrieve an article. On the first, the dog will retrieve a 1000 gram (2.2 lb.) dumbbell over a flat ground. On the second, the dog will be required to retrieve a 650 gram (1.5 lb.) dumbbell with a free jump over a hurdle 39½" high. On the third, the dog is required to climb over a 64" wall and retrieve an object belonging to the dog handler. The dog must also leave his handler on command, going at least 30 paces in the indicated direction in a fast gait and drop on command. The last exercise is the long down, with the handler 40 paces away and his back turned toward the dog. The dog remains while another dog goes through his paces.

In *Protection,* the dog must first locate the agitator hiding in the field and just bark, not bite. In the next exercise, the dog handler will leave the dog guarding the suspect while he investigates his hiding place. The suspect then attempts to escape and the dog stops him by seizing him. After the suspect has come to a halt the dog releases. At this time the decoy threatens the dog with a stick. The dog has to seize the suspect's sleeve firmly and it will be hit twice. The next exercise is the transport of the decoy with the dog

Negotiating the "new" wall. Ch. Mason vom Odenwald, AD CDX. Breeder: Margot Schmidt. Owners: Sol Oven and Patricia Hellmuth.

and handler approximately 5 paces behind. Following the transport, the dog handler will be attacked by the suspect, which the dog is to prevent. On the courage test, the dog is sent after the suspect who is about 50 paces away, and he is to firmly seize the suspect until called off by his handler. A side transport to the judge concludes this part.

Schutzhund III

To compete for this most advanced degree a dog must have earned the SchH II title. There are three sections: Tracking (A), Obedience (B) and Protection (C).

In *Tracking,* the dog must search for three lost articles on a track approximately 1,200 paces long and at least 50 minutes old. The dog may be worked off leash or on a 10 yard lead.

Obedience starts with heeling off leash at normal, fast and slow paces, including a walk through the crowd and a test for gun-shyness. There are two exercises in which the dog sits and downs while heeling. On the sit out of motion, the handler picks the dog up. On the down out of motion, the handler hides for one minute and then calls his dog. The dog will also stand-stay out of a normal and a running pace. In the first instance the handler will return to the dog, in the other he will call his dog. There are three

Unidentified picture of Rottweiler winner of Working Dogs of America trial.
— *Photo, courtesy Hilda Weihermann*

retrieves: a 2,000 gram (4.4 lb.) dumbbell on flat ground, a 650 gram (1.5 lb.) dumbbell with a free jump over a 39½″ jump, and his handlers article climbing over a 71″ high wall. The go-away is similar to SchH II, except that it is 40 paces. For the long down the handler goes 50 paces away out of sight of the dog. The dog remains while another dog goes through his paces.

In *Protection,* the dog must first locate the agitator hiding in the field and just bark, not bite. While the handler searches the decoy's hiding place, the suspect tries to run away and the dog stops him. After the decoy has come to a halt the dog releases. At this time the decoy attacks the dog with his stick and the dog apprehends the decoy again. During a back transport of the suspect with the dog and handler about 10 feet behind, the handler is attacked by the suspect. His dog comes to the rescue. In the courage test the dog catches a fleeing suspect who—after the release—attacks and strikes the dog. The dog holds this suspect and transports him—together with his handler—to the judge.

Throughout this examination the dog must show courage and fighting instinct.

F H (Advanced Tracking Degree)

Only dogs with at least a SchH I degree can compete in this test. The track is laid by a stranger. It is about 1,500 paces long, with six angles, and three hours old. It must also intersect with a misleading cross-track at three places, laid by a second stranger. Four articles, with the first stranger's scent on them, are to be found. The dog may be worked free or on a 30 foot leash. The track should be laid over different kinds of ground and over a well-used roadway.

SCORE CARD

Schutzhund A, I, II, III

date .... Club ....

dog's name .... m/fem

breed .... reg. # ....

owner ....

handler ....

Exercise	Points			
B. OBEDIENCE	**A**	**I**	**II**	**III**
heel on leash	15	15	10	-
heel off leash	20	20	15	10
sit/motion	10	10	5	5
down/motion and recall	10	10	10	10
stand walk/run	-	-	-	15
retrieve flat	10	10	10	10
retrieve hurdle	15	15	15	15
retrieve wall	-	-	15	15
send away	10	10	10	10
long down	10	10	10	10
sub total	100	100	100	100
C. PROTECTION				
search	-	-	5	5
find and bark	5	5	10	10
attack on handler	35	35	-	-
escape and defense	-	-	50	35
pursuit/courage test	60	60	-	-
transpoort	-	-	5	5
attack/courage test	-	-	30	45
courage and hardness	-	-	-	-
sub total	100	100	100	100
A. TRACKING				
handler's track, 400 steps, 20 min. old	-	100	-	-
stranger's track, 600 steps, 30 min. old	-	-	100	-
stranger's track, 1200 steps, 50 min. old	-	-	-	100
sub total	-	100	100	100

TOTAL POINTS ....

RATING .... DEGREE ....

....

TRIAL CHAIRMAN   DVG SchH JUDGE

CARTING

Regretfully, my personal experience in carting is limited to one episode when dire necessity required a test of my Rottweiler's native willingness to pull.

We left the Eastern Dog Club Show in Boston after Group judging this particular December night. It was freezing cold and windy. In addition, while attending the show the weatherman had treated us to just enough of a snowfall to make the streets and sidewalks a sheet of ice. Our entourage consisted of two Rottweilers, their two crates, our two suitcases and a dolly. Having carefully loaded the one dog in the bottom crate, secured the top crate with our suitcases ensconced, we optimistically set off for the parking garage only three blocks away. It wasn't too long before we realized what had been a short downhill walk on clear pavement at 10 a.m. that morning was now, at 10 p.m., a hazardous, freezing cold, mountain-scaling challenge back to the car. Valiantly we pushed, pulled, slipped, fell, gasped for air, but when we started to slip backwards, more drastic measures had to be taken. I unsnapped Maxie's lead, attached it to the corner of the two crates, snapped it back on the dead ring, attached the second lead to his collar and without further ado, took a step forward and simply said, "Now, Maxie, pull." He knew exactly what was expected and other than our having to guide the dolly to keep it going straight, he did the job with no apparent effort. You can believe, he was rewarded with lavish praise plus more tangible evidence of our gratitude in the form of an ice cream cone at the first highway stop. His willingness to perform without any previous training really impressed us and we came to the conclusion the act of pulling might well be another inherited characteristic.

In any event, it is beneficial physical exercise for dogs needing further development and it also serves to stabilize rambunctious or insecure dogs.

The following two articles have been written by experienced "carters" Gwen Chaney and Judy Wilson, and the series of photographs provided by Stephen Johnson are invaluable aids. I am grateful to all. Their enthusiasm is abounding. Hopefully you will share it and benefit by their expertise.

TIPS ON CARTING (1)

by Gwen Chaney

Carting is one segment of the Rottweiler heritage which our family has found to be enjoyable as well as useful.

It has given us an opportunity to introduce a working Rottweiler to the masses. People have a chance to meet and observe the stability of mind, soundness of body, and the fortitude of character which is the essence of the Rottweiler.

A dog for all seasons—at a Fourth of July parade.

A dog for all seasons—and a very merry Christmas.

— *Chaney photos.*

Training

We have found that we can introduce a young pup, four months old, to harness by teaching him to track. The unrestricted pulling, while tracking, provides a perfect way to expend all that puppy energy along with educating his nose.

Beginning carting is *not* a one man job. Always have another adult present. We have made it a practice of using two choke collars and leads set up for an adult on either side of the dog.

At 12-18 months, begin by harnessing and hitching to the cart. Never, at this age ask him to pull anything heavy; a small child will do. All that is needed is enough weight to keep the cart from bouncing and making unnecessary noise. Lengthen the distance (i.e.: 1 block, 2 blocks, etc.) each day.

Harness

There are two basic types of harness: leather and nylon web. The most important aspect of the harness is the correctness of the fit. It should be snug and comfortable, not tight or loose. Most carts come with their own harness.

Cart

How you choose your cart depends upon what your plans are for its use. There are three basic types. 1). A two wheel with seat, built like a sulky or pony cart. Sometimes it is available with runners and double yoke. We use this type for parades. 2). A two wheel with box which we use for yard work as well as parades. 3). A four wheel which can be all purpose. This type is usually used with double or multi-dog hitches resembling the old time stagecoach.

The most important aspect of the two wheel cart is its balance; the weight must be on the axle of the cart, *not* on the dog.

Carting is an excellent technique for conditioning your dog. Gradually build distance, speed, and amount of weight pulled.

Never forget the overall welfare of your dog by keeping these factors in mind: 1). temperature and time of day; 2). type of road surface and the temperature of the road surface; 3). your dog's overall condition. Follow these common sense rules and you will have a happy Rottweiler and happy carting!

Our family has spent many happy hours carting in parades and demonstrations, or by ourselves on quiet country roads. We take turns riding in the cart while the rest of us bicycle. In the snow-covered winter, with runners attached, we continue our adventures only this time the rest of us become joggers.

A happy Rottweiler is a working Rottweiler fulfilling his heritage.

The following series of 8 pictures showing the steps in teaching a dog to pull have been provided us by Charlotte and Stephen Johnson of Frolic'n Kennels.

The first 7 pictures are of Stephen with Ch. Frolic'n Darth Vader, CDX, TD. The 8th photo is of Am., Bda., Can., Mex. & Intl. Ch. Jack von Emstal, Am. & Can. CD, Mex. PC, SchH1, owned by the Johnsons and Linda Schuman.

We begin with putting the harness on dog and walking with lead—no load.

Harness on dog and guiding from behind.

Introduction to skate board. (Pulling it is easier than balancing cart between shafts.)

Walking along with skate board, which handler pulls to accustom dog to sound.

Introduction to cart. The log is used for balance, not weight.

Walking along on lead beside cart to accustom dog to sound of cart and route for training.

Pulling the cart on familiar route.

Jack vom Emstal is in harness and waiting to go.

156

Margareta McIntyre
"riding in class."

Everybody's happy—and the dog most
of all. Dennis and Judi Wilson's Halvar
with friends.

TIPS ON CARTING (2)

by Judi Wilson

Regarding my carting experiences, I own one of Asa's puppies and we have been carting for about a year and a half. I was very interested in carting but knew no one with previous experience, so had to resort to looking at photos. I also attended the Desert Dog Drivers races to see how they trained. I wanted to start with a minimal investment and made my cart myself using the rear axle and wheel assembly of an adult tricycle purchased from a manufacturer. A borrowed pipe-bender turned electrical conduit into shafts and scrap lumber was used to construct a small wagon-type box. There was no machining or welding necessary. The unit is light enough that I can lift it myself and as the shafts are easily removable it will fit into the trunk of an automobile. My pulling harness and traces are of very heavy, wide nylon web with a fleece-lined breast collar.

Halvar (Ch. Gatstuberget's Halvar, U.D.) loves using his muscles and pushing and pulling seem to be part of his nature, so cart pulling was made to order for him. It took two slices of leftover Spam to teach him to pull with the shafts in place. Halvar has given cart rides to pre-school classes, at an Easter Seal fund raising and he and I take the children to school, which means we return with an empty cart. It occurred to me how practical it would be were I able to teach him to pull without a "handler" up front to guide him. This is very difficult for an Obedience dog but with lots of praise and encouragement I am now able to get into the cart and he will pull me for about a city block before he stalls out. We use a familiar route so the dog has no doubt as to where he is going. I will not start training with the reins until he is confident to pull without guidance. When I do, it will be done with a rein attached to each side of the collar and through the harness rings.

I would not attempt cart work with a dog who did not have a good command of basic Obedience. A high degree of control and self-confidence are necessary for safe carting and good character is a must. The dog must be able to keep calm and work in spite of cats, loose dogs, traffic and unusual noises. I use the commands "forward," "easy" (to slow down or steady) and "whoa." These are the same commands I have always used when doing road work with the bicycle and yet do not duplicate any of my Obedience commands. I feel that the carting has been especially good for the chest and back muscles; however, our primary reason for doing it is the sheer pleasure of yet another activity together.

Learning young.

HERDING

Although herding was originally the principal occupation of the Rottweiler, this is not true today. In some foreign countries where cattle and sheep are raised, an occasional Rottweiler will still work the farm animals. This is true in Australia and included are pictures to substantiate this statement.

One also might find this in Germany where the combination of Rottweiler breeder by avocation and butcher by vocation is not uncommon. In cases where the butcher raises his own cattle, the dogs can be seen bringing in the herd daily. In fact, some of the outstanding show specimens are so employed.

In the United States lately there has been an interest in reviving this time old talent of the Rottweiler; particularly in Texas where a few breeders working with Australian Cattle Dogs and Border Collies decided the Rottweiler should also be given a chance. The correct instinct still persists and with no training some dogs seem to know just what to do.

The ensuing article was provided by Nina Seifert in answer to my request for material authored by an expert.

Show Dogs Retain Herding Instincts

by Martha Dahly

On the weekend of September 1 and 2, 1980, the Texas Rottweiler Club hosted a stock working clinic open to all breeds. I was asked to instruct at the seminar, having some experience with working ranch dogs and some success with my late trial dog. I have taught several seminars throughout Texas, but was very impressed with the turnout for the Rottweiler Club. Entries included over 20 Rottweilers and six Australian Shepherds. For demonstration purposes I worked two Bouviers of my breeding and my eight-year-old Australian Shepherd. Many of the entries were champions of record and several had Obedience and tracking titles.

Some of the dogs present had worked cattle previously, but most of them were first-timers. It was fascinating and rewarding to see how many of the dogs still retain stock working instinct. I was personally interested to see how the different breeds characteristically have different working styles. Of course there were a few dogs with absolutely no interest in the cattle, and several that chased rather than herded. It is challenging to me to try to explain to an enthusiastic owner that his dog is really more of a menace than a help.

Typically the Rottweilers work in a very upright and calm attitude, seemingly confident of their strength and size in controlling the herd. The Aussies work further back from the stock, constantly moving back and forth to drive (wearing) the cattle, darting in very low to nip at the heels of stragglers. Interestingly, my littermate Bouviers fell somewhere in between the other two breeds in style. They were active like the Aussies, but worked in an upright posture like the Rottweilers. I was of course tickled to see that both my Bouviers were quite enthusiastic and showed real instinct in their first exposure to cattle.

I always start my seminars by informally gathering the participants together for some basic principles and vocabulary. Then each handler and his dog join me in the pen to test for instinct. Initially, the dog is kept on a long line to avoid trouble. If the dog is responsive and remains calm and controlled, then the line is removed. Individual sessions are usually less than 15 minutes at a time. The dogs get tired or over-excited, and the stock get tired and uncooperative, if worked too long. A great deal of the success of a working clinic lies in the livestock. Never work inexperienced dogs on mama cows with calves.

Generally speaking heavy calves are the best stock for working larger breeds. However, in a seminar in Corpus Christi using ducks and cattle, a German Shepherd proved very efficient with the ducks but uninterested in the cattle. In contrast, a Pembroke Welsh Corgi refused to look at the ducks but then stole the show when it came time to work the cattle. Caution should be exercised when working sheep as they are prone to injury and heat exhaustion. Sheep also tend to panic easily, which encourages the dogs to get too rough with them. There is nothing like a couple of solid kicks to dampen over-enthusiasm. Geese are to be avoided by all but very experienced working dogs. Their bites are extremely painful and can blind a dog. I never let my dogs work horses. Their kicks are calculated to kill. It would be far better to never know if your dog will work livestock than to have his teeth kicked out or become completely frightened by a situation he lacked the experience to handle.

Comments on Instinct

The ability to herd livestock is a natural, inherited ability. It cannot be taught. Dogs with the natural herding instinct can have their abilities refined through training, but unless a natural desire to herd is present, no amount of training will make the dog a useful worker.

The herding instinct is actually a refinement of the wolf-like hunting-killing instinct. The desire to keep the animals bunched and moving stems from the hunter's techniques of wearing the herd down and pinpointing stragglers. In the domestic herding dog, training and a full belly keep the ancient kill desire at bay. However, that instinct is always present and it is the dog owner's responsibility to keep that instinct suppressed.

There are several ways to do this. First, discourage roughness while working the stock. Force should be used on the stock only as a last resort. In addition, do not allow a dog (of any breed, but particularly a herding breed) to run unsupervised around livestock. It is also better to work dogs singly until they respond to basic commands. An uncontrolled pair is inviting trouble.

Obedience Training and the Herding Dog

There are pros and cons regarding formal Obedience training for a dog to be used for herding. Of course, a great deal depends on the individual dog. Specimens with a very strong desire to herd and work livestock will usually not be affected by formal Obedience training or competition.

Temperament also plays a part in how Obedience training will effect herding. Strong-willed or stubborn dogs will definitely need some basic Obedience training before facing livestock. Control of the working dog is vital. Timid or insecure dogs are sometimes adversely influenced by formal Obedience. They may tend to rely entirely on the handler for direction and courage. They often visualize all problems in relation to the handler. This may be excellent for Obedience work, but a herding dog must be able to think for himself and make decisions without consulting his handler.

One final remark on Obedience training. A dog's trainability and desire to "work" for his handler must not be confused with the instinctive desire to "work" livestock. Many very trainable breeds make excellent Obedience or protection dogs, but do not have the ability to herd livestock. The desire to serve and protect home and master does not necessarily extend to tending livestock.

What Breed?

There are as many breeds of herding dogs as there are groups of people to prefer one over the other. When selecting a dog, do not be easily swayed by one owner. Each breed has merits and faults. Look for the breed that will best suit your purpose. Just as in choosing any breed of dog, a buyer must have an idea of what he wants from the animal.

Some of the breeds available are recognized by the American Kennel Club (AKC) and are included in the Working Group. A few of the breeds that were originally herding dogs have become primarily guard type dogs. Of these, German Shepherd Dogs and Belgian Sheepdogs are most notable. Occasionally, a German Shepherd will display a desire to herd, but if herding is to be a large portion of the dog's function, a buyer should look into some of the other breeds available.

Breeds developed and used exclusively for farm and livestock work include the Border Collie, the Briard, the Collie, the Shetland Sheepdog, the Corgis and the Bearded Collie. These dogs are widely known for sweet temperaments and easy going ways. They make excellent pets as well as useful herders.

Two breeds currently spotlighted by their excellent guard and protection duties are often overlooked in the herding ability class. Both the Rottweiler and the Bouvier des Flandres were developed for cattle herding and general farm work. In both breeds, their size and generally aloof attitude and strong protective instincts make them excellent guard dogs. However, these very characteristics result from their herding dog origins.

Training Your Herding Dog

The most important command for a herding dog is some form of "stop." The only way to control both the dog and the herd of livestock is to be able to stop the dog. Some breeds will tend to drop in a "down" position while working. This is again instinctive. The low silhouette provided from this position is less threatening to the stock. Other breeds prefer to remain standing; the down position being a submissive posture. Try to discover a position that the dog will hold on a stay command. Then be consistent in making the dog hold the position until given a release command.

Work with the dog's natural instinct. Some dogs are "headers" and others are "heelers." Headers are not dogs that bite at the stock's faces. Headers are "fetch" dogs. They prefer to bring the livestock to you. This position will leave the stock between you and the dog. Fetch dogs are handy in open pasture land and for general gathering of stock. Heelers, or drovers, drive the stock ahead of them to you. They will prefer to work between you and the stock. Drovers are exceptionally handy in tight places like working in pens or stockyards.

162

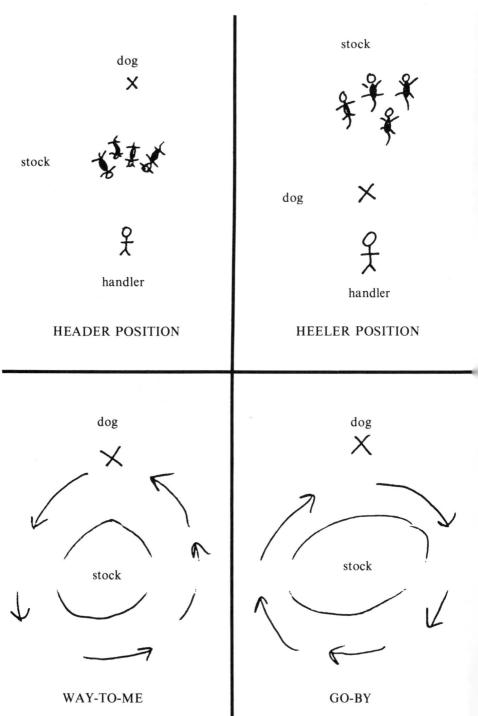

HEADER POSITION

HEELER POSITION

WAY-TO-ME

GO-BY

Basic commands aside from some form of stop include directions for left and right. Traditional sheepherders commands are "Way-to-me" and "Go-by." Understand that the commands must always be in relation to left and right for the *dog,* not the handlers. It may be easier to understand by thinking clockwise or counter-clockwise around the stock. Counter-clockwise is "Way-to-me" while "Go-by" is clockwise.

When applying these terms and techniques, try to give the dog a job. Creating a sense of purpose will enable the dog to apply the commands in situations that can be related to. Move the stock from one pen to another, or put them in a smaller pen. This helps the dog understand that he is working, not just aimlessly chasing the stock from one end of the field to the other.

A final comment on training. Be patient. Loss of temper can cause you to set your training sessions back by weeks. Work your dog only short periods of time and end each session on a happy note.

GOOD LUCK!!

GUIDING THE BLIND

Years ago in Germany it was not an uncommon occurrence to see a Rottweiler engaged as a "Blindführer," leader of the blind. Pictures from the German Stud Books document their use for this purpose.

Today one does not generally find the Rottweiler engaged in the duty of leading the blind. Their size and consequently their need for larger amounts of food make them less desirable candidates to train for this work than other breeds, viz. the German Shepherd Dog, Golden Retriever or Labrador Retriever.

Exemplifying excellence in phenotype and genotype. Int. Ch. B/S, Am. Ch. Harras v. Sofienbusch SchH1, owned by Rodsden's Rottweilers, Reg.

Ch. Rodsden's Kluge v.d. Harque, CD, RO-50, son of illustrious sire, Harras (above)—and himself a top producer. Sire of the first two Rottweilers to win Best in Show in America. Owned by Rodsden's Rottweilers, Reg. (P. G. Rademacher and R. F. Klem).

10

Breeding Precepts

"A little learning is a dangerous thing;
Drink deep or taste not the Pierian Spring:
There shallow draughts intoxicate the brain,
and drinking largely sobers us again. . . . .
For fools rush in where angels fear to tread."

Pope — *Essay on Criticism*

THE CHALLENGE to establish the ideal breeding program is an on-going struggle. It is small wonder so much has been written on the subject. Books on genetics are available in any library. The care of the Brood Bitch and the Stud Dog, the whelping and care of the litter are subjects covered in readily available texts. It is, therefore, not the province of this book to deal with those areas in depth, but rather to outline certain irrefutable principles, to generalize and only be specific when a thought is germane to the Rottweiler.

Proceeding on that premise we recognize three distinct courses of action to be considered in a breeding program:

1. *The outcross* — wherein partners must be totally unrelated in four to five generations. The reason for employing this method is to establish the dominants which will surface. Care must be taken not to breed faults common to both lines.

2. *Inbreeding* — the breeding of close relatives such as mother to son, father to daughter, sister to brother, etc. In the hands of experienced breeders able and willing to cull—capable of discerning the problems at birth, at seven weeks and then adolescence—it is the road to establishing a bloodline. In the hands of the ignorant, it spells the eventual demise of the breed.

3. *Line Breeding* — at least one common ancestor is to be found in the third generation. Line breeding is, of course, the safest and the most

Class is not an accident. Ch. Rodsden's Axel v.h. Brabant, RO-582, owned by Jayne Harstad. Medallion Rottweiler Club Top Producer 1978. MRC Hall of Fame Honor Roll. Axel is a son of Ch. Falco v.h. Brabantpark, a MRC Top Producer, who in turn was a son of Ch. Erno von Wellesweiler, SchH1. Erno's sire was Ch. Harras von Sofienbusch, SchH1, also an MRC Top Producer.

Class is not an accident—continued.
Am. & Can. Ch. Rodsden's Zarras v. Brabant, Am. & Can. CD, RO-1167, owned by Gwen and Earl J. Chaney. Zarras, a son of Ch. Rodsden's Axel v.h. Brabant (pictured above) was Best of Breed at the 1978 Medallion Rottweiler Club Specialty.

commonly practiced procedure. The common ancestor or ancestors must necessarily be of excellent phenotype and genotype, devoid of any serious faults. It should also be determined through previous breedings that these individuals are prepotent in passing on their desirable characteristics. Grandparents, then, will strongly influence the litter as the genes have been set by them.

What can be achieved? The inbreeding reveals recessives, good and bad. We must eliminate from the program any animal displaying undesirable characteristics and we must note these characteristics and be certain that any individuals used in the program are genetically devoid of these particular undesirables. Of course, the opposite is practiced with the good characteristics.

The outcross provides us with access to desirable dominants. Prepotency for these desirable traits can be achieved by line breeding.

Line breeding then is the logical sequel to inbreeding and/or outcrossing. By this method we reduce the gene pool to admit those characteristics considered to be desirable.

Specifically, when one undertakes the breeding of Rottweilers, the "modus operandi" must be constant vigilance on the part of the breeder to reinforce those characteristics which are the mark of our breed—namely, correct temperament, intelligence, natural fidelity to master, good health, willingness to work and the circumspect demeanor befitting a dog of the Rottweiler's heritage.

The following diagram demonstrates a planned breeding which has withstood the test of time:

DIAGRAM OF BRUCE-LOWE THEORY OF BREEDING

Litter:
Bred according to the theory

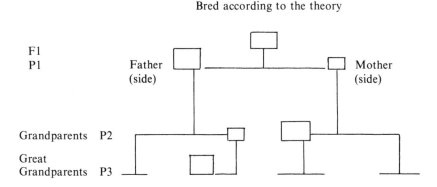

The Sire of the dam and the grandfather of the Sire from the dam's side should be one and the same individual.

"This theory, predicated upon matings between blood relatives, was in use and practical application long before the discoveries of Mendel

Exemplifying distinguished bloodlines. Lore von der Hobertsburg, by Caro vom Kupferdach ex Adda vom Dahl. A great-granddaughter of Ch. Harras v. Sofien-busch, and a granddaughter of Ch. Erno v. Wellesweiler. Breeder: Friedrich Berger. Owner: Ida Marcus.

A bitch of correct size, with type. If you start with one like this, you're ahead of the game. She is badly posed, with front legs too far forward, and her overall length could be shorter, but she has much to offer.

brought about its modification. It had brought about good results whenever and wherever used, particularly in England where it was intensively practiced in the breeding of horses, and availed itself of the Mendelian laws of heredity even before the great monk formulated them.

"The greatest care must be exercised in the selection of mates for close inbreeding and every individual of obvious and congenital defect must be relentlessly eliminated. It has been experimentally proven dozens of times that inbreeding not only fixes and makes permanent the subject's virtues, but also brings out latent defects in an aggravated form.

"Notice must be taken of the fact that the entire type of a breed subjected to persistent inbreeding will be adversely affected unless the degenerating influence is forestalled by careful selection. The Dobermann, but forty years ago, showing more than a casual resemblance to the Rottweiler, has been transformed into his present state by the purposeful breeding for this type and appearance."*

THE FOUNDATION BITCH

To be a successful breeder requires study, sacrifice, experience, a large portion of good luck, patience, farsightedness and, just between you and me, a few bucks can be a great help also. Steadfastness, a willingness to acknowledge mistakes, or to admit failure, and the ability to persevere in the face of adversity when a principle is involved, are also prime requisites. Then, beyond all these very basic qualities is that indefinable something called "talent." In this frame of reference let's call it a "feel." Some have it and some don't. It is what separates the men from the boys, and perhaps it accrues to those who are intuitive and basically relate to their dogs, rather than the most learned scholars in the group.

Having generalized, the next step is to explore (of course, in a superficial manner) the way one proceeds towards the goal.

The first step must be to select the very best bitch one is capable of buying. It is an irrefutable rule that the choice of the foundation bitch is the most important step one ever makes. With a good bitch you have something on which to build; with a poor bitch a lifetime is spent breeding out faults before one can ever start on a constructive breeding program. Beg, borrow or steal, but start with a good one—or don't start at all!

To make the point, we are going to indulge in a bit of fiction. Two and a half years ago our hypothetical breeder selected a puppy bitch out of a litter which he considered to be excellent breeding stock. He personally knew both the sire and dam of his puppy as well as the dam's sire and dam and her four grandparents. This breeder was ahead of the game.

He raised his puppy sensibly, took her to a few match shows, worked her in Obedience, and when she was about a year old he had her hips X-

---

*Gruenig, Philipp, *The Dobermann Pinscher—History and Development of the Breed,* Orange Judd Publishing Company, Inc., New York, 1947.

Follow the line of descent:

Ch. Missy v. Stahl was the foundation bitch of Felice Collesano Luburich's Srigo Kennels. "The majority of my best stock came down from her."

Srigo's Constance v. Missle (at 3 mos.), daughter of Ch. Missy v. Stahl. Dam of Srigo's "E" litter.

Ch. Srigo's Econnie v. Lorac, CD, daughter of Srigo's Constance v. Missle. Srigo's Econnie enjoyed a very successful show career but her outstanding contribution came in the whelping box.

Ch. Srigo's Madchen v. Kurtz, daughter of Ch. Srigo's Econnie v. Lorac, in direct line of descent on dam's side from foundation bitch. Madchen was one of the loveliest bitches ever to grace the Rottweiler ring in America. She was impeccably shown by her breeder Felice Luburich to multiple BOB and BOS wins. Madchen was dam of Srigo's "X" litter of 3 champions, and the "Z" litter of 4 champions.

Ch. Srigo's Xclusive v. Kurtz, daughter of Ch. Srigo's Madchen v. Kurtz. Xclusive is dam of 3 AKC champions and 1 Bermudian champion.

Bermudian Ch. Srigo's The Jig Is Up, son of Ch. Srigo's Xclusive v. Kurtz, and 5th generation in direct descent on dam's side from Srigo's foundation bitch, Ch. Missy v. Stahl.

rayed for a preliminary evaluation by OFA. Results were favorable.

At 15 months she had a C.D. degree. She had in the meanwhile attended some conformation matches with varying success. She was a slow maturer. Between 15 and 18 months, after her second season, she began to blossom giving fair warning that "the apple had not fallen far from the bough." At 18 months our breeder thought her ready and entered her in some point shows. Owner-handled, she acquired her championship, encountering very few setbacks.

Time for the family to go on vacation. This summer it was to be a camping trip in Maine. Our bitch (let's call her "Ideal" as it sounds like the stuff dreams are made of) swam, walked through the woods, chased deer and learned to avoid porcupines for one reason and skunks for another.

She returned home and within two weeks celebrated her second birthday. The day of reckoning was at hand. An appointment to X-ray Ideal for OFA evaulation was made. Our breeder put in 3 or 4 bad weeks awaiting the verdict. (We could have told him Ideal would pass because otherwise there's no story). Indeed, our breeder had a brood bitch!

This is the end of the fairy tale. From now on, it's cold hard facts. If Ideal is to be bred, she must be assessed (both her phenotype and her genotype). Our breeder is now ready to seek the advice of Ideal's breeder regarding known faults and strong points in the line. He has also spoken to knowledgeable people regarding inadequacies in Ideal's phenotype. He will speak to the owner of Ideal's sire. Hopefully the feedback will be accurate.

Our breeder is now at his first crossroad. In order to make use of the information he has received he must record it in a manner which lends itself readily to interpretation. This means charting the facts. (One such chart is described in the following section dealing with the Stud Dog.) In order to do this, categories which are important to him must be selected because obviously not every quality can be covered. Whereas character, temperament, soundness, type, are mandatory, the option to monitor the color of the eyes, or the firmness of the back, or the length of the foreface, etc., remains with the breeder and is indicative of his values and the direction his breeding program will take. As no dog is perfect, there has to be some compromise in every breeding. It is this choice of where to stand pat, and where to give which reveals the knowledge and creativity of the breeder and spells his eventual success or failure.

The breeder is now armed with the facts concerning the phenotype and genotype of his bitch and consequently ready for the next step which is to select the appropriate stud dog.

TELEGONY — Telegony is defined in Webster's *New International Dictionary* as "the supposed carrying over of the influence of a sire to the offspring of subsequent matings of the dam with other males." It is appropriate at this stage to dispel any apprehension a bitch owner may have in this regard. The only possible carry-over from one mating to another is infection which may have been imparted at the time of mating and which remains uncured.

SELECTION OF THE APPROPRIATE STUD

Articles have been written on the subject of the proper management of the stud dog, but regrettably, they are too few and far between. This much neglected, but vital facet of the dog game, is overlooked due to ignorance and shunted aside to avoid treading on someone's toes.

We are constantly bombarded with warnings to breeders, but how often do we admonish the stud dog owner? He has his responsibilities to our breed, ill-defined as they may be. Just because a dog is an overwhelming winner in the show ring does not make him a suitable mate for every bitch. Far from it! Yet how many stud dog owners undertake to research the background of their dog in order to honestly represent him? Surely there must be some of those "gremlins" we referred to earlier present.

Every stud dog owner owes to the breeder approaching him for service an accurate evaluation of his dog's ancestors in the three preceding generations. To point to Grand Champion so and so, and Champion so and so, or SchH3 Working Champion or UD bitch in the fifth generations is very picturesque, but not too influential in the making of the stud dog's genes. It's all very well to sport a superb show record. Unfortunately, show records are not hereditary. There is more to it than that. Many an outstanding show dog, although given ample opportunity, never made his mark as a sire. Too few good dogs with the potential to be great sires ever achieve that distinction if they have not attained status in the show ring, as they remain untried.

Unfortunately, because the United States is so vast, most people are able to see very few of the dogs available for breeding in other sections of the country. Thus, advertising plays a disproportionately big part in the presentation of a stud dog. Pictures are deceiving. Character, gait, color, dentition, etc., cannot be seen in a picture. So it behooves the stud dog owner to accurately present both the phenotype and the genotype of his dog. This means if a dog is being advertised at stud, to circulate a picture taken in high grass if the dog has flat feet and weak pasterns, is hardly cricket.

In order to honestly offer a dog at stud, the owner should have available all information on the dog in question, detailed information on the parents and grandparents and some knowledge of the great-grandparents. Certainly any outstandingly good or bad characteristics must be presented in a straightforward manner. I have said it many times and repeat, there is no perfect dog. So the facts should be presented accurately.

Charting your stud dog's characteristics is a clear, concise method of recording the facts. Here's one suggestion of how you might do it:

Take a ruled page, 8½ x 11, and turn it so that the longer side is horizontal. The ruled lines are now vertical separators. Leaving about ¾" at top, draw 16 horizontal lines across the page, ½ inch apart.

At the left of the page, list the dogs of your stud's 4-generation pedigree down the column, as per:

Great grandsire
Grandsire (paternal)
Great granddam
Sire
Great grandsire
Granddam (paternal)
Great granddam
YOUR STUD DOG
Great grandsire
Grandsire (maternal)
Great granddam
Dam
Great grandsire
Granddam (maternal)
Great granddam

Then, at the head of each of the vertical columns, note a characteristic to be monitored. As mentioned earlier, the list of characteristics is almost endless, so the stud dog owner must include those which are of importance to everyone—namely, character, soundness, etc., and as many denotations as possible. The breeder making a chart for his bitch must make certain to include the characteristics with which he will not compromise, as well as those which are faults in his bitch or line which he cannot double.

Characteristics which you might want to monitor include:

1. Conformation titles	11. Mouth and Gum pigment	21. Set of Pelvis
2. Working Titles	12. Neck	22. Stifle Angulation
3. OFA status	13. Shoulder angulation	23. Hocks
4. Character	14. Forelegs	24. Rear Feet
5. Overall soundness	15. Pasterns	25. Coat
6. General head shape	16. Feet	26. Markings
7. Foreface	17. Chest and Ribs	27. Gait
8. Eye Shape and Color	18. Back	28. Free Choice
9. Ear Size and Set	19. Loin	
10. Dentition (Bite and Teeth)	20. Croup	

Those items included in the chart can be rated "g" for good, "m" for mediocre and "p" for poor or lacking.

When all possible boxes have been marked, the stud dog owner can count the pluses and the minuses in each column, make a summary and in this way will have more than a reasonable idea of the good characteristics and bad characteristics for which the stud dog is prepotent. He is then in a position to honestly and knowledgeably offer the dog at stud. When a bitch owner makes inquiry, he can now ask, "What do you expect my dog to bring to the breeding?" If the bitch owner replies with characteristics for which the dog is strong, the next question must be what "gremlins" lurk in her background and, if the same problems are not present in the dog's, well then it could probably be a desirable mating.

One more salient point must be made. The mating of extremes with the expectation that things will average out is fallacious thinking. We are dealing with genes which for the better part are dominant or recessive so if, for example, a short-muzzled dog is bred to a long-muzzled bitch, an average-length muzzle will not result. The gene for inheritance of the under jaw and the gene for the inheritance of the upper jaw are different. The progeny resulting from the mating of diverse jaw types may well inherit one jaw from one parent and the other from the other parent. The result is an undershot, overshot or otherwise incorrect jaw. The stud owner must understand this and not expect miracles of his dog. He must advise any misguided breeder that moderation must be practiced. Breeding out faults takes intelligent thinking, time and patience. No magic wands are available.

The first few breedings of any dog are more or less test breedings and only after the puppies are on the ground for a couple of years can the verdict be made as to the true value of the mating. Remember, no matter how great the animals may be as individuals, and no matter how sincere, knowledgeable and honorable we may be as breeders, there is always one factor beyond our control: *"L'homme propose, Dieu dispose."* Translated from an old French proverb this means, "Man proposes, God disposes," and the breeder who does not recognize His omnipotence will be taught religion the hard way.

So if with all the correct tenets observed and all precautions taken, things do not work out for the best for the breed, don't wait to recognize a mistake when you make it *again.* Profit by the first experience. Another bitch from a different line may be just the "nick" which produces six Bests in Show, Utility Dog, OFA registered Rottweilers. We can always hope— it's what keeps us going.

CARE OF THE BITCH PRIOR TO BREEDING AND WHILE IN WHELP

Never breed a bitch unless she is in optimum health and then only if the circumstances are such that time can be devoted to her and her litter. We must not look upon motherhood for the bitch as "a big deal", any more than the average healthy woman has a right to expect a medal when she delivers. Nevertheless, we must be somewhat prepared for eventualities and that always spells time out of the breeder's schedule. So set it aside just in case.

Some two months before the anticipated breeding the bitch should be tested for parasites. This leaves sufficient time for treatment should she be found in need of it. Vaccinate for distemper, hepatitis, leptospirosis and kennel cough at the same time. Test for brucellosis. Parvo shots must be current.

Continue her daily exercise and be careful not to overfeed the bitch for the first 5 to 6 weeks after the breeding. Presuming she has been on a balanced diet and fed two times per day, maintain her on same, adding two teaspoons of edible bonemeal to that diet. At seven to eight weeks, depending upon the individual bitch, it may be desirable to feed her the

American, Dutch & Belgian CH. OSCAR van het BRABANTPARK.

American, Dutch & Luxembourg CH. QUANTO van het BRABANTPARK.

American, Dutch & Belgian Ch. Oscar van het Brabantpark, WE110402, RO-1428. Whelped 10/2/73. Breeder, Mej. A. Huyskens (Holland).
and
American, Dutch & Luxembourg Ch. Quanto van het Brabantpark, WE46606, RO-1935T-Excellent. Whelped 10/1/74.
Breeder: Mej. A. Huyskens (Holland).
Both dogs owned by: Mrs. Clara Hurley and Michael S. Grossman.

<pre>
                                    Bsg. Ch. Harras v. Sofienbusch/I
                        Brutus v.d. Kurmark
                                    Biene v. Felsenquelle
            Moritz v. Silahopp—H.D. Free Utrecht
                                    Droll v.d. Brotzingergasse/II
                        Queen v.d. Solitude
                                    Fanny v.d. Solitude
    Gerlach v.h. Brabantpark—H.D. Free Utrecht
                                    Hektor v.d. Solitude
                        Fetz v. Oelberg/I—RO-25 H.D. Free
                                    Dora v.d. Brotzingergasse
            Ch. Burga v.h. Brabantpark—H.D. Free Utrecht
                                    Duco v.d. Brantsberg
                        Ch. Rona v.d. Brantsberg
                                    Ch. Anka v. Sudpark
</pre>

<pre>
                                    Mirko v.d. Solitude II
                        Axel v. Leitgraben/III
                                    Bsgn. Cora v. Lindeck/I
            Einar v.h. Brabantpark—H.D. Free Utrecht
                                    Fetz v. Oelberg/I—RO-25 H.D. Free
                        Ch. Burga v.h. Brabantpark—H.D. Free Utrecht
                                    Ch. Rona v.d. Brantsberg
    Ch. Onsbessy v.d. Brantsberg—H.D. Free Utrecht
                                    Ch. Balder v. Habenichts
                        Ajax v.d. Brantsberg
                                    Nicolette v.d. Brantsberg
            Capsones v.h. Brabantpark—H.D. Free Utrecht
                                    Duco v.d. Brantsberg
                        Ch. Rona v.d. Brantsberg
                                    Ch. Anka v. Sudpark
</pre>

Oscar and Quanto are full brothers from different litters. They exemplify the excellence which results when intelligent line-breeding is the tool for selection. Consult the pedigree. The dogs are further written about in Chapter 8 saluting Distinguished Winners, and their ancestors are mentioned throughout the text. (Incidentally, the v.d. Brantsberg prefix identifies the kennel owned by Mrs. Brinkhorst, author of our Holland chapter.)

same amount overall, but divide it into three meals. If liver agrees with her, add a small amount to her daily food ration. If she seems to be carrying a large litter and is very hungry, increase the amount of food by about one quarter. Keep on with the exercise until the ninth week when caution should be observed.

Average gestation period is 9 weeks (63 days), but many bitches will whelp from the 57th day on, so be prepared and build the whelping box well in advance of her due date. The "style" and dimensions are discretional. Be certain it is sturdy, is raised off the floor, has a pig rail of sorts and the sides are sufficiently high.

For guidance in building your own whelping box, we have included a plan designed by Rottweiler breeder Clara Hurley in the Appendix.

Start to accustom the bitch to the whelping box at least one week prior to anticipated delivery. Line the floor of the box with four or five layers of newspaper. For sanitary reasons, remove any excess hair around the nipples. Have on hand:

1. Scale
2. Thick white thread for tying cord if necessary
3. Bandage scissors for cutting cord if necessary
4. Antiseptic soap
5. Lots of old turkish towels
6. Thoroughly rinsed gallon plastic bottle (to be filled with hot water)
7. Laundry basket or similar container
8. Plenty of light and heat (85° must be maintained a couple of days)
9. Lots and lots of newspaper
10. Big bags for garbage
11. Bouillon cubes for broth for the bitch
12. A bit of cognac to use as stimulant if necessary
13. Esbilac or 6 cans of goat's milk, baby bottles and/or feeding tube in case of a problem with bitch's milk
14. Red nail polish for identification or any other device to differentiate one puppy from another
15. Pen and paper for recording whelping data . (*See sample,* P. 182.)
16. WHEREABOUTS OF YOUR VET

Average normal canine temperature is 101.5°. On or about the 58th day, the bitch's temperature should be taken A.M. and P.M. If it drops below 98°, the pups should start to come within 12 hours. If the temperature is over 102.5°, call your vet. Most bitches will refuse the meal just prior to the onset of labor but neither that nor the temperature drop are infallible rules.

Routinely, bitches scratch up the papers to make the "nest." They can do this days in advance of delivery, or last minuteish. When they begin to shiver and shake, visible signs of labor are at hand. Keep a watchful eye but trust her animal instincts to carry her through. If she actively labors and no pup is delivered over a period of more than two hours, CALL YOUR VET.

Just as certain bitches may deliver somewhat prematurely, others may go over the usual 63-day term. However, if such is the case, the bitch must be very carefully monitored and your vet should be consulted.

WHELPING AND CARE OF THE LITTER

This part of the text dealing with whelping is only meant to acquaint the novice with what most likely will transpire and remind the experienced breeder of what he already knows. Novices, after an introduction to the subject, will do well to purchase one or more books dealing specifically and/or scientifically with the subject.*

When the bitch showed signs of being ready to whelp, you called your vet and alerted him. He will now be more readily available should you need his help. Clear the whelping area of strangers and young children, and of other animals. The bitch should have no distractions. She is entitled to peace and quiet. This is not a side show for the entertainment of children. When they are old enough to be of help, it's a different story. She must concentrate on the business at hand and especially a maiden bitch can easily be confused. She is operating on instinct. Each step follows the last rather automatically if she is left to her own devices. Undue interference by humans only complicates the issue. Give her the chance to do it her way. Rottweiler bitches especially can be very independent. They have their own ideas about many things, not the least of which is whelping. Some are very protective the moment the puppy is born. If that is the case, do not constantly hover over her and her puppies. Just see that they are nursing and she is cleaning them. Once the first one is born, normal intervals are anywhere from five minutes to one to two hours between the rest. However, if she is in active labor for more than an hour and no puppy is delivered, CALL YOUR VET.

Some of the things you should know about and be prepared to carry out:

1. How to help in a breech birth.
2. Some of the placentae can be removed after separation as ingesting too many in a large litter often gives the bitch diarrhea.
3. How to remove the sac if the bitch does not.
4. How to get a puppy going if it is not breathing.
5. If she is in labor and you feel pups are in danger of being crushed, remove them to the basket beside her. The basket should be lined with towels, and the plastic bottle filled with 85° water should be in it for them to nestle against. Put the basket where she can see

*1. Delbert G. Carlson, D.V.M. and James M. Giffin, M.D., *Dog Owner's Home Veterinary Handbook,* Howell Book House.

2. Leon F. Whitney, D.V.M., *The Complete Book of Dog Care,* Doubleday & Co.

3. Dr. Herbert Richards, *Dog Breeding For Professionals,* T.F.H. Publications, Inc.

4. Hilary Harmar, *Dogs and How To Breed Them,* T.F.H. Publications, Inc.

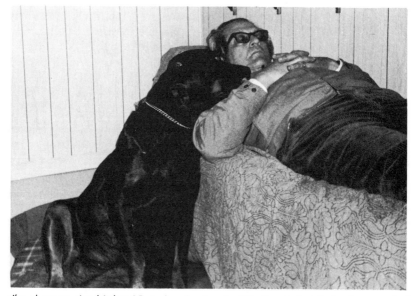

"I'm about to give birth to 15, and you're sleeping! That's not what the book says to do."
— *Photo, courtesy Wayburns*

it—right under her nose—as any whining where she cannot see what is going on might upset her. Return all pups to her when the next pup is delivered. It gets to be an "in again, out again Finnegan" game after a while, but the bitch, if she accepts the routine, is free to care for the last born. One of my bitches, after two go-arounds, picked them up in her mouth and stuck them in the basket herself when another pup was on the way. You know our dogs are the smartest!

6. Offer her warm bouillon at intervals. It's a tiring procedure and the bouillon will give her energy.

7. If things come to a halt, put the pups in the basket and try to get her up and out for a moment. If she will relieve herself, the stirring around may get things going. A word of warning—put her on a lead and take a towel along. Some bitches may entertain ideas of going under a bush or behind a rock to complete the job. Use the towel to grasp the newborn if one plops out on the way. They are extremely slippery, so handle it with care. On the other hand, if the bitch refuses to leave the box, do not force her.

8. Any puppy consistently falling off the nipple should be examined for cleft palate or other serious congenital fault. Provided none are apparent and the puppy is otherwise worthy of saving, it can be tube or bottle fed with a formula of goat's milk and a drop of brandy or an available product such as Esbilac. Tube feeding is

preferable by far, but only in the hands of a person knowledgeable on the subject. Have your vet or an experienced breeder describe or demonstrate the method in advance of the whelping date.

9. Make certain all pups to be retained get their fair share of the first milk called colostrum. It provides them with passive immunity to the various diseases for which the dam has been vaccinated or otherwise has active immunity. This passive immunity is short-lived. Many factors affect the length of time protection is provided. Later on your vet must advise you as to the necessary course of vaccinations for the litter.

10. The assumption up to this point is the whelping has gone smoothly. (Again, this text in no way presumes expertise on whelping problems. They must be referred to your vet.) If and when you think the bitch has finished delivering, inform your vet. He most probably will want to examine her and administer a shot to clear the uterus.

11. Young Rottweiler bitches in good health customarily produce litters of from six to ten puppies. In my view, ten puppies are too many for any dam to raise. Rottweiler whelps are very demanding. A breeder has but to observe a two-week old litter in action when the dam returns to the box after even the shortest sojourn. All hell breaks loose! It is my posture that to raise eight good healthy ones is sufficient task for any bitch. This is, of course, a personal opinion but having been trained by a German, I am influenced by their thinking. It is fair to say many American breeders do not agree.

12. Notwithstanding and regardless of the size of the litter, there are some pups which should be automatic culls. There is absolutely no sense in raising a Rottweiler when from day one it exhibits congenital or disqualifying breed faults. The cleft palate has been mentioned as one. A puppy without eyebrow markings or with a large white spot on the chest or white on the feet or long fringe on the ears or any color pattern other than described in the Standard (I personally have never seen that condition), should be culled immediately.

After the ordeal of whelping is over and the bitch has been checked out and fed and the box has been cleaned up, make certain the puppy room is warm enough (85° for the first couple of days) and free of drafts. Make sure every puppy has suckled, as a hungry puppy is a cold puppy and shortly a dead puppy.

It is now time for you to relax and leave the bitch to her own devices for a short while.

While lactating, the bitch should be fed on a high protein diet with lots of liquid available. I feed three to four times per day. The amount depends on the size of the litter and the individual bitch. She must be observed and if she is obviously losing weight, her rations must be increased.

Whelping Data

Puppy #	Time	Sex	Weight	Identity	Placenta	Vitality	Dewclaws	Remarks
1	10:30 PM	M	15 oz.	blue	yes	good	left rear	active nurser
2	10:40 PM	F	14 oz.	pink	yes	good	no rear	long body, good bone
3	10:55 PM	M	18 oz.	orange	yes	excellent	both rear	cobby, large head
4	11:30 PM	M	16 oz.	dark green	yes	fair	left double	small white spot on chest
5	12:15 AM	F	15 oz.	purple	yes	excellent	no rear	good bone, few white hairs on chest, cobby
6	1:30 AM	F	12 oz.	light green	yes	excellent	both rear	smaller, nice head
7	3:00 AM	F	14 oz.	white	yes	good	no rear	breach, good proportion
8	3:20 AM	F	14 oz.	brown	yes	poor	both rear	ears (low set), slow nurser, bitch not interested. Cull?
9	5:00 AM	M	18 oz.	grey	yes	poor	both rear	nicest male, a bit hard to get started

Sample of a record you might want to keep.

Keep a daily chart noting particulars about the pups. I weigh each puppy every day at the same time. This provides a check, as loss of weight or failure to gain are indications of trouble afoot.

Cut the tips off the puppies' nails at four days and regularly thereafter to prevent their scratching the dam's breasts. Normally, at four days tails are docked and dewclaws are removed. Tails should be docked leaving one and a half to two vertebrae. This is extremely difficult to determine at so young an age. If the vet does not know Rottweilers but has successfully docked Giant Schnauzers which call for docking at second and third joint (approximately 1½" to 3" long at maturity), and Bouviers des Flandres (2 to 3 vertebrae), then he must be informed to dock the Rottweiler on the short side of these two breeds. The ordinary Doberman, Boxer or terrier tail is not comparable, nor is the Pembroke Welsh Corgi or the Old English Sheepdog.

It is well to go into this thoroughly with the vet as exceeding consternation for a new owner, unnecessary pain for the puppy and considerable expense for the breeder are incurred when tails are incorrectly docked the first time and must be redone.

There is an alternative to having the tail surgically docked by the veterinarian and for those breeders who have courage (although at first it may sound barbaric), it has much to commend it. Through the courtesy of Mrs. Eileen Smith, the author of the article, I have permission to reprint the method as she described it in the *Rottweiler Club of Canada Newsletter*. Neither your author, Mrs. Smith, nor Howell Book House assume any responsibility for its success. So you are on your own if you wish to try.

TAILS—Do You Dock or Tie?

by Eileen Smith

My father being a "terrier" man, I am very familiar with the surgical removal of tails and the traumatic experience this is for the whelps and more so, the bitch. Having whelped her litter, and having had the puppies and herself examined by that 'strange smelling' intruder (our veterinarian always made housecalls), then a couple of days later they all have to go through this other ordeal.

Invariably when a large breed is involved, the veterinarian will insist that the bitch be removed and placed either in a strong crate or behind a locked door, out of earshot of the litter. I have known bitches to jump through windows in an endeavor to return to protect their young in such cases. Try also to imagine her thoughts when she is finally allowed to return and finds her babies bloody, mutilated and with a variety of smells on them—and her thoughts towards you, her family, who allowed this to happen! One other factor to consider is that many vets refuse to dock as short as our standard indicates.

I'm all in favor of tying off tails—and having had much experience with both methods, would never revert to the surgical removal of tails.

How is it done?

Swiftly, always with the bitch in attendance, with little or no fuss and *maybe* a couple of hours whimpering from the whelps.

Usually this is carried out around the third day after birth and involves two persons; a third person might well prove an asset if the litter is particularly strong and the 'operator' inexperienced. Need I say that absolute cleanliness is a must, both in the nest and around the rear ends of each puppy. If I have any doubts, a veterinarian is asked to check out the litter to ensure we have only strong, healthy puppies to work with.

I use size-12 elastic bands, cut through to make a single length of elastic; small, sharp scissors are used to trim off excess ends of the band after it has been tied. The inexperienced may well prefer two elastic bands of the same strength but longer. During the three to five days the tails are shrivelling up I use cornstarch and cotton wool to dust around the tied area where there might be a little seepage. Cornstarch is used on babies who prove to be allergic to talcum power—do not use anything else!

 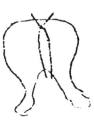

| Tail up; | Tail level — | Tail tied off, |
| Band placed above anus. | tie off now. | band ends cut off. |

One person—the assistant—will hold the puppy, back up with the rear facing the 'operator', who will do the actual tying off. The tail is held above the back to enable the operator to place the center of the band immediately above the lip of the anus. The tail is then lowered so that it is level with the back; the ends of the band are brought over and tied directly above in a single tight knot. At this stage a check can be made to ensure that the band is correctly under the tail—if not the band can easily be cut off. With the tail on a level with the back, a second very tight knot is tied and the ends of the band cut to within half an inch of the knot.

It is that simple.

I find that tying prior to a feed is most satisfactory; with the puppies lifted from the nest and tied off, they can then be returned for a feed and will settle down easier despite the obvious discomfort for the first few hours.

This method is used extensively for Pembroke Welsh Corgis, with a slight variation due to the different tail length, and this is how we came to use it. The only times we have heard of problems with infections is when cleanliness has not been a priority of the owners involved. We have never had any problems, but then again we whelp and raise our litters within the house—why should a bitch be banished when she is a member of the family? It is not a method I would recommend if the bitch is in a kennel or is on any type of straw bedding.

Of late, Brian and I have tied off the tails for litters of Rottweilers other than our own. Although not 'known' to the bitches involved, the entire operation has been carried out with those bitches in attendance; indeed in one case the bitch and I shared her whelping box while I tied off her litter's tails and her owner sat outside the box!

Having written the above I hasten to add that the veterinarian we now have would never banish Cleo when attending her puppies—they have a bond based upon mutual respect and understanding but alas all too often our breed does put off some veterinarians.

Our first litter of Rotts was done using the Corgi method and although their tails are somewhat short I still find their appearance more pleasing to the eye than the 'handles' we are seeing on many of the Rottweilers today.

If at first, using the above method, your Rott tails appear very close to the body, do not despair—at a later date you will see those stubs begin to appear and will know all is well.

Other than to administer a few drops of an all-purpose vitamin product, for the first three weeks the bitch should be able to care for the food intake of the litter successfully, presuming, of course, she is not over-burdened with too many whelps, was in good health to start and is being fed appropriately while nursing. (This can be just about double her normal intake.) At 12 days some breeders feed the puppies a tiny amount of *lean* top round from the tip of the fingers. This is just about when the eyes are starting to open, but the sense of smell is incredibly well-developed. This becomes evident the second day the meat is "served." Their manners as they dive for it would not meet Amy Vanderbilt's standard.

At about 3½ weeks some supplemental food should be given. There are as many theories as to what is the best as there are stars in the sky. Some Germans believe in oatmeal and raw liver juice, gradually adding minced liver. Rice cereal and various puppy chows mixed with diluted milk (or just water) are other possibilities. I use the top round mixed with oatmeal and diluted milk. Just be careful of the consistency and don't let a puppy dive into it. The only puppy I ever lost was the biggest and strongest in the litter. He wolfed his first meal down right into his lungs. Neither his dam nor I could get his lungs cleared. We tried everything. It was horrible!

Once the puppies start to eat solid food it is the exceptional bitch that will keep the box clean. Although not previously mentioned, the surface on which the litter is kept is thought to have a definite bearing on the eventual hip status of the puppies. Line the whelping box with a surface that can be kept clean, but yet on which the puppies can get a footing.

Stool samples should be taken at 3 weeks of age and if indicated, pups must be de-wormed. The vaccination schedule and the timing of further stool checks should be set with your veterinarian.

At this point, I wish to stress again the instructions suggested are by no means meant to be all-encompassing. They merely include recurring situations, conditions, peculiarities, minor difficulties, call it what you wish, which accrue to Rottweilers. For any considerable departures, consult your veterinarian.

By the 5th week or before, it is normal to remove the bitch at intervals from the litter. This should be done after the puppies have been fed a meal and have had a time to nurse on her. This is the beginning of the weaning process and, again, the rate at which they are weaned is variable. To some degree it depends on the bitch's predisposition to nurse them. Her food intake should slowly be reduced in order that she not produce as much milk.

The puppies should have play time out of the box and, depending upon the weather, can have time in the open air. Children in the family should be encouraged to play with them. Toys should be introduced. They should be accustomed to vacuum cleaner noises and other household goings on.

When they are 5 to 6 weeks old, the bitch should be out of the box all day with an occasional visit for the pups to drain her and for her to see all is well. By 6 weeks they should be weaned and the process of drying her up should begin.

Give her nothing to eat for 24 hours and restricted water. Rub the breasts with camphorated oil and apply hot towels 2 to 3 times per day. Massage lightly. Resume feeding lightly. Keep water restricted and exercise her.

Some bitches will tuck up neatly and in a few weeks look like maidens; others take longer and still others never regain their girlish figures. Follow the preceding instructions and you will have done the utmost for her.

If the puppies are to go to their homes at 8 weeks of age, at about 7 weeks they should be checked by the vet, and whatever vaccinations are in order should be administered. It is wise to have the vet check for two testicles on the males. Sometimes they are a bit difficult to detect, but they should be down. Unlike some other breeds, a Rottweiler male without two testicles at 7 weeks is likely to remain that way.

If the suggestions put forth have been followed, at 7 weeks the breeder should have a very good idea of the character and temperament of each puppy. The development should have been recorded daily or at regular intervals, i.e. whose eyes opened first, who grabbed the ball away from the other, who got to the feeding dish first, who was on top in the fights, who had the biggest mouth, who wanted to be cuddled, who bit the ankles hardest, etc., etc.

All these observations should be determining factors when it comes to placing the puppies. Naturally the conformation as well as the temperament of each individual must be assessed by someone of experience.

If any of the pups are definitely of pet stock (not to be shown and not to be bred), the question now arises as to whether or not to neuter them.

Having fun out of the box. Puppies, 6 weeks old, from a litter by Ch. Igor v. Schauer ex Ch. Anka von Gailingen. Breeder: C. M. Thompson.

Preparing to be a woodsman. Doroh's Jaegerin v. Noblehaus at 7 weeks. Breeder, Dorothy Wade. Owners, M. and P. Schwartz.

"What big teeth you have, Grandma!"
—Courtesy, Frolic'n Kennels

8-week-old promising bitch puppy. Few white hairs on chest should disappear.
— *Courtesy, Gun Sharp*

This "sleeping angel" (8 weeks old) grew up to be Ch. Birch Hill's Hasso Manteuffel, CDX.

What's that? Puppies by Am. & Can. Ch. Rodsden's Elko Kastanienbaum, CDX, TD, Can. CD, ex Ch. Reza Birs vom Hause Schumann.
— *Photo, courtesy Mrs. B. Murray Tucker*

This can be done safely by experienced vets—a tubal ligation for the bitches and a vasectomy for the males. Breeders desiring to perpetuate only the best and insure protection of their good name, will interest themselves in this avenue of escape.

RESPONSIBLE PLACEMENT OF PUPPIES

Perhaps the most hazardous task a breeder faces is the selection of puppy owners. Not everyone is a psychiatrist capable of on-the-spot interpretation and evaluation of another's words or actions. Thus, the prospect of entrusting a stranger with one of the "babies," when first faced, becomes a rather awesome proposition.

Careful screening of each potential buyer is one of the contributions a breeder makes to protect his breed, which incidentally enhances his personal reputation. Careless, unconcerned or ineffectual selection puts the dogs in the hands of the wrong people. A Rottweiler is a special dog only suitable for certain homes. So if all a prospect wants is a dog, then he will not make a proper Rottweiler owner.

The question arises as to how to make the determination of what is and what is not potentially a good home. Buyers can be screened in one of three ways: personal interview, over the telephone or via the mails. The overwhelmingly more desirable route is personal interview. A lot more can be accomplished face to face, and especially if the entire family is present. Ill-mannered children are fair warning. If people cannot properly raise their children, it is unlikely they will do a better job with a Rottweiler. A disinterested wife with an enthusiastic husband, or vice versa, is a ticklish situation. Both adults should be "full speed ahead" for the puppy. A Rottweiler is a family dog and appreciates some attention from every member of the family. Children old enough should participate by grooming the dog, filling the water dish, offering the food, sweeping the run, getting the leash, etc. What better way to teach a child a sense of responsibility for animals? The likelihood of an involved family situation for a puppy is ideal.

No matter which of the selection methods is employed, it is businesslike and prudent to have established a set of guidelines by which each prospect can be evaluated. The following pertinent questions can be asked. The answers are revealing.

1. What do you know of the Rottweiler and what attracts you to the breed?

Desirable answer: Very little, only what I've read in books. It sounds as though they are good with children. As I travel a great deal, I would feel more secure knowing a Rottweiler was in the house.

Undesirable answer: They bite hard.

2. Have you ever owned a large dog?

Desirable answer: (a) Yes. (b) No, but I like big dogs and realize the need for discipline.

Undesirable answer: No, but one dog is the same as another, and I've owned lots of dogs.

3. What facilities do you have for housing a Rottweiler?
Desirable answer: We have a house with a fenced-in dog run.
Undesirable answer: We live in the country with plenty of room for the dog to run.

4. Will you keep the dog in the house at night?
Desirable answer: Yes.
Undesirable answer: It looks like a rugged dog. Can't it stay out most of the time?

5. How do you feel about a children-dog relationship?
Desirable answer: A dog has its rights and my children must learn to respect that, within reason.
Undesirable answer: No dog of mine had better ever even growl at my kids.

Suggested further questions:

6. Have you time each day to devote to the training of a puppy?

7. Have you time to go to Obedience Class?

8. Have you any interest in showing a dog?

9. When all is said and done, what do you expect the dog to do for you?

It must be established that Rottweilers require both love and discipline. They cannot be allowed to grow up like "Rover". From 1 lb. to over 100 lbs. in just over one year is rapid growth and if control has not been established from the outset, by the time the need for it is realized, it could be too late. The protective aspect of the Rottweiler's nature must be correctly channeled. So attendance at Obedience Class should be forcefully recommended and in some cases required.

A fair estimate of the cost of feeding and approximate cost of veterinary care should be discussed. Hip dysplasia should be explained and the limits to which a breeder can be responsible should be defined. (See Code of Ethics in the Appendix.)

If a prospect is interested in showing a dog, special note should be made of that fact. In selecting for such a home, the breeder must weigh one asset versus another, i.e. very outgoing puppy of good phenotype or a duller individual of excellent phenotype. Although it should not be the case, personality and bearing have a great influence on decisions in the conformation ring.

In any event, for a breeder whose aim it is to assure a permanent home for the puppy, there must be selection for individuals primarily seeking a companion. The show dog aspect must be secondary.

The conversation or correspondence, whichever the case may be, will have provided other areas to explore. The more little feelers put out, the more secure the breeder can be in making a decision to sell or not to sell. If the prospect has qualified, then a thorough explanation of the care and raising of a Rottweiler puppy (see Chapter 11) should be given to the future owner.

He'll study same and be prepared for the day the puppy goes to its home. This is a happy occasion for the new family and the most eventful thus far in the puppy's short life. Having followed the previously referred to instructions, the new owners have all in readiness. Still, it is wise for the breeder to again go over details making certain no misunderstandings exist. The transition must be as smooth as possible. Following this procedure will help to make it so.

Assuring the new owners of a desire to be of help at all times will open the door to their seeking timely advice and avert possible problems in the future. For the involved breeder this is a difficult moment. Provided he has chosen his owner wisely, he can take solace in the fact the puppy will have the best opportunity to arrive at its full potential.

Here are points breeders should check with puppy buyers:

PUPPY CHECK LIST

VET
Health certificate, shots and worming:
Stress to carry into Vet's office and no exposure to other animals.
Caricide—discuss what dosage with Vet before three months of age.
X-Ray—at one year of age is optional but helpful to breeder.

FEEDING
Proper feeding arrangement. Be sure puppy just reaches dish.
Carrot juice for moistening food.
Egg once or twice per week.
Bone Meal—Use 3/4 of what is on the instruction sheet ("Care").
Kelp—Start with a half tablet of .015 mg and work up gradually to two tablets per day by one year of age—continue through life.

OPTIONAL—according to climate and need.
Vitamycin (amounts corrected) 3/4 teaspoon up to three months; 1 to 1½ teaspoons three to five months; 1½ to 2 teaspoons five months to one and one half years; then cut back gradually to 1 teaspoon per day for lifetime maintenance.
(or Pet Tabs)

*PLEASE NOTE—SUPPLEMENTS ARE GIVEN ONCE A DAY
ONLY*

"My mistress put my collar on upside down, so I tried to adjust it."
— Courtesy, Gun Sharp.

8 WEEK TRAUMA (*See* P. 200)

SLEEP—Alone during day

CRATE TRAINING—At the start of house breaking do not use any pad, newspaper, etc. in the crate. Buy Masonite board. Fit it exactly to bottom. Turn rough side up for non-slippery surface which can be readily cleaned with Lysol and water. Always remove collar. Nylon bone is the only toy left with puppy.

TEETHING—Alert about permanent teeth at three months of age.

EAR MANIPULATION—As per demonstration and BFI powder as in "Care."

TOE NAILS—Snip a bit off—once or twice per week.

NO JUMPING OFF FURNITURE—NO STANDING ON HIND LEGS—NO TUG-OF-WAR.

PEDIGREE, AKC REGISTRATION, CONTRACT, if applicable. Get name in which dog is to be registered.

SUGGEST CLUB MEMBERSHIP

CONSULTATION—Conferring with breeder should be on a regular basis, over the telephone, if not in person. Advise immediately of any difficulty before it becomes a problem.

11

Care and Feeding of Your Rottweiler Puppy

TRAINING is naturally everyone's first concern with a new puppy. Results are obtained in direct proportion to the amount of intelligent handling employed (always assuming that the pup is healthy). To do the job quickly you must devote two weeks of concentrated effort and then your pup will be well on its way, if not completely trained. The following is the method I recommend:

Obtain a Safari crate #904, or the equivalent size (36" long x 27½" high) in another make. This size crate will be useful throughout the dog's lifetime. Your crate will be the puppy's bed until such time as it is housebroken and trustworthy in other areas as well. Crate training is not cruel. As a matter of fact, dogs like their crates and will very often go into them out of choice. The purpose they serve is to make the most of the dog's natural tendencies, viz. dogs do not like to mess in the immediate vicinity of where they lie. So, confinement helps to make them control themselves and that is housetraining.

And this is how your day must be planned: take the puppy out the minute it stirs. After it makes, return it to the crate until you have time to feed it and take it out for all duties. Mission accomplished, bring the puppy in and it is now playtime. Take it out again in an hour and back into the crate for sleep. Mid-day, out again and then lunch and then playtime for a while; then out again and then dinner and playtime. Out again and to sleep until 10 P.M. Out again and then supper and the usual routine of play, out and sleep. Good night. Amen.

You have your work cut out for you. Stick to the schedule. Be intelligent, be observant and you will be rewarded with a pup that is housebroken in record time.

While this housebreaking is going on, another form of training should be in progress. The puppy should be required to spend a good part of the day sleeping. This is as important to its well-being as food. It should go to sleep alone in its own quarters and learn right from the start that when you put it somewhere, that is where it is to stay. Do not neglect to do this at the outset because later on it is not easy to teach a dog to stay alone. And if your pet needs constant companionship, this obviates the possibility of ever traveling with it or leaving it alone in the house.

Put a choke collar on your puppy. This is not cruel and makes the dog easier to handle. Remove it when you are not in attendance, so it does not get caught on anything. You will need three or four collars in the growing process. Snap a lead on at least once a day and start to teach your puppy to come when called. If it does not respond, give a slight tug on the lead and pretty soon it will get the idea to come to you and avoid the tug. As an added incentive when it comes, give a reward. Do not let children drag the pup around. This completely confuses the issue. Walk around the house with the pup on the lead and see if you can get it to walk without crossing in front of you. Later on, when you take it out walking, it will be leashbroken.

The need for discipline is essential. Your puppy is an adorable fuzz-ball, but remember that within the year a male will weigh about 100 lbs. It will be clumsy, over-zealous and loving. If you have not insisted on obedience from the beginning, you may find this an impossible time to start. A disobedient Rottweiler is a menace and a disgrace. Never give a command that you are not willing and able to enforce. If you say SIT, it must be SIT and not DOWN. If you mean DOWN, then say it. Use short commands. Rottweilers are very intelligent dogs and for generations they have been doing a job for their masters. *You* start in right away being "Boss" and giving lots of love. This is a language your Rottweiler will understand.

Feeding

Note: Meat and kibble measurements listed here are for a 7 to 8 week old puppy and must be gradually increased as the puppy grows.

Breakfast: 1/4 pound of uncooked chopped meat. Use only best quality canned meat or a good grade of fresh meat. 1/3 cup of kibble. I prefer a combination of Ken-L-Biskit and Wayne. Pre-moisten with hot water or carrot juice. 1 tsp. Mazola oil (increase to 1 tblsp. by 1 year). 1/4 tsp. of bonemeal (increase to 2 tsps. by 8 months). At 1 year eliminate bonemeal. 1/2 kelp tablet (6.5 gr. providing .15 mg. iodine) (gradually increase to 2 tablets by 8 months for lifetime maintenance). 1 raw egg 2 times per week. A small amount of liver may be added occasionally.

Lunch: 1/4 cup kibble pre-moistened with 6 oz. skim milk. If diarrhea occurs, stop milk and when you start again, dilute milk with water. Gradually increase milk content.

Dinner: Same as breakfast, except no kelp and no bonemeal. You may substitute cottage cheese 1 day a week for the meat, or use it in combination.

10 p.m.: Until 10 weeks old, same as lunch and then eliminate and substitute 1 or 2 small Milkbone biscuits. Increase biscuit size from puppy size to medium, and finally to large size as the dog grows. Compensate for 10 p.m. feeding by adding a bit to the other three meals.

Supplements (Optional): Pet Tabs or similar multi-vitamin product (according to poundage).

By the time a male puppy is 3 months old, it should be eating 1/2 lb. of meat and 2 cups of kibble per day. A female needs a bit less. At 5 months the male pup should be eating 3/4 lb. of meat and 3 cups of kibble per day. Keep on with the 3 meals per day for 8 months, then you can eliminate lunch and feed twice per day. At 8 or 9 months, a large male may well need as much as 1-1/2 lbs. of meat per day, and upwards of 6 cups of kibble in this growing stage. You must be guided by good sense. We do not want the pups to starve, but on the other hand, we now know that overweight is a definite factor in hip-dysplasia victims. *DO NOT LET THE PUP GET FAT!*

Do not make a fussy eater of your pup. If it does not eat a meal, take the food away and offer nothing until the next meal. Eventually, it will eat if you have patience, presuming of course, that it is not ill.

Please feed high off the floor. This procedure makes a cleaner eater, helps strengthen pasterns, helps prevent protruding elbows, and encourages the dog to stand up. At all stages, the dog should have to reach slightly to get the food. Refer to the diagram of the feeding arrangement herewith.

Adult dogs should be fed twice a day. Never give more than 1 lb. of meat per day and after 1-1/2 years old cut back to 3/4 lb. These amounts are for a large, active male. Smaller males and bitches should get somewhat less. The amount of kibble is determined by how much is necessary to maintain proper weight.

FEEDING DISH ARRANGEMENT

Somewhat amended from original submitted to CRC *Newsletter* by Bill Logan, February 1968.

This arrangement has weathered the test of time and inflation. It makes possible, with minimum effort, feeding your Rottweiler off the ground. Adjustment of height of dish is accomplished by removing two screws requiring only a few seconds. Thus one is able to start a puppy a few inches off the ground and feed the growing dog at one-inch intervals.

KIT: A. Woodworking shops or lumber yards usually carry them. Two 2' or 3' strips with two 12" or 14" brackets in blonde wood or walnut.
    B. Piece of plywood with a hole cut in it to accommodate feeding dish, and sufficiently thick to remain firm.
    Cost of materials — about $5.50.

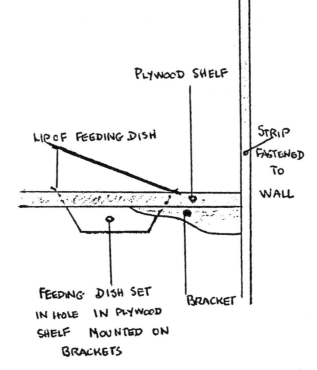

PLYWOOD SHELF

LIP OF FEEDING DISH

STRIP
FASTENED
TO
WALL

FEEDING DISH SET
IN HOLE IN PLYWOOD
SHELF MOUNTED ON
BRACKETS

BRACKET

Mount strips on wall in kitchen, preferably in an out-of-the-way spot, where dish can remain in place without projecting out into room.

Then mount plywood piece to brackets, fitting placement to space between strips. Screws placed at proper level for dog to stretch a bit to eat. Put shelf in place on strips and place feeding dish in cutout.

Added thought from Freeger Kennels: Cut two holes in one piece of plywood, one for food dish and one for water. Use the 14" brackets for support.

Additional thought from John Wehrle: Laminate your plywood shelf with vinyl coordinated to your kitchen motif — elegant!

Grooming

Buy a rubber curry, a steel comb and a Resco Nail Clipper at your pet shop. Curry the puppy daily, or as often as you have time. After the loose hair is out, take a damp turkish towel and rub it back and forth through the coat. Bathing a Rottweiler is almost never necessary if you keep it groomed in this way.

Buy a very small can of B.F.I. powder at your drug store. Shake a bit into each ear once per week. This will help to eliminate mites and the danger of caked ear wax (a tendency of all floppy-eared dogs).

Learn to cut your dog's nails at an early age. Be very careful not to cut too short, but a styptic pencil or a piece of white bread held firmly against the nail will arrest any bleeding. Electric grinders are also available and

DOING THE NAILS

Puppy with stocking muzzle—sometimes necessary for training puppy to submit to nail clipping. Stocking is wrapped around puppy's muzzle, then crossed underneath the chin and tied at the nape of the neck.

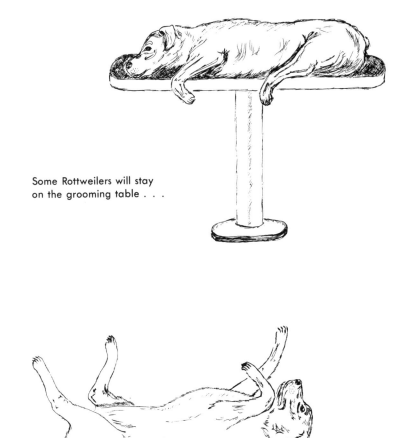

Some Rottweilers will stay on the grooming table . . .

Others prefer the comfort of wall-to-wall carpeting!

— *Drawings by Mary E. Stringer*

some find this an easier method than nail cutting, but caution must be used not to let it overheat the nail.

Teething

At about three months of age the permanent teeth start to erupt. There is a possibility that the deciduous (baby) teeth have not fallen out. If this situation occurs, in order not to deflect the bite, the deciduous teeth must immediately be worked loose. If that is not possible, a vet's assistance must be enlisted.

Teething is a stress-filled stage and trying situations should be avoided at this time. Rest, proper food on schedule and no exposure to ill dogs is mandatory when resistance is at this very low ebb.

Ear Carriage

Further indication of the depletion of reserves can be observed in the ear carriage of some puppies. The ears will fold and hang in an unsightly manner as a result and if in addition the pasterns seem suddenly to weaken, the veterinarian should be consulted as to whether the puppy should be further supplemented. It is at this stage the tendency is noticed and immediate attention must be given to massage the ear in such a manner as to encourage proper carriage.

With the puppy's back to you, start by massaging the top of the skull between the innermost corners of the ears. Then turn each ear flap back, observe the protrusion of cartilage near the base and place the index finger of each hand above it on the corresponding ear. Place both middle fingers just beneath the protrusion. Gently grasp the ear with the thumb on the outside, acting in opposition to the other two fingers. Gradually pull the two ears apart with a motion that should be out, up and then over. Thus ending with the inner edge of the ear hugging the cheek as described in the standard. This procedure should be followed as many times as possible each day and results can be seen almost immediately. Illustrations of the technique and a picture of an adult with the improper ear carriage appear on the facing page.

Veterinary Care

Seek out the best veterinarian in your area, not the nearest one. This choice may one day be the difference of life and death for your dog. So choose wisely.

Have the vet examine your new puppy and get acquainted as soon as possible. A word of advice: when you go there, leave the puppy in the car until it is your turn and then carry it directly into the examining room. Remember, sick dogs go to the vet and the puppy's shots are not as yet completed.

Examine for worms periodically and be sure to get the shots on schedule.

THE EAR MASSAGE

1. Out

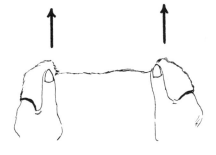

2. Up

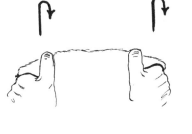

3. Over

— *Drawings by Mary E. Stringer*

This kind owner has photographed her other-wise lovely bitch to show the ear carriage we deplore. This can be avoided, in most instances, if the instructions given on caring for the puppy's ears are followed.

200

Some vets are not accustomed to handling big dogs. They are not for you. Rottweilers are tough and do not take to being pushed around. The vet who cares for your dog must have respect for this sort of animal. On the other hand, it is up to you to teach your dog proper manners at the vet's. He must learn from the outset to submit to innoculations and all the usual routine. A vet will appreciate your regard for him and treat your dog all the more kindly.

Helpful Hints

1. Do not put paper in the crate. Many breeders raise pups on paper and they have gone in their box, which is paper lined as long as they can remember. So, if you lay paper down, the puppy may think it is meant to go in its crate. The only suitable toy to be left in the crate is a nylon bone.

2. Do not vary the diet.

3. Keep a regular time schedule.

4. Do not let mistakes occur. It's easier to instill good habits than to break bad ones. Say a sharp "no" if the pup makes a mistake but *never strike it*. Bear in mind that when the pup makes a mistake, it is your fault. You were not attentive enough.

5. Encourage the puppy with lots of praise.

6. When the puppy is just about eight weeks old a rather common phenomenon of erratic behavior may occur. A minor setback in housetraining, in appetite, personality, learning ability is not unusual. This stage is sometimes referred to as the "eight-week trauma." It passes in a few days and the return to normal behavior is apparent.

7. IMPORTANT. Do not force exercise until after one year old, and then start gradually. And do not play tug of war. It will ruin the bite.

A Finnberg puppy, by Am. & Can. Ch. Birch Hill's Governor, CD, TD, ex Can. Ch. Finnberg's Anneli. Breeder: Lars Rekola.　　　　— *Photo, Gerard J. Gregory, Jr.*

12

Some Health Problems

$\mathbf{H}$EALTH PROBLEMS which seem to occur with a degree of regularity in Rottweilers will be singled out for discussion. This does not imply the incidence is more or less frequent than in any other breed unless such is specifically stated, but simply that they are a factor. The hope is that by identifying some of the symptoms, early detection and immediate treatment will permit of a cure, whereas ignorance or neglect might otherwise cause serious consequences.

3 - 8 weeks

Parvo: Symptoms are listlessness, vomiting, bloody diarrhea. Immediate veterinary care is mandatory. To neglect even one day could well result in death.

This is one disease from which Rottweilers are believed to suffer a disproportionate number of fatalities as compared to other breeds.

Vaginitis and Cystitis: Quite common in female puppies. First signs are sticky discharge in vaginal area followed by pussy discharge. Frequent attempts and excessively long squatting to urinate with only a few drops being passed.

Veterinarian must prescribe the specific drug as cure. Sufficient drinking water must be available. The area must be kept clean, bathing with warm water. I find the administering of vitamin C daily is an aid in avoiding this problem.

I know of no other problems incurred at this stage which are endemic to the Rottweiler.

8 weeks - 4 months

Usually a relatively trouble-free time with a Rottweiler puppy. However, severe cases of hip-dysplasia will manifest symptoms this early. Bunny-hopping, difficulty in arising, crying out when rear legs spread are suspicious symptoms. Get to the vet.

4 months - 8 months

This is a period of severe stress in a Rottweiler puppy's development. Great caution must be taken. Teething and rapid growth rate diminish resistance. Rest is mandatory and random exposure to other dogs should be kept to a minimum between 4-5 months. Parvo shots must be up-to-the-minute for maximum protection.

If rear lameness appears, consult your vet.

SKIN PROBLEMS. **Mange (demodectic):** Generally recognizable by appearance of small circular areas of hair loss in head area and on forelegs without itch. Thought to be passed from affected dam to puppies. Therapy must include stress-free environment. Get to the vet.

8 - 12 months

This is the usual stage when **forequarter lameness** first surfaces. If it persists for more than a few days and no known injury is the cause, consult the vet.

Panosteitis or *Osteochondritis dissecans* are common causes of forequarter lameness in all large, rapidly-growing breeds. The Rottweiler is not an exception. The condition must be treated with rest, or in some cases surgically, before the acute stage progresses to a chronic ailment. Do not neglect.

Sarcoptic Mange appears in many cases at this age or even earlier. It is recognizable as small red bumps on the skin which cause incessant scratching and hair loss on face, hocks, elbows and ears. Treatment after diagnosis generally consists of three, or more if necessary, dips at weekly intervals. Do not neglect. Get to the vet.

Hindquarter lameness or gait disorder: Severe or moderate hip-dysplasia victims will usually give evidence of their problem at this age. Even some dogs with only a mild divergence will manifest a degree of lameness or difficulty in rising or negotiating slippery surfaces.

The magnitude of the problem cannot be defined by the amount of discomfort visible. The individual's pain tolerance level is a very large factor in this determination. Therefore, the one and only solution is to have the hips x-rayed, and for an authoritative opinion, sent to the OFA for evaluation. This is known as a preliminary evaluation and a lesser charge is made than for OFA clearance.

Owners of dogs diagnosed as moderate or mild should realize that their Rottweilers are not potential breeding stock, but have no reason to despair of their future as successful pets. Many go on to do advanced Obedience requiring jumping. This is, of course, dependent upon factors which require individual analysis.

Also, it must be realized that many dogs which are severely lame at eight months will between 14 and 17 months manifest a radical change for the better. This is not as a result of any change in the hip status, but rather is attributable to the musculature development which has taken place and is now better able to compensate for the imperfect bone structure.

18 months - 3 years, or possibly earlier

If a stilted front movement exists, if there is a sudden unwillingness or inability to negotiate stairs, if an unsteadiness in the gait occurs, consult your vet.

Unfortunately, a new problem has been recently discovered in Rottweilers. The name it has been given is *Neuro Axonal Dystrophy.* Positive identification has not been established, at this time. Autopsy seems to reveal some means of identification. Work on this disorder is in progress at Johns Hopkins University by Dr. Linda Cork. She is certainly willing to field any question by Rottweiler owners.

18 months - 3 years

Food Intake: Most Rottweilers seem to be possessed of a bottomless pit for their stomachs. We must be careful not to let them dictate their alimentary needs to us. By 18 months of age, they have passed the period of rapid growth. Their caloric needs are greatly diminished. Superfluous food only puts on fat. It is highly undesirable from the point of view of health and appearance for a young dog to achieve the proportions of a mature adult simply as a result of over-feeding. Owners who are misguided into thinking otherwise are doing their dogs a great disfavor. It takes a good three years for a Rottweiler male to achieve maturity, not much less for a Rottweiler bitch. It is a slow process of broadening of the frame and building of muscle which creates the desired mass. Fat is not an equable substitute; and if the purpose is to compete with mature dogs in the show ring any judge worth his or her salt is not fooled into thinking it is.

Adulthood

Bloat, or torsion as it may be called, is a digestive disorder common to horses as well as dogs. In horses it is called foundering. As has been stated many times, this is not a veterinary handbook so you will be spared all technicalities. Suffice it to say, if a swelling of the abdomen occurs, obvious discomfort in lying down is present, difficulty in breathing, whimpering, are noticed, GET TO THE VET HOSPITAL AS FAST AS YOU CAN!

Time is of the essence or you will lose your dog.

In my opinion this dreaded problem can in many cases be avoided if the following precautions are taken:

1. Feed your dog twice in the day. Two smaller meals do not overload the stomach, then leave it empty to fill with gas.
2. Never feed under stressful conditions (at a dog show, before an airplane trip, etc.).
3. Never feed an hour before nor an hour after heavy exercise.
4. Never allow a dog to drink large amounts of water within an hour before or after feeding.
5. Do not feed unmoistened kibble to older dogs.
6. Do not ever feed indigestible foods to older dogs, viz, frankfurters with the skin on, peas, corn, etc.
7. Discourage any dog from lying on its back with the four feet in the air right after eating.

Acute Moist Dermatitis *(Hot Spots)* is a skin condition rather common in Rottweilers. Most often it occurs in warm weather. Perhaps the most common cause is an allergy to flea bites, which sets up an itch-scratch-lick cycle, resulting in an ulceration. In due time, the area becomes hairless.

Home treatment, if a small area is involved, consists of applying a soothing preparation which is also drying. A camphor or menthol base has been suggested. The licking-scratching syndrome must be eliminated for healing to take place. Larger, or areas which seem to be spreading, require veterinary attention.

Our Older Dogs

Rottweilers, if well-bred, correctly fed, adequately exercised and maintained under proper veterinary supervision during their lifetime, may be expected to live 9 to 11 years with relatively few problems. Their eyesight and hearing remain comparatively keen. Their teeth, if kept clean, are seldom a problem. They are, as they get older, subject to the ordinary arthritic discomforts which accrue to man and beast alike in the aging process. A couple of Bufferin one to four times a day will go a long way toward alleviating arthritic pain. Some individuals, as time goes on, will require more drastic medication.

It is my experience that the senior citizens provide far and away the best companionship. They are wise to all our ways, anticipate our moves, cater to our peculiarities and demand only to be by our side. This would be the perfect stage were it not for our sub-conscious fear of time running out on them. The wise owner obliterates such thoughts and enjoys to the fullest whatever time is allotted.

It is at this stage I must give the last of my warnings. Rottweilers are more prone to suffer from cancer than most other breeds. It is a common cause of death. Usual forms are bone cancer, pancreatic cancer, mammary cancer in bitches and prostate cancer in males. Heroic surgery, such as the

"I'm assuming the 'low profile' for now, but when we grow up you had better follow my instructions." Frolic'n Darth Vader and lamb. — *Courtesy, Frolic'n*

amptuation of a leg, is ill-advised. Recurrence elsewhere in the body is usual within a few months. Operating on mammary cancer, if caught in time, can be very successful. Chemotherapy has not proven to be productive, but this is a personal decision each owner must make.

Do watch the inside of the mouth and should any growths appear, they should be removed with alacrity, and analyzed for malignancy.

All of this leads me, inevitably, to the "day of reckoning." If an owner is fortunate enough to be spared the making of a decision, he is indeed relieved of a great burden. It has been my misfortune never to have lost a Rottweiler from natural causes, and I mention this only because I could not bear to be thought of as callous, when nothing could be farther from the truth.

In a discussion on this subject, it is only natural there be a variety of opinions as to how the problem is best solved. It is a time when advice and moral support are required. The criterion must be the "quality of life" which remains. I shall never forget my first encounter with such a loss. Dr. Skelley called me from the operating room with these words: "Mrs. Freeman, if you love this dog as much as you say you do, you will never let him wake up."

What a shock! And what a spur of the moment decision with which to be confronted. The way it was put to me I really did not have a choice and perhaps that was best. Gerhardt was the first one and I might otherwise not have gone through with it.

Subsequently, with each additional year I lived with these dogs, I came to a fuller realization of their great dignity and the premium they put on "being in control" under all circumstances. It is this latter deeply ingrained facet of their character we must consider. If they are no longer in control, when pain, incapacity, senility or circumstances are such that they are subject to indignity, the time has arrived. It takes courage, but we are able to do for our dogs what we are not able to do for our human loved ones.

"He passed the OFA!"

A progenitor dominant for good hips. Fetz vom Oelberg, SchH2, ADRK 38416, RO-25 (Hektor v.d. Solitude ex Dora v.d. Brotzingergasse). Breeder: Herman Reiling. Owner: Paul Harris.
— Photo, courtesy of Joan Klem

13

Hip Dysplasia, The OFA and the Rottweiler Registry

In EACH and every breed of dog certain anomalies exist. They are known to the knowledgeable breeder whose responsibility it is to do all within his power to avoid the expression of these latent "gremlins." The mode of inheritance, the prenatal influence, the environmental effect all must be understood and evaluated.

In the Rottweiler one such "gremlin" is the predisposition to canine Hip Dysplasia (HD).*

1. *What is HD?* HD is a hereditary disease of polygenic character generally associated with dogs maturing over 40 lbs. It implies faulty conformation of the head of the femur and the acetabulum.

2. *How is it manifested?* Lameness, inability to negotiate slippery surfaces, apparent difficulty in rising from a sitting position or vice versa, refusal to jump, hopping gait, withered rear, inappropriate resistance to activity are all possible indications of HD.

3. *How can a breeder avoid HD in his puppies?* Unfortunately, to date, that is not possible. However, by selective breeding a greater percentage of normal puppies should result.

---

*Those interested in a detailed scientific discussion are referred to published studies by the following authorities: Dr. G.B. Schnelle; Dr. Sten-Erik Olsson; Dr. Wayne B. Riser; Fred Lanting, *Canine Hip Dysplasia;* The James A. Baker Institute for Animal Health, *Cornell Research Laboratory for Diseases of Dogs,* Laboratory Report Series 2, Number 8, June 1977; and untold numbers of papers circulated by OFA.

4. What is meant by "selective breeding"? In this context, the breeding of dogs with normal hip joint conformation.

5. What constitutes normal hip joint conformation and how can a breeder determine the hip status of one of his dogs? All authorities agree a live dog's hip status can only be determined by X-ray.

6. Is the problem of HD solely attributable to heredity? Absolutely not. It has been shown "pups raised and confined in 3' x 3' x 3' cages after 30 days of age seldom develop hip dysplasia."** The predisposition can be hereditary, but the environment has a great bearing on the end result. Overweight, slippery floors, over-exercise at an early age, stairs, standing on hind legs are all negative factors which most certainly contribute.

THE OFA

It is now appropriate to tackle one of, if not *the* most controversial issues confronting Rottweiler breeders—the question of what constitutes correct evaluation of a dog's hips. In other words, the positioning of the dog for X-ray, the quality of the film which results, the ability of the person reading the film to properly interpret the results are all variables. It seems there must be some attempt made to minimize the interpretation of these variables in order for a program to be workable.

The background material on the recognition for the need of HD control in Rottweilers is unknown to many now active in the breed, conveniently forgotten by some, but gospel to those of us who initiated the program and have faithfully supported it despite the personal sacrifice involved.

Back in 1958-59 when your author first exhibited a Rottweiler, an entry of one, two or three dogs constituted the normal complement of Rottweilers at a show. Sexes were combined at many shows for even one championship point to be in contention. As the years passed there was a gradual increase in the number of Rottweilers being shown with a disproportionate number of dogs manifesting stiffness or some other irregularity of gait in the rear limbs, if not outright lameness.

By 1965, the number of afflicted dogs to be seen in the ring had increased to an alarming statistic. Being closely connected with the University of Pennsylvania Veterinary School, I made inquiry regarding available information, and happily discovered that one of the recognized authorities on the subject of HD was on the staff. As Vice President of the Club, I invited Dr. Wayne H. Riser to speak to the Colonial Rottweiler Club (CRC) members at their semi-annual meeting held in conjunction with the Kennel Club of Philadelphia all-breed show. As an intended service to all breeds, we placed posters around the arena inviting anyone

**Wayne B. Riser, DVM, MS and Harry Miller, *Canine Hip Dysplasia and How To Control It,* Copyright 1966, page 24.

interested to attend the lecture. Indeed, we had breeders from "all walks of dog life" present.

Needless to say, Dr. Riser was a convincing speaker, armed with sound theories which have withstood the test of time. He spoke on cause, effect, prognosis for future control, etc. He demonstrated normal and dysplastic hips, both on slides and on bones which were preserved from necropsied dogs. He told us of research programs being funded in England, Sweden, Holland and Germany, as well as here at home.

We learned of the establishment of the Orthopedic Foundation for Animals, Inc. (OFA), thanks to the efforts of several progressive breed clubs aided by funds from charitable individuals. We discovered our speaker was none other than the Project Director of the OFA and the University of Pennsylvania Veterinary School was to house the project.* The objectives of the OFA were defined:

"1. To collate and disseminate information concerning diseases of the bones and muscles with first and major emphasis on hip dysplasia.

2. To devise and encourage the establishment of control programs to lower the incidence of musculoskeletal disease.

3. To encourage and finance research in musculoskeletal diseases.

4. To receive funds and make grants to carry out these objectives."**

We had the answer to many of our questions. We had an awareness of the nature of the illness and the magnitude of the problems facing us in our effort to control it. Furthermore, out of that meeting came the resolve of the Board of Directors of CRC to embark on a course of action, principally via the *Newsletter,* to educate our membership. We were groping for a program.

Within a very short time the word had spread across the country. Rottweiler people were thirsty for knowledge on the subject.

In October of 1967, Rottweiler #1, Champion D'Artagnan of Canidom, C.D., owned by your author, was certified by OFA.

Up to this point there had been unanimity of opinion. Everyone acknowledged existence of HD. The hereditary factor was accepted and the need for selective breeding was recognized.

The great schism occurred between those who on one side opted for OFA certification as the only valid authority, and those in the other corner who felt their personal veterinarian was equally competent to interpret the findings. This same argument persists today.

Here is the issue:

Certification by OFA requires a dog be two years of age or older, be X-rayed in a prescribed position on a specified size film, and that the film be identified with the date, veterinarian's name or hospital, the dog's AKC registered number, sex and age. Unfortunately, to date, OFA is remiss in not requiring tattoo numbers for positive identification of each dog.

---

*The OFA is presently at the University of Missouri, Columbia, MO 65201.
**Riser, Wayne H., DVM and M.S. and Miller, Harry, *Hip Dysplasia and How to Control It,* p. 98.

GROLL VOM HAUS SCHOTTROY
name
ROTTWEILER
breed
RO-891-T
certificate no.

WD-517950
registration no.
MALE
sex
MARCH 4, 1975
date of birth

Based upon the radiograph submitted, number   70599
no evidence of hip dysplasia was recognized.

owner

MRS. BERNARD FREEMAN
SHELTER ROCK ROAD
MANHASSET, NY 11030

This certificate issued with the
right to correct or revoke by the
Orthopedic Foundation for Animals

MARCH 18, 1977
certificate issued

DYSPLASIA CONTROL REGISTRY

This is the old OFA form which defines the OFA ratings and reveals the category into which the individual dog falls on a separate sheet (see below).

ORTHOPEDIC FOUNDATION FOR ANIMALS · DYSPLASIA CONTROL REGISTRY · CONSENSUS REPORT

GROLL VOM HAUS SCHOTTROY
registered name of dog
ROTTWEILER
breed
BLACK & MAHOGANY
color
MARCH 18, 1977
date of report

WD-517950
registration no.
MALE
sex
49513
tattoo
RO-891-T
OFA certificate no.

owner

MRS. BERNARD FREEMAN
SHELTER ROCK ROAD
MANHASSET, NY   11030

veterinarian

DR. WAYNE G. RISER, SCHOOL OF VET. MED.
UNIV. OF PA., 39 TH & PINE
PHILADELPHIA, PA   19104

RADIOGRAPHIC EVALUATION OF PELVIC PHENOTYPE WITH RESPECT TO CANINE HIP DYSPLASIA

Application No. _____ 70599 _____ Age at evaluation _____ 24 _____ months

✓ **EXCELLENT HIP JOINT CONFORMATION***
superior hip joint conformation as compared with other individuals of the same breed and age

GOOD HIP JOINT CONFORMATION*
well formed hip joint conformation as compared with other individuals of the same breed and age

FAIR HIP JOINT CONFORMATION*
minor irregularities of hip joint conformation as compared with other individuals of the same breed and age

BORDERLINE HIP JOINT CONFORMATION
marginal hip joint conformation of indeterminate status with respect to hip dysplasia at this time

MILD HIP DYSPLASIA
radiographic evidence of minor dysplastic change of the hip joints

MODERATE HIP DYSPLASIA
well defined radiographic evidence of dysplastic changes of the hip joints

SEVERE HIP DYSPLASIA
radiographic evidence of marked dysplastic changes of the hip joints

*Eligible for the assignment of a breed OFA number if 24 months of age or older at the time of radiography

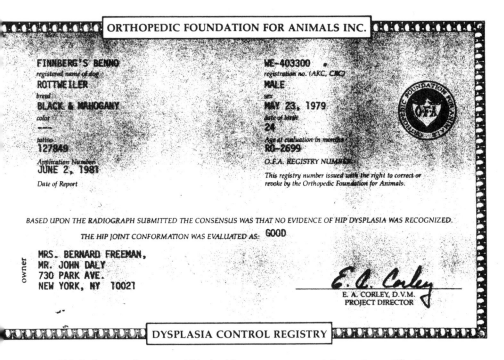

This is the new form, on which the hip status appears right on the certificate.

The film is submitted to the OFA for evaluation accompanied by a fee of $15, which defrays the cost of the processing. It is read by three different radiologists. They render their opinions independently and the consensus is the verdict handed down on the dog.

OFA has somewhat changed the format of its findings. At this writing, certification is issued to those dogs whose hips are considered to be excellent, good or fair as compared to others of the breed at the same age. Borderline cases are asked to re-X-ray at a later date and resubmit with no additional charge. Dogs found to be dysplastic or displaying other related abnormalities are rejected, with those abnormalities defined.

As against the above procedure, we have the personal veterinarian taking the film, reading and interpreting the film and then in the final analysis rendering a quantitative opinion on a subject in which he may or may not be well versed. In addition, the factor of personal relationship can most certainly color an opinion. One's own veterinarian, knowing of the problems involved when an animal is rejected, is loath to be the "bad guy."

To summarize the pros and cons, I warn my readers of my bias in favor of OFA certification. There can be no question of the superiority of an opinion which is the consensus of three experts in the field having as a basis of comparison 3000 other individuals, versus the opinion of one person whose experience is limited both in the reading of X-rays and the number of Rottweilers presented for evaluation. There can be no denying the desirability of anonymity. To charge that errors have been made is begging the issue. More errors are made by the private veterinarians, but no one checks on them.

In the final analysis, payment of a $15 fee for OFA certification cannot be the objection. Anyone breeding Rottweilers of quality spends many times that figure on a dog. What it comes down to is fear of rejection.

Were that not the case, "people in the other corner," armed with their veterinarians' favorable conclusions and certifications by OFA, would be blessed with double indemnity—a very pleasant prospect.

Those claiming OFA certification is "the breeding of numbers" are off the wall. OFA certification is not of itself a reason to breed any dog, but *the lack of certification is a reason not to breed a dog.*

In this day and age we are not lacking in numbers of Rottweilers. What we need is fewer dogs of better quality. The gene pool for good phenotypes with good hips exists. There is no need to accept less than what is best for the future of our breed and there should not be forbearance for those who do less than the most they can do to breed sound Rottweilers.

From the desk of the OFA Project Director

CANINE HIP JOINT CONFORMATION

Consensus reports on pelvic radiographs from the OFA contain information for serious breeders and concerned owners. The consensus is the result of independent review by three veterinary radiologists and is reported as one of the following categories. The first three are considered within normal radiographic limits for age and breed and are eligible for assignment of an OFA breed number if the dog was 24 months of age or older at the time of radiography.

1. EXCELLENT HIP JOINT CONFORMATION
   Superior hip joint conformation as compared with other individuals of the same breed and age.

2. GOOD HIP JOINT CONFORMATION
   Well formed hip joint conformation as compared with other individuals of the same breed and age.

3. FAIR HIP JOINT CONFORMATION
   Minor irregularities of hip joint conformation as compared with other individuals of the same breed and age.

The following categories are not eligible for an OFA breed number:

4. BORDERLINE HIP JOINT CONFORMATION
   Marginal hip joint conformation of indeterminate status with respect to hip dysplasia at this time. A repeat study is recommended in 6-8 months.

5. MILD HIP DYSPLASIA
   Radiographic evidence of minor dysplastic change of the hip joints.

6. MODERATE HIP DYSPLASIA
Well defined radiographic evidence of dysplastic changes of the hip joints.

7. SEVERE HIP DYSPLASIA
Radiographic evidence of marked dysplastic changes of the hip joints.

Hip joint conformation (phenotype) is the radiographic appearance of the hip joints and is the outcome of interaction between a dog's hereditary make-up (genotype) and its environment. Hip joint conformation can be represented as a range from excellent to very dysplastic and shades in between these two ends of the spectrum. Traits such as this are referred to as quantitative characters and are thought to depend upon the interaction of many genes (polygenic).

Modern breeds of dogs vary widely in body size and shape and in pelvic conformation. Because of these differences, OFA classifications are based on comparisons among other individuals of the same breed and age. Knowledge of a dog's pelvic phenotype can be a valuable guide for the breeder in selection against hip dysplasia and understanding a dog's pelvic phenotype can be a useful means of estimating an individual dog's potential for an active working life.

The Rottweiler Registry

As aforementioned, when the Colonial Rottweiler Club, through its *Newsletter*, disseminated information on OFA, several very active members of the Golden State Rottweiler Club in California embraced the issue and lent early support to the promulgation of a program whereby only dogs with OFA certified hips could advertise in the Club Newsletters. It must be noted that in the very beginning dogs with near-normal hips were also considered acceptable.

One of the first individuals to support the desirability of OFA certification was Mrs. Clara Hurley. To my knowledge in 15 years she has never wavered in her opinion on this subject. In fact, her conviction of the need for a program led to her establishing the "Rottweiler Registry" which Mrs. Hurley has maintained to date. This is truly an outstanding contribution to our store of knowledge and to the welfare of our breed. "The Registry" serves not only as a roster of dogs passing OFA with their sires and dams listed, but also, because of the data included, serves as a sort of specialized Stud Book. Mrs. Hurley truly deserves appreciation from all of us for this "labor of love".*

The Registry is available from Mrs. Hurley directly, 3320 Wonderview Plaza, Hollywood, CA 90068.

Ch. Rintelna the Dragoon, RO-2312, first Canadian-bred Rottweiler to win an all-breeds Best in Show in Canada (1979). Pictured here later in the same year winning BOB at the Rottweiler Club of Canada Specialty under author Mrs. Bernard Freeman. Breeder: James Miller. Owners: Pat Johnson and James Miller.

Ch. and O.T. Ch. Don-Ari's Baron, the first Canadian-bred Rottweiler to win this dual title. Pictured at 7½ years. Breeders: Mr. and Mrs. Matthew Donaghy. Owners: Mr. and Mrs. L. Graham.

14

The Rottweiler
in Canada

by Brian Smith

Our Canadian reporter, Brian Smith (of Cantass Kennels, Reg.), and his wife Eileen, emigrated from England where they had first made the acquaintance of the Rottweiler. Though they were unable to bring their dogs along, they did not waver in their devotion to the breed and in due time again shared their home with a Rottweiler.

Brian has always been equally interested in Obedience and conformation and both he and Eileen have devoted much time to helping people with all breeds in the matter of Obedience.

Brian is a former Secretary of the Rottweiler Club of Canada. I am especially grateful to him for the effort he made to compile the statistics on Canada. Apparently they were not readily available.

The report on the seminar is made by the irrepressible but all too modest former president of the Rottweiler Club of Canada, William H.C. Marsh. He and Mrs. Marsh are also from England. They have been breeding Rottweilers since 1969 using the registered kennel name Fairvalley, and have had much pleasure and success with their Rottweiler family.

Assuming more than his fair share of responsibility for the successful functioning of the Club, Bill Marsh served as president during two very formative years. He did, so to speak, make history by foreseeing the need for education in Rottweiler circles and by implementing his foresight with conviction and extraordinary effort.

Thank you both, good neighbors.

ALTHOUGH the Rottweiler has been known in Canada since the late 1930s, the present dog can only trace its origins to a litter born in 1964. According to the Stud Book published by the Canadian Kennel Club in 1939, the first Rottweiler registered in Canada was Baya von Jakobsbrunnen (Hackel von Kohlerwald ex Cilla von Rotenwald) bred by

Erwin Bofinger and imported from Germany. After passing through three owners, this bitch was finally registered as being owned by The Commissioner, Royal Canadian Mounted Police. The same stud book also lists the male Bachus vom Universum (Ido von Zuffenhausen ex Afra von Reutlingen), bred by Richard Gutenberger as being imported and finally registered with the Royal Canadian Mounted Police as owners.

There is no record of any litters registered with the Canadian Kennel Club.

In a letter dated April 9, 1981 S.W. Horrall, Historian for the Royal Canadian Mounted Police, writes:

> I am enclosing for your information some copies of excerpts from the published reports of the R.C.M.P. for 1939 and 1940 which mention the acquisition of Bachus and Baya, as well as some of their subsequent history. Also enclosed is a copy of the registration for Bachus and a newspaper clipping on one of his exploits.
>
> After training at Rockcliffe Bachus was sent to New Brunswick. He developed a bronchial infection and was later transferred to Yorkton, Saskatchewan where the dryer climate was found to be better for him. In 1940 he was back in Rockcliffe. An inflammation of the prostate gland was found. It was not considered serious but in 1942 a blood disorder was diagnosed, and he was destroyed on June 16, 1942.
>
> Unfortunately, the records on Baya have not survived. Other than what is in the published reports all I can tell you is that she was either sold or destroyed sometime before April, 1941.
>
> As to their suitability, they were not considered as sharp in nose work as the German Shepherds or Dobermans. This may explain why no others were purchased. Of course, they would not have been so readily available as the others, especially after the outbreak of war.

Extract from The Commissioner's Report, 1939:
> Under your instructions I visited the Wilsona Kennels and purchased five dogs, two Rottweilers, two Riesenschnauzers (Giant Schnauzers) and one German Shepherd . . .
>
> Other than Baya, a female Rottweiler, the dogs on the strength of this force are males. Baya was bred shortly after arriving at the kennels but for some reason destroyed her young. She whelped the second time on March 6, and delivered two well formed pups; both however were dead and it is considered that there is probably some internal deformity which has caused this mishap.

Extract from The Commissioner's Report, 1941:
> On April 18, 1940, a child was reported lost in the Fenwood District, Saskatchewan, and after a search party had covered considerable ground without success, Police Dog "Bachus" was called in and despite the fact that the trail had been greatly fouled by the searching party, he led them through bush and swampland to a ploughed field where the child was finally located.

"Bachus"
> Born November 1936, in Germany; he was acquired by this Force in June, 1938. "Bachus" and his mate, "Baya" are the first Rottweiler dogs registered in the Dominion of Canada. "Bachus" has an average weight of around 100 pounds and "Baya" around 107. These dogs, from experience, have been found to be very thorough in their tracking and searches, but are slower in action than others.
>
> "Bachus" was first transferred to New Brunswick for duty but proved physically unsuited to the climate and soon became ill, being placed under the care of the provincial veterinary. When he was pronounced fit, he was again transferred to

Rockcliffe Kennels for further training, and from there to Saskatchewan, where the climate appears to agree much better with him and he now shows very keen interest in his work.

"Bachus'" first case in the West was assisting in solving a case of theft of wheat. He was allowed to search around the granary from which the wheat was stolen, but the ground had been well trodden by horses and also marked by wagon tracks. However, he picked up a trail which he followed along a road for two miles, and from there turned off into a field. "Bachus" appeared to be following some sort of scent and, when trail came to a ploughed section, it was seen that he had been following a wagon track recognized as one of those tracks seen around the granary. He continued the trail to a farm where the wagon was found and the owner arrested.

This is an unusual case in that it is the first time the trail of a vehicle has been followed by a dog. The age of the trail at this time was approximately 20 hours old.

Copy of Newspaper Clipping dated April 23, 1940 from the *Regina Leader Post* (This relates to the item in the Commissioner's Report 1941):

DOG FINDS LOST BABY
(Special Despatch)

MELLVILLE, April 23—A trained police dog "Bachus" in charge of Const. W. Pitcher of the Yorkton detachment R.C.M.P. succeeded after an all-night search in locating Valery, two-and-a-half-year old son of Mr. and Mrs. Fred Trelenberg, missing from his farm home northeast of Fenwood. The animal was found standing guard over the sleeping child in a field of summer-fallow three-quarters of a mile from his home about 9 o'clock the morning of April 19. The child had evidently wandered around until exhausted, then laid down and gone to sleep in the open field, but when found he was little the worse for his experience.

The child was missed about 6:30 the night before and a search of the immediate surroundings by the parents and neighbors failed to locate him. The Melville police were called at 9 o'clock and Constables T.G.G. Raisbeck, G. Morton and Abbott Brown went out to organise a search party of neighboring farmers. The dog and his master were also called from Yorkton, but the young animal, though he worked well when on the leash, kept losing the scent of the child because the members of the search party had wandered all round the vicinity of the farm home of the lost child. The search went on all night unsuccessfully and the following morning Const. Pitcher unleashed the dog, calculating that if the animal was allowed the run of the vicinity he might pick up the scent, and in the daylight he could be watched and followed. That is what happened and the dog was followed and found beside the sleeping child in the field.

There is then a gap of twenty years before the next dog is recorded with the Canadian Kennel Club—Marlene of Alberta by Skipper Royal out of Schatz v. Eichen. Two years later in 1961, Britta v. Eberstein, born June 4, 1960, imported to Canada in August 1960 by George DeYoung, was registered. This bitch by Asso v. Kaasbruch out of Mucke V. Kohlwald was later transferred, in 1962, to S.W. Ingmar Remmler. Also registered in 1961 was the male Othello v. Hohenreissach, Sire: Hektor v. Burgtobel, Dam: Numa v. Hohenreissach. This dog, born in June 1960, was also owned by Mr. H. George DeYoung.

The Canadian Kennel Club Stud Book for 1962 records the following registrations: Follow Me's Noah (wh. 2/6/61 by Follow Me's Jhan ex Natitia v. Hohenreissach); Follow Me's Odin (wh. 3/8/61 by Arras v. Stadthaus ex Flame of Wynnedale); Norse King (wh. 4/3/61 by Hard-Guy ex Lyda); Panamint Antje and Panamint Christal (wh. 5/21/60 by Emir v. Kohlenhof ex Panamint Ragnarok); Panamint Ragnarok (wh. 11/3/58 by

Claus v. Schildgen ex Kezia v. Heidenmauer); and Quitt v.d. Schwarzwiese (wh. 3/29/62, by Eddi v.d. Hobertsburg ex Cilli v.d. Schwarzwiese).

The first litter registered in Canada was the result of the mating of Othello v. Hohenreissach and Britta v. Eberstein. This litter was born on July 11, 1962 and consisted of seven males and two females and was registered with the Falkenhof's prefix. This litter was recorded in the Stud Book of 1963 as were the following dogs: Angelique v.d. Heid (wh. 8/3/62 by Arras v. Stadthaus ex Numa v. Hohenreissach) and Panamint Sunday Special (wh. 8/5/62 by El Fago Baca ex Panamint Ragnarok).

In 1964 the second litter was born. This was an incestuous breeding between Falkenhof's Arras and Britta v. Eberstern and resulted in one male and nine females. This litter was born on February 18, 1964 and was the Falkenhof 'B' litter. Also registered in 1964 were: Bullino v.d. Neckarstroom, wh. 11/8/62, by Harras von Sofienbusch ex Recora v.d. Brantsberg. This is the first record of Harras progeny in Canada. Fernando v.d. Sheriff (wh. 10/8/62, by Balder v.d. Habenichts ex Bauxite v.d. Woelwijk). Lyngsjons Sindy (wh. 1/9/63 by Ricki ex Lyngsjon's Molly).

However, 1964 was most important for it saw the first litter born to a kennel which is the basis of many of today's dogs. This litter was bred by Patricia Lecuyer (now Hickman) of Northwind's fame. The dam of the litter was the foundation bitch of the Northwind's kennels—Northwind's Tina bred by D.S. Maslund, whelped 5/31/63 by Dervis v. Weyershof ex Katherina's Adorn of Townsview. The sire of the litter was Quitt v.d. Schwarzwiese which was also only the second Canadian Champion (the first being Panamint Sunday Special). Interestingly, the first Northwind litter of three males and six females did not follow the normal practice of the dogs being named with the first letter of the alphabet; indeed, two of the dogs did not carry the Northwind's prefix. The second, third and fourth Northwind litters were born on May 2, 1966, April 22, 1968 and July 12, 1970 respectively and were repeat breedings to Rodsden's Kluge v.d. Harque. These three breedings produced the 'B', 'C', & 'D' litters which appear on many Canadian and American pedigrees and include such names as Northwind's Barras, Cilli, Citta, Darras, Deena and Danka.

The Northwind's 'C' litter is recorded in the Canadian Kennel Club Stud Book for 1968. Also recorded in that issue is the registration of the dog Drauf vom Molzberg, born November 22, 1967 by Kuno vom Kronchen (also recorded as Cuno) out of Do-Jean's Adventurous Miss, to Mr. & Mrs. J. McCormack. This dog, bred to Babette vom Molzberg (Kuno vom Kronchen out of Centa vom Krainberg) started the Jaheriss line. The Jaheriss 'B' litter again saw Drauf as the sire with the import Kathi v.d. Hobertsburg as the dam and the 'C' litter was a repeat of the 'B.' The Jaheriss dogs include such names as Jaheriss' Anejoh, Baer, Baaca and Chayley. The 'D' litter was sired by Blitz von Lucas out of Jaheriss' Anejoh which resulted in the well-known Jaheriss' Drummer Boy and the lesser-known Jaheriss Doraye at Delisa (see later). Many Jaheriss dogs form the basis of other kennel names; for example, Jaheriss' Baaca bred to

219

Ch. Rodsden's Freda of Fairvalley, CKC 862473, AKC WB-404559, RO-160. Wh. 6 July 1969, by Ch. Rodsden's Kluge vd Harque ex Ch. Franzi v. Kursaal. Foundation bitch of Mr. and Mrs. William Marsh's Fairvalley Kennels in Canada. BOB at the first Rottweiler Club of Canada Booster Show in 1973.

Ch. Don-Ari's Brigitte, CD (RO-719T—Excellent), Best of Breed at the Rottweiler Club of Canada Specialty in 1976 under Stan Whitmore, and in 1977 (pictured) under Muriel Freeman. By Graal's Anton ex Ch. Delisa's Bona Dea. Breeders: Matthew and Elena Donaghy. Owner-handler: Eileen Smith.

Ch. Gamecard's Ninette, RO-1771. By
Ch. Jaheriss Drummer Boy ex Ch.
Quintessence of Gamecard's. Breeder:
H. J. McCullough. Owner: Andrea Miles.

Simson vom Heidenmoor, prominent sire
in the Fairvalley and Chrisstenbrad
breeding programs. Bred by Olavi
Pasanen (Finland) and imported to
Canada in 1974 by Lars and Rita Rekola.

Fairvalley's Jago, JH 18721, RO-2403-T,
sire of Fairvalley's "M" litter in 1981.
Jago (wh. 1977) is by Simson von Heiden-
moor ex Ch. Fairvalley's Daphne.
Breeders: Mr. and Mrs. William Marsh.
Owner: Kurt Gatringer.

Sonja von Heidenmoor, litter sister to
Simson, prominent in the Finnberg
breeding program. Owned by Lars and
Rita Rekola.

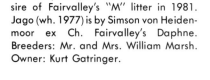

Rodsden's Heiko produced the Trollegen's 'A' litter of Maureen Wilkinson; Jaheriss' Drummer Boy and Jaheriss' Baaca produced Cord (Trollegen's Cord) which was bred to Jaheriss' Chayley to produce the Koskemo 'B' litter.

Having looked briefly at two of the foundation kennels of the Rottweiler in Canada, let us now look at the third kennel which has an important bearing on today's dogs, that of William & Phillipa Marsh's Fairvalley line. Their foundation bitch was Rodsden's Freda of Fairvalley born July 6, 1969 by Rodsden's Kluge v.d. Harque out of Franzi vom Kursaal. The first Fairvalley litter was sired by Rodsden's Goro vom Sofienbusch and born May 2, 1971. The most important of this litter were Fairvalley Anna and Fairvalley Achsah, both kept by the Marshes as breeding stock to continue their program; in addition Fairvalley Alice went to Peter Mehnert's Konigsberg kennel to be used in his program. The second Fairvalley litter, born in December 1971, was also out of Freda but sired by Rodsden's Rhett von der Barr; because of illness only two puppies survived. The third litter sired by Dux vom Hungerbuhl out of Romona von Muskoka was also hit by sickness and only three survived; this litter was born June 2, 1972. The Fairvalley line became established with the first "mixing" between kennels, when Northwind's Darras was used to sire the 'D', 'E', 'F' & 'G' litters. The 'D' litter was born January 31, 1973 out of Fairvalley Anna and included Fairvalley Daphne and Fairvalley Drummer of Dunbarton. Anna and Darras also produced the 'E' litter on February 25, 1974 and the 'G' litter on January 18, 1975. One week prior to this Fairvalley Achsah produced the 'F' litter.

The Don-Ari prefix started in 1960 but it was not until 1972 that the name became associated with Rottweilers. Delisa's Bona Dea was their first bitch that was used in a breeding program. This bitch was bred by D. Morin and sired by the German import Donar v. Lindeck out of Northwind's Cilli. The second Don-Ari bitch was also purchased from D. Morin but was bred by the McCormacks. She was Jaheriss Doraye at Delisa, a litter sister to Jaheriss' Drummer Boy. Both bitches were bred to Graal's Anton, a dog born in Canada out of English stock by Gentris Jerontius and Retsacnal Chesara Dark Zinnia owned by Harm Graalman at the time of importation. The first Don-Ari litter was produced by Doraye on April 20, 1974 and one day later Bona Dea whelped the 'B' litter which included Don-Ari's Baron and Don-Ari's Brigitte. The third litter was also out of Delisa's Bona Dea, this time sired by Northwind's Darras. This litter was born April 3, 1975 and one month later on May 20, 1975 the 'D' litter by Northwind's Darras and Jaheriss' Doraye at Delisa was born— this last litter includes Don-Ari's Deidre and Don-Ari's Donar.

The Millerhaus prefix of Gerald and Shirley Miller is another which has been on the books for a number of years. A few of their progeny have been used in other breeding programs although their main success has probably been in the States rather than Canada. The Millerhaus name starts with Millerhaus Igor, a male by Igor vom Kursaal out of Follow Me's

Burga. He was then bred back to his mother to produce Millerhaus Adam (amongst others). Once again we see an amalgamation of bloodlines with Millerhaus Adam being bred to Northwind's Citta, a breeding which was repeated. Perhaps the most notable offspring were Millerhaus Senta and Millerhaus Fritzgerald who was later the sire of Doonesbury's Myria Angeline. The Millers then imported from England Phasels Seclusion, a male sired by Ero vom Bucheneck out of Chesara Dark Czarina. This dog was bred to Millerhaus Senta which resulted in several more litters with the Millerhaus prefix.

In British Columbia, James Miller's Rintelna prefix was started out of Australian stock. When Mr. Miller returned from Australia, he brought with him his foundation bitch Rintelna the Jubilant and Rotvel Cyllene. Rotvel Cyllene was bred to Rotvel Hermes which produced Rintelna of Cork, to Angus vom haus Kalbas which produced Rintelna Kona (in 1975) and to Rodsden's Rough Diamond which produced Rintelna the Dragoon in 1976.

In Saskatoon, Saskatchewan, the Janlynn kennels of Don & Madge Flury have used a wide base to establish their lines. In the first place Veran's Bon Terra (Jaheriss' Drummer Boy out of Rodsden's Hera Vom Norden) was bred to Rintelna of Cork to produce in November 1975 Janlynn's Megan Merrymaid and to Rintelna Kona to produce Janlynn's Big Shadow of Kona, Janlynn's Bon Katrina and Janlynn's Bon Adonis in May 1977. Janlynn's Merrymaid later produced the 'C' litter sired by Jahriss' Cord in October 1977 and in 1978 Veran's Bon Terra whelped the 'D' litter sired by Cantass Wendigo.

The Glockenhof line of Marilyn Bell is based upon the bitch Ilse vom Schauer who was bred to Drauf vom Molzberg to produce the 'A' litter, to Northwind's Barras for the 'B' litter and to Fandango's Werner (Gamegard's Far & Wide out of Fandango's Gudrun) for the 'C' litter. From the 'A' litter, Glockenhof Anita became the foundation bitch for the Winterland prefix of Karl Eggebrecht. Anita produced many litters mainly from Bruno 3rd (Fandango's Werner out of Stina), an import from Denmark, but also from Admiral—the same way bred as Bruno 3rd.

Having looked briefly at the establishment of some of the early kennels, let us now, without mentioning every litter born, take a look at the progression from then to now.

Northwind's Della produced the Northwind's 'G' litter sired by Rodsden's Goro von Sofienbusch, while the 'H', 'I', 'J' and 'K' litters were all out of Northwind's Danka sired by Rodsden's Kato v. Donnaj, Igor von Schauer, Ero von der Mauth and Igor von Schauer respectively. Ero von der Mauth was also the sire of the 'L' litter out of Graal's Brikka of Northwind.

Fairvalley Daphne produced the Fairvalley 'H', 'J' and 'L' litters all sired by von Heidenmoor Simson born in April 1976, April 1977 and November 1979 respectively while the Fairvalley 'I' and 'K' litters, also sired by vom Heidenmoor Simson were out of Fairvalley Achsah and were born in December 1976 and March 1978.

The Don-Ari line continued with the 'E' litter which was an incestuous breeding between Northwind's Darras and Don-Ari's Deidre born June 30, 1977. The 'F' litter was a repeat of the 'D' litter, namely Northwind's Darras out of Jaheriss' Doraye at DeLisa born December 31, 1977. Don-Ari's Baron sired the 'G' litter out of Don-Ari's Deidre and the 'I' litter was a repeat of this breeding. The 'H' litter was sired by Arras von Majorhausen out of Don-Ari's Elisha.

The Don-Ari's 'B' litter produced Don-Ari's Barda who became the foundation bitch for Peter and Joyce Snider's Wynfield kennel, Don-Ari's Baron—used in the Donaghy's own breeding program and Don-Ari's Brigitte, the foundation bitch of Eileen Smith's Cantass line. Brigitte was first bred to Arras von Kohlerwald. This first Cantass litter was named with Chippewa Indian words. It is interesting to note that the Fairvalley 'H' litter and the first Cantass litter have been bred together four times. Fairvalley Happiness and Cantass Mitigami, both owned by Leigh Semple's Burlynleigh kennel have produced two litters while Fairvalley Hearty Tanya (owned by Gloria Piron's Solera kennels) was bred to Cantass Nibi who was also used to Fairvalley Huncamunca owned by Barry and Donna Verlinde's Blackburn kennel. Cantass Wendigo went to the Flury's Janlynn kennel and Cantass Wabun was the foundation bitch for Aime and Adele Brosseau's Kyladie kennel. The second Cantass litter was an incestuous breeding between Cantass Bekwuk and Don-Ari's Brigitte while the third, also out of Brigitte, was sired by Groll vom Haus Schottroy.

The foundation bitch for Clifford and Lorraine Underwood's Chrisstenbrad's kennel was Millerhaus Alana (Phaesel's Seclusion out of Millerhaus Senta). She was bred to von Heidenmoor Simson to produce the 'A' litter. The 'B' litter was out of Vom Chrisstenbrad's Alexia and sired by Finnberg's Arto Black Bear. There have been two further Chrisstenbrad litters, one sired by Chrisstenbrad's Benjkennoby out of Vom Chrisstenbrad's Alexia and the 'D' sired by von Heidenmoor Simson out of a Finnish import Joukonheimo Domina (Faunus Demon ex von Heidenmoor Lorelei).

Both vom Heidenmoor Simson and vom Heidenmoor Sonja—littermates—were imported from Finland in 1974 by Lars and Rita Rekola. These dogs sired by Artemis out of Krambambuli vom Heidenmoor were bred by Mr. O. Pasanen. Simson has been used in both the Fairvalley and Chrisstenbrad breeding programs while Sonja has produced two litters under the Finnberg's prefix. The first litter was sired by Arras von Kohlerwald and the second by Groll vum Haus Schöttroy.

The Majorhausen kennel of Jacques and Patricia Major used Northwind's Juno as their foundation bitch and their first two litters were both sired by Donnaj Vt Yankee of Paulus. Northwinds also supplied the foundation bitch for the Meyerhof kennel of Ruth Meyer. Northwind's

Jewel was used by both Harriet Gonske's Koskemo kennel and by Don and Sheila O'Brien's Heidegruen kennel in their breeding. Koskemo's first litter was sired by Cord and the Heidegruen litter by Trollegen's Frodo. Trollegen's Fable was the sire of the first Cantymere litter of Marion Postgate, the dam of this litter being Ganseblumchen Von Asgard.

The Vom Weilerhaus kennel of Gilles and Christianne Caumartin used Fairvalley Jalna as their foundation bitch and used Vom Chrisstenbrad's Bacchus as the sire of their first litter. Fairvalley also produced the foundation bitch for the Hallenhof kennel of Henry and Charito Hall with Fairvalley's Fare-thee-well. This bitch, bred to Glocken of Archimedes, produced the 'A', 'B' and 'C' litters for Hallenhof in 1976, 1977 and 1978. Hallenhof Gentleman Bayre was the sire of Kyladie's first two litters out of Cantass Wabun.

The Show Scene

Before looking at the success of various dogs in the Show Ring let me first describe the method by which a dog becomes a Champion in Canada. Prior to January 1, 1980, a dog had to accumulate ten points under at least three different judges and, in addition, one win had to be a "major" which means that a dog had beaten another! The number of points available at a show depended upon the number of dogs in the breed being shown (the number of points being offered were different between breeds) and the location of the show. For example, in Ontario south of 46° North latitude the number of points offered for Doberman Pinschers and Rottweilers were:

		Number of Points				
		1	2	3	4	5
Dogs required	Doberman Pinschers	3	8	11	17	22
	Rottweilers	1	2	4	6	8

This means that a Rottweiler could attend nine shows, be the only Rottweiler present and accumulate nine points towards his title. All that was then required was to attend one more show and beat another Rottweiler. It has been known for dogs to have 14 points and still not be a Champion.

From January 1, 1980 the points structure was amended and points are now awarded on the following basis for all breeds throughout the country:

Number of dogs competing	1	2	3 to 5	6 to 9	10 to 12	13 or more
Points allocated	0	1	2	3	4	5

In addition points are awarded at group level depending upon the number of breeds shown in the group but in no case will more than five points be awarded at a show.

A brief look at the number of dogs entered in competition throughout the country in the early 1960s will give some idea of the scarcity of the breed at that time.

	Ontario	B.C.	Alberta	Quebec	Total
1961	0	15	1	0	16
1962	0	0	2	0	2
1963	11	36	0	0	47
1964	10	11	0	0	21
1965	24	39	0	2	65

These statistics, from *Dogs in Canada,* relate to the number of entries. As the first Champion was not made up until June of 1964 it can be seen that many shows had only one dog in competition. Unfortunately similar statistics for recent years are not available.

The first champion in Canada was Panamint Sunday Special (June 1964) followed closely by Quitt v.d. Schwarzwiese in September of the same year. The early champions were all "imports" and we have to wait until 1967 for the first Canadian bred champion—Northwinds Barras. Incidentally, in the same year Priska vom Kursaal earned her Canadian title.

It is difficult to assess "important" show wins in Canada due to the poor entries of the breed. The Rottweiler Club of Canada has held booster shows and Specialty shows and these results probably reflect those shows which were better attended; however, one must bear in mind the location of the show and the proximity of some kennels to the show sites. The first boosters and Specialties were all held in Ontario and entries from the West were, in the early days, non-existent. The first Specialty of the Rottweiler Club of Canada was held in 1975. BOB was Ch. Achsah of Fairvalley (885634) bred by Mr. & Mrs. William H.C. Marsh

Dogs in Canada, the national dog magazine in Canada produces an annual list of Top Dogs. Points are awarded for every dog beaten at the breed level. Since 1977, the Rottweiler Club of Canada has also produced a list of top dogs; this list is also based on points awarded for dogs beaten but from the "winners" level upwards. In fact both *Dogs in Canada* and Rottweiler Club of Canada produce two lists—one at breed level and one for all breed competition.

The records of the Canadian Kennel Club do not lend themselves to ready interpretation of all breed competition. It would appear though that Rottweilers did not make any impression in the Group ring until the 1970s when Jaheriss' Anejoh obtained several Best Canadian Bred Puppy in Group placements. The following year on September 25, 1971 at the Burlington show, Rodsden's Duke du Trier, owned by Dr. & Mrs. N.O. Olsen, won the first Best in Show award for a Rottweiler in Canada. The next Best in Show award for our breed, and the first for a Canadian bred dog, was on May 6, 1979. This time, under judge Irving Diamond, Ch. Rintelna the Dragoon owned by Pat Johnson of Winnipeg and James Miller of Vancouver won the honors. Later the same year, Mrs. Bernard

Freeman awarded this dog Best of Breed at the Rottweiler Club of Canada's Specialty Show.

In recent years, several Rottweilers have found their place in the Group ring. The Canadian bred dogs to achieve this feat are:

		No of Group Placings			
		1	2	3	4
in 1977	Ch. Doonesbury's Myria Angeline		1		5
in 1978	Ch. Northwind's Kaiser of Mallam	1			
	Ch. Fairvalley Happiness		1	1	
in 1979	Ch. Cantass Wendigo				2
	Ch. Cantass Nibi			1	
	Ch. Fairvalley's Kluge				1
	Ch. Rintelna the Dragoon	1			
in 1980	Ch. Bryloukis Alexander		1		1
	Ch. Cantass Kitigami	1		1	
	Ch. Gamecard's Ninette	1			1
	Ch. Northwind's Jewel				1

It may be interesting to note that all three Cantass dogs listed are litter brothers.

In the Obedience environment participation has been extremely poor, although again, in recent years, the trend has been to more dogs being seen in competition. From the records of the Canadian Kennel Club for the years 1963 to 1970 only nine dogs obtained their C.D. degree—none of them Canadian bred. The first Canadian bred dog to attain a C.D. was Northwind's Cilli, in 1971, and in 1972 this title was earned by Aliwaki's Atticus of Fairvalley. In Canada, to become an Obedience trial Champion a dog only has to earn its Utility Degree, whereas in the States a dog has to campaign and earn points and be placed in competition. The first and only Canadian bred Rottweiler to earn the Obedience title and also the first dual champion is Ch. & Ob. Ch. Don-Ari's Baron. The first U.D. Rottweiler in Canada was Rodsden's Goro von Sofienbusch in 1973. More recently this title has been earned by Dasso v. Geeren, owned and trained by Peter Navratil.

Dogs in Canada produce a top dog list for Obedience—this list relates to the number of points earned in C.D.X. and U.D. competition only; since 1977, the Rottweiler Club of Canada has also produced a top ten list for Obedience but this list relates to all levels of Obedience.

THE FIRST ROTTWEILER SEMINAR

by William H.C. Marsh
President, Rottweiler Club of Canada 1975-1976

In the late winter of 1976 the Directors of the Rottweiler Club of Canada struck upon the idea of holding an educational forum for the benefit of owners and judges who were serious about improving their knowledge of the breed. After much discussion and groping around for ways and means of providing, presenting and paying for such a venture we approached Mrs. Bernard (Muriel) Freeman with the idea of heading up a team of experts in various aspects of dogdom.

Our planning eventually evolved into a very full one day Seminar with a panel of three speakers: Muriel Freeman of Long Island, N.Y., a Rottweiler breeder and international judge with the distinction of being the first American to have earned the privilege of judging the breed in Germany; Catherine (Casey) Gardiner of Milton, Ont., also a dog breeder, an established authority on dog movement (gaiting) and the originator, developer and promoter of the Community College courses entitled, Dogs a Hobby or a Profession; Dr. Edward S. Gibson, M.D., of Burlington, Ont., a Professor at McMaster University, Hamilton, Ont., a dog breeder, trainer and a student of the Anatomy of the Dog.

The programme consisted of an exhaustive review and discussion of the Rottweiler Breed Standard led by Mrs. Freeman with suggestions on how it might and should be improved. Dr. Gibson and Mrs. Gardiner combined talents to demonstrate measuring bone lengths and joint angles at the same time, explaining the significance of these measurements in determining the structure of the animal. After luncheon Mrs. Gardiner spoke on the Movement of the Rottweiler using a film on gaiting which had been produced by Club Vice-President Matthew Donaghy. A Judging Clinic was conducted by Mrs. Freeman which gave those present an opportunity to apply some of their new found knowledge in a very practical manner. This clinic was designed to teach one how to assess the total dog.

The Seminar was held on Sunday, October 3, 1976 at the Howard Johnson's Airport Hotel in Toronto. Invitations were sent to all members of the Rottweiler Club of Canada, other known owners and to one hundred and fifty Canadian Group III, permit and All Breed judges. It appears that we were ahead of our time, as attendance was poor to say the least. Those who did attend were loud in their praise of the programme and the marked ability of our three guest speakers.

Apparently our basic concept of a worthwhile educational programme was correct, as evidenced by the success of a series of similar and subsequent Seminars or Symposia held in the USA, Canada, Australia and England.

Members of the Group Brandenburg parading with their Rottweilers. Photo from Stud Book 10 of the ADRK, closed December 31, 1926.

15

The Rottweiler in Germany

As will be noted, the articles on the Rottweiler in foreign countries have been authored by eminent authorities in each one of those countries. I am deeply indebted to my contributors for their response to my appeal for information.

Unfortunately, the same cannot be said for the Germans. Despite many solicitations on my part, and promises to comply on theirs, no material has been forthcoming. It is regrettable inasmuch as Germany is the country of origin of the Rottweiler and as such, information from this source is vital to any book on the Rottweiler.

Failing their cooperation, I will present the case as best I can from my vantage point which is limited. Except for the experience of apprentice judging, prior to my acceptance as a German Rottweiler Specialist Judge, I have been an observer at all functions, which is very different from being a participant.

CHAMPIONSHIP DOG SHOWS world-wide are under the jurisdiction of an organization called the Federation Cynologique Internationale, which we will hereafter refer to as the FCI. Notable exceptions to this jurisdiction are the United States of America—where the ruling body is the American Kennel Club, Canada—where it is the Canadian Kennel Club, and England—where the sanctum sanctorum is The Kennel Club. These three national clubs are autonomous in their respective countries, whereas the national clubs of most other countries are subject to FCI regulations. This is a very important fact to bear in mind in any discussion of cynological regulations on an international basis.

For Germany, the national club is the *Verband für das Deutsche Hundewesen* (VDH). The VDH does not keep the Stud Books as does our American Kennel Club. It does publish a monthly all-breed magazine entitled, *Unser Rassehund*. Also, among its functions is the selection of important show dates and the designation of the locale for the Bundessieger Show (with FCI approval).

Die Rassekennzeichen des Rottwe

Ziel der Rottweilerzucht ist ein harmonisch, fest und stark gebauter, den Rassekennzeichen entsprechender Begleit-, Schutz- und Gebrauchshund von höchster körperlicher und charakterlicher Leistungsfähigkeit. Das Streben des Züchters muß stets darauf gerichtet sein, die Rasse nicht nur zu vermehren, sondern Form und Wesen auf breitester Basis zu erhalten und zu festigen.

Unter Rassekennzeichen versteht man die durch den berechtigten Zuchtverein erarbeitete Zusammenstellung von Merkmalen und Eigenschaften, die jeder Hund dieser Rasse möglichst ausgeprägt aufweisen soll. Dabei legt man das erstrebenswert erscheinende Idealbild, den sogenannten Musterhund, zugrunde. Zuständig für die Festlegung, Ergänzung oder Berichtigung der Rassekennzeichen ist der Zuchtverein des Landes, dem der Ursprung der Rasse zuerkannt worden ist; in unserem Falle der **Allgemeine Deutsche Rottweiler-Klub e. V. (ADRK)**, Sitz in **Stuttgart**. Alle übrigen Länder, soweit sie der Federation Cynologique Internationale (FCI) angehören oder mit diesem Verband unter Vereinbarung stehen, sind verpflichtet, die Rassekennzeichen des Ursprungslandes einzuhalten, wodurch eine weitgehende Gewähr für übereinstimmende Zucht-, Beurteilungs- und Bewertungsmaßstabe gegeben ist.

Der ADRK schickt den Kennzeichen seiner Rasse folgenden Leitsatz voraus:
Die Rottweilerzucht erstrebt einen kraftstrotzenden Hund, schwarz mit rotbraunen, klar abgegrenzten / chen, der **bei wuchtiger Gesamter nung den Adel nicht vermissen läßt sich als Begleit-, Schutz- und brauchshund in besonderem Maß net.**

Äußere Erscheinung

Gesamtbild:

Der Rottweiler ist ein über mitt ßer, stämmiger Hund, weder noch leicht, nicht hochläufig ode dig. Seine im richtigen Verhältni hende leicht gestreckte, gedru und kräftige Gestalt läßt auf Kraft, Wendigkeit und Aus schließen. Seine Erscheinung Urwüchsigkeit, sein Verhalter selbstsicher, nervenfest und schrocken. Sein ruhiger Blick b det Gutartigkeit. Er reagiert m her Aufmerksamkeit gegenüber Umwelt und seinem Herrn.

Größe:

Widerristhöhe Rüden 60 bis 68 c

60 bis 61 cm klein
62 bis 64 cm mittelgroß
65 bis 66 cm groß
67 bis 68 cm sehr groß

Widerristhöhe Hündinnen 55 bis

55 bis 57 cm klein
58 bis 59 cm mittelgroß
60 bis 61 cm groß
62 bis 63 cm sehr groß

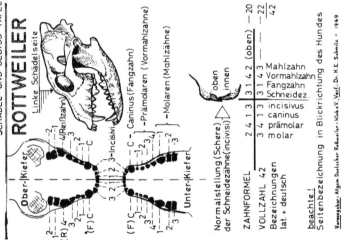

A page out of *Die Bestimmungen* (see P. 231).

Progressing down the ladder of authority, on the next rung one finds the various breed clubs which correspond to our parent clubs. The one concerning us is:

Allgemeiner Deutscher Rottweiler Klub e.V. (ADRK)

The ADRK performs all the important duties of our most active parent clubs, adopts the standard, and, in addition, keeps the Stud Book, issues the pedigrees, approves all tests and trials and monitors the results, confers all titles and degrees and licenses any and all Rottweiler Conformation and Working Dog Judges. Controlling these functions assures the direction the breeding program will follow and therein lies the core of the Germans' ability to improve their stock in a manner quite impossible for us, under our present system, to emulate.

Adopts the Standard

"Die Bestimmungen" is the book containing the Standard of the Breed and the rules and regulations pertaining to the breeding, showing and training of Rottweilers.

Glancing at the page reproduced, the eye travels to the diagram of the jaws, which shows the correct number and placement of the teeth and proper occlusion.

The text on the facing page gives a general description of the desired "type" and the purpose for which the Rottweiler is bred. The ADRK takes the position that Germany, being the country of origin, Rottweilers world-wide should be judged by its Standard. This is followed by the exact stipulations of the Standard. The figures which can be seen are the acceptable height at the withers of males and females and the category (small, medium, large, very large) into which these numbers fall.

The entire Standard is accurately defined as are all the rules pertaining to breeding, showing and training of the Rottweiler which follow.

The Stud Book

Study of old ADRK Stud Books can be very interesting, as well as informative. For example, the page that I'm looking at, from a pre-1950 volume, includes names of breeders still well-known to us today, 35 years later. Jakob Köpf (von Gaisburg) was an outstanding breeder of his time. His Vroni v. Gaisburg 29911 Sch H2 was Bundessiegerin in 1952. Mr. Köpf was a highly regarded judge with vast knowledge of the breed. He was the mentor of much respected Friedrich Berger (von der Hobertsburg), who judged in the United States on several occasions. Friedrich passed away in 1981 after serving the ADRK for 17 years as Head Breed Warden and Director. He will be remembered as an outstanding judge possessed of a faultless memory for dogs he had seen and their pedigrees.

Christian Armbruster (vom Burgtobel) was one of few breeders in his area still owning a Rottweiler after World War II. The bitch, Dora, listed as

GEBRAUCHSHUNDEZUCHT

AHNENTAFEL
für den
Rottweiler

Der Hund darf erst zur Zucht verwendet werden, wenn er auf seine Zuchttauglichkeit geprüft ist und das Alter von 24 Monaten erreicht hat.

Eingetragen in das Zuchtbuch des ADRK

Band: **XLVI**   Nummer: **39 499**

Name des Hundes: **E r n o   von Welleweiler**

Geschlecht: **Rüde**

Farbe und Abzeichen: **schwarz mit braunen Abzeichen**

Wurftag: **26.August 1962**

Wurfziffer in Buchstaben: **Neunundhundertzweiundsechzig**

Züchter des Hundes: Name: **Karl Baekes**   Wohnort: **Castrop-Rauxel 4, Feldstraße 1**

Erläuterungen über den Wurf, zu dem dieser Hund gehört		Rüden	Hündinnen
Wurfstärke b.d. Geburt		5	2
Totgeboren			
Gefallen		1	1
Im Wurf belassen		4	1
Verendet b.z. Eintragung			
Zum Zuchtbuch gemeldet		4	1
Nicht nachgewiesen			

Die Ahnentafel hat nur Gültigkeit, wenn sie mit dem Siegel des Klubs versehen, vom Zuchtbuchführer beglaubigt und vom Züchter eigenhändig unterschrieben oder vom Zuchtbuchführer als Abschrift (Duplikat) bezeichnet ist. Sie gilt als Urkunde im juristischen Sinne. Wer Ahnentafeln fälscht, abändert oder mit ihnen Mißbrauch treibt, wird strafrechtlich verfolgt. Beim Tode des Hundes ist die Ahnentafel an das Zuchtbuchamt zurückzugeben.

Bei Verkauf des Hundes ist die Ahnentafel dem neuen Eigentümer unter Eintragung des Eigentumswechsels auszuhändigen, beim Eingehen des Hundes sie an das Zuchtbuchamt des ADRK zurückzugeben.

Ergebnis der Zuchttauglichkeits-Prüfung

in Ansbach a.d.R. am 19.April 1964

Zuchttauglich - zur Zucht nicht geeignet

Körmeister bzw. Richter: Hermann Diehl, Erfelden

Bestätigung des Zuchtbuchamtes des ADRK
Stuttgart W, den 22.April 1964

1. Körung in Kaiserslautern am 27.Mai 1965

Für die Dauer von zwei Jahren angekört
(bis einschl. 22.Mai 1967)

Körmeister: Hermann Diehl, Erfelden/Rhein

Bestätigung des Zuchtbuchamtes des ADRK
Stuttgart W, den 3.Juni 1965

2. Körung in Heppenheim am 23. April 1967

Auf Lebenszeit angekört

Körmeister: Hermann Diehl, Erfelden

Für die Richtigkeit der Angaben an das Zuchtbuchamt zur Ausfertigung dieser Urkunde bürgt als Züchter durch Unterschrift

7.Januar 1963   Kurt Baekes
(Ohne Unterschrift des Züchters nicht gültig)

Eintragungs- und Prüfungsbestätigung

Der obenbezeichnete Rottweiler ist am 30.Dezbr.1962 in das Zuchtbuch des Allgemeinen Deutschen Rottweiler-Klub unter Nr. 499 eingetragen worden. Die Abstammungsangaben sind nachgeprüft und ihre Richtigkeit wird hiermit bestätigt.

Das Zuchtbuchamt des ADRK

I Eltern	II	III Ur-Großeltern	IV Urur-Großeltern	V	Ururur-Großeltern
1 **Internat.Champ. Bsg 1960,1961,1962 Harras von Sofienbusch 36 474 SchH 1**	3 **Arno von der Hemmerpaote 35 107 SchH 3**	7 BS Igor vom Kohlwald 32 149 SchH 1	15 Eros v.d.Morgstadt 30 171 ZDH	31	Nestor Marschbrünnle 26101 SchH 1
				32	Erni von der Platte 26196
			16 BS Dora v.Naubebel 27 644 SchH	33	Bruno v.Jakobsbrunnen 24975/I
				34	Nila von Rebensbach 25031 SchH 3
		8 Carin v.Zicksackhausen 33 557	17 Dolf von Gerstetten 32 037	35	BS Bruno v.Rehen-Dach 28789 SchH 3
				36	Alma von Sebatien 27166 SchH 1
			18 Citta vom Cilebrunnen 29 810 SchH 1	37	Lord von Birkenbusch 27142 SchH 3
	4 **Afra aus den Mayen 33 914 SchH 1**	9 Arko von Schmiedebrunnen 30 090 SchH 3	19 Claus v.Silberhagen 28 849 SchH 1	38	Senta v.d.Amerquelle 25869 SchH 1
				39	Hold von Gaisburg 25579
			20 Birbel v.Jakobsbrun- nen 27 127	40	Carin von Habichtswald 24917
				41	Hold von Gaisburg 25579
		10 Antje von der Insenruh 31 075	21 Edi v.Jakobsbrunnen 27 278 SchH 3	42	Alex v.Ostenbach 25911 SchH 3
				43	Pia v.Jakobsbrunnen 24315 SchH 3
			22 Ida v.Schloß Kilchberg 28 596 SchH 3	44	Xanthippe v.Jakobsbrunnen 24975/I
				45	Glass vom Waisbachtal 26086 SchH 3
				46	Belka vom Wurtel 25542
2 **Alke von Gomaringen 37 398 SchH 2**	5 **Castor vom Schnasental 34 476 SchH 1**	11 Alex vom Röntgenweg 31 407 SchH 2	23 Genius v.d.Siebhalde 30 487 SchH 1	47	Kilu vom Lämmiblick SHSB 94157
				48	Arna von Jülffweg SHSB 91250
			24 Rita v.Jakobsbrunnen 29 136	49	Olana vom Weisbachtal 26086 SchH 3
				50	Xanthippe v.Jakobsbrunnen 24975/I
		12 Anni vom Forchenkopf 33 158	25 Arras von der Schwei- zergrenze 29197	51	Tillo von Hohenzollern 24062
				52	Musa von Gaisburg 26736
			26 Bose v.Falkenstein- Schramberg 26335	53	Arko von der Hohenstaig 24982
				54	Polka v.Falkenstein-Schramberg 2366
	6 **Flora vom Butzensee 35 733**	13 Arno von der Tanne 32 041 SchH 2	27 Genius v.d.Siebhalde 30 487 SchH 1	55	Kilu vom Lämmiblick SHSB 94157
				56	Arna von Jülffweg SHSB 91250
			28 Anny vom Salamander 28 673 SchH 1	57	LS Pluto v.Jakobsbrunnen 26355/III
		14 Centa vom Butzensee 33 580	29 Arras von der Schwei- zergrenze 29197	58	Dora v.Hohn-Aspen 26228 SchH/I
				59	Tillo v.Hohenzollern 24062
			30 Bona vom Hohenzoller	60	Musa von Gaisburg 26736
			29 583	61	LS Pluto v.Lohengrinfel 25101
				62	Bila von Burstal 24495

27644 became Bundessiegerin in 1951 and is pictured on Page 2 of this book in illustration of an ideal head.

Richard Schmidgall (vom Kursaal) was one of the most successful breeders in Germany throughout the '60s and '70s. Very few pedigrees of that era exist in which a dog bred or owned by him does not appear.

Studying the Stud Book, we note the detailed information provided on each litter—the sire, dam, grandsires, granddams, with their registered numbers and earned titles to date. The date the breeding took place (DT), whelping date (WT), the number of pups produced (W), the number culled (††), the number expired, when such occurred (†), and the number registered are included. This information is gathered from the litter applications submitted to the Stud Book Office.

Other important sections to be found in the Stud Book are results and critiques of the *Zuchttauglichkeitsprüfungen* (explanation follows) and a list of those dogs rejected as unsuitable for breeding, including the reason for rejection, i.e., entropion, missing teeth, poor temperament, etc. Results and critiques of the *Körung* (explanation follows) can be found, as can the scores obtained in the working trials along with the degrees earned. An alphabetic index by kennel name of litters registered in that year is also included. A new addition to the Stud Book is a list containing the results of those dogs X-rayed for HD in that year.

It can be noted here, Rottweilers in Germany are eligible for permanent hip evaluation after they are a year old. All dogs are tattooed, in the ear, with their ADRK number and this identification is included on the film when the vet takes the X-ray. The X-ray is sent to the University for interpretation and the results are sent to the Stud Book Office. Should the vet be remiss in any way and not comply with ADRK regulations, his name is forthwith published as having been deleted from the approved list of veterinarians—proof of the Club's control of the program.

ADRK Issues the Pedigree (*Ahnentafel*)

The pedigree reproduced herein was selected because it is one of my dogs and, therefore, permission was not needed to reproduce it. In addition, it contains many interesting facts not appearing on all pedigrees. Recorded on every pedigree is the individual dog's name, whelping date, breeder with address, an enumeration of the littermates, the sex, Stud Book number assigned to the individual, the volume of the Stud Book in which it appears, plus a five-generation pedigree wherein all Stud Book numbers and earned degrees of the forebears are recorded. Space is reserved to enter the results of the *Zuchttauglichkeitsprüfung,* the *Körung,* Working and Conformation titles and degrees, if and when they are earned.

This pedigree is approximately twenty years old. Some minor differences occur in the forms used today, i.e., only four generations appear, but critiques on the parents and grandparents are included, space is allotted to enter the results of the hip X-ray, and some dogs' pedigrees are issued on pink paper, denoting select breeding stock.

Allgemeiner Deutscher Rottweiler Klub e. V.
(ADRK), Sitz Stuttgart

Ort: Herzogenrath
Tag: 27. November 1976
XXXXXX Dr. Schmitz
oder Richter

Ergebnis der Zuchttauglichkeitsprüfung

für die Hündin ▮▮▮▮▮▮▮▮▮▮

gew. am ▮▮▮▮▮▮ Zuchtbuch Nr. ▮▮▮▮▮

Vater: Elko y. Kaiserberg Zuchtbuch Nr. 44 342

Mutter: Carmen v.Liebersbacher Hof Zuchtbuch Nr. 47 325

Züchter: ▮▮▮▮▮▮▮▮

Besitzer: ▮▮▮▮▮▮▮▮

Name ▮▮▮▮▮▮ Vorname

PLZ Wohnort ▮▮▮▮▮▮ Straße Nr.

Körpermaße

Widerristhöhe: 58 cm. Brusttiefe: 29 cm
Rumpflänge: 73 cm. Brustumfang: 83 cm

I. Erscheinung und Verfassung, Gebäude und Ganganlagen:

Mittelgroß, harmonisch, austrainiert, typischer Kopf, sattbraunes Auge, mittleres Ohr, mäßiger Stop, natürlicher Aufbau mit mittleren Winkelungen, spannkräftige Bänder, guter Aufknöchelung, kräftige Keulen, kurzes, robustes Stockhaar, schön gefärbte, gut verteilte Abzeichen, leicht gehemmtes, hinten breittretendes Gangwerk, gutes Geschlechtsgepräge.

Leichte HD - zuchttauglich.

Wesen:	gering	mittel	hoch	sehr hoch
Selbstsicherheit		X		
Unerschrockenheit		X		
Temperament			X	
Ausdauer				
Aufmerksamkeit				X
Führigkeit		X		
Mißtrauen	X			
Schärfe		naturschärfe		
Mut			X	
Kampftrieb			X	
Schutztrieb		X		
Härte			X	
Reizschwelle	X			

	gleichgültig	leicht	scheu
Reaktion auf den Schuß	X		

HD-Nr. ....

Zucht- und Körfähig	X	zur Zucht geeignet		Zuchtverbot	
X	zuchttauglich		zurückgestellt		zuchtuntauglich

Paarungen, die zu Würfen geführt haben, in denen sich Hunde mit erbbedenklichen Fehlern befinden, dürfen nicht wiederholt werden.
(Abschnitt IV Absatz 5 der Zuchtbestimmung.)

.... den .... 19... Zuchtrichter: ....

Hauptzuchtwart: ....

Bestätigung der Zuchtbuchstelle

Umstehendes Ergebnis ist für den Hund eingetragen.

Porta Westfalica, den .... Zuchtbuchstelle des ADRK

167

Place: _____
Date: _____
Kör Master
or Judge _____

RESULTS OF TEST FOR BREEDING SUITABILITY

For, male
female
Wh. on _____ Reg. #
Sire: _____ Reg. #
Dam: _____ Reg. #

Breeder: _____

Owner: _____

Address _____

BODY MEASUREMENTS

Withers Height: _____ cm. Depth of Brisket: _____ cm.
Body Length: _____ cm. Chest Circum.: _____ cm.

1. Appearance, condition, conformation and movement:

Character or Nature	Low	Medium	High	Very High
Self-sufficiency			X	X
Fearlessness			X	X
Disposition		X		X
Endurance, persistency			X	X
Watchfulness				X
Tractability			X	X
Mistrustfulness	X			X
Sharpness			X	X
Courage				X
Fighting Drive				X
Guarding Drive				X
Hardness			X	X
Point of Arousal		X		X

	Ignores	Slight	Shy
Reaction to the Gun	X		

H.D. #

Breedable, Elig. Körung		Breed Endorsed		Breed Forbidden
Breedable		Eligibility Held Back		Unbreedable

Breed Judge:

Head Breed Warden:

ENDORSEMENT OF THE BREED BOOK BUREAU

At top, copy of a marked test sheet (*Zuchttauglichkeitsprüfungen*). Below, an Anglicized version for your understanding. (See P. 235.)

ADRK Confers all Titles and Degrees

Interpreting the titles, Bsg and BS stand for *Bundessieger*, meaning Champion of the Bund. Only one dog and one bitch can achieve this title each year. International Champion is a title conferred by the FCI on dogs which have competed successfully in the breed ring in at least three different countries.

Sch H, with the number after it is the Working Degree, varying from one to three in ascending order of difficulty. *Leistungsieger* (LS) is the dog making the highest score doing Sch H3 work at the Championship Working Dog Show of the year. Another interesting detail to remember is that German dogs carry the kennel name as a suffix, and the first names of all dogs in the litter begin with the same letter keyed to the number of litters the breeder has had. Thus, in a breeder's first litter all names begin with A, in the second litter all names begin with B, etc.

Beneath this is a space for recording sales of the dog with all owners' signatures to be entered. Today, the hip status is also recorded on the pedigree. Compared to our AKC registration, we can only appreciate and admire the overwhelming superiority of the information offered on the pedigree by the German method.

The Breed Warden

Many of you have undoubtedly heard of the German Breed Warden system, but are unfamiliar with its function. Simply stated, a Breed Warden is a person deemed by the ADRK to be sufficiently experienced in the breed to advise others as to suitable matings, care of the expectant dam, whelping and culling of the litter, cropping of tails and dewclaw removal, care and raising of the pups, etc.

There is a hierarchy of Breed Wardens from the Head Breed Warden, who is a member of the Board of Governors, down through what would be our State Breed Wardens to a Sectional Breed Warden, and finally, a local Breed Warden. Each one is responsible to report to the person in authority over him and finally the "buck stops" with the Head Breed Warden, who is responsible for overseeing the accuracy of the data which appears on every dog's pedigree besides his required other duties, the most important of which is guidance of the breeding program.

ADRK Approves and Monitors All Tests

Another function of some select breed wardens is to preside at *Zuchttauglichkeitsprufungen*. These are the tests for breeding suitability which must be passed before a Rottweiler can be bred in Germany. The penalty for non-observance of this regulation is simple—the litter cannot be registered, a rather effective method of exercising control.

A copy of a marked test sheet, and the same sheet with the terms in translation are presented. You will note bodily measurements have been

Körschein für Rüden

als Bestätigung der vom Allgemeinen Deutschen Rottweiler-Klub (ADRK)
durchgeführten Körung für den Rottweiler

Körort: Kaiserslautern
Körtag: 23. Mai 1965
Körmeister: Herm.Diehl, Erfelden

Gebrauchshundezucht/Körzucht/Leistungszucht

Angekört für 2 Jahre

[Name]: Erno von Welleweiler

Wurftag: 26.August 1962 , ZB Nr.: 39 499 , Ausb.-Kennz.: SchH I bis einschließlich 22.Mai 1967

Vater: BS Harras vom Sofienbusch – 36 474 – SchH 3

Arno von der Hammerposte – 35 1o7 – SchH 3

Afra aus den Mayen – 33 914 – SchH 1

Mutter: Alke von Gomaringen – 37 398 – SchH 2

Castor vom Schussental – 34 476 – SchH 1

Flora vom Butzensee – 35 733

Inzucht:

Züchter: Karl Backes   Wohnort: Castrop – Rauxel

Eigentümer: Erwin Mohr   Wohnort: 614 – Bensheim a.d.B.

Straße: Wilhelmstr. 9

(Bei Änderung des Eigentumsverhältnisses ist dem Zuchtbuchamt Stuttgart innerhalb längstens acht Tagen unter gleichzeitiger Einsendung dieses Körscheines Mitteilung zu machen.)

Nacheigentümer: (Zeitangabe) .... Anschrift: ....

Feststellungen bei der Körung:

I. 1. Gesamturteil über allgemeine Erscheinung und Verfassung, Gebäude und Gangvermögen, Gefügefestigkeit, Wesen und Kampftrieb:

Starkknochiger gut proportionierter Rüde von edlem Ausdruck, typischer Kopf, dunkle Augen, richtige Ohrenhaltung, breite u. tiefe Brust, straffer Rücken, richtige Winkelungen, freies Gangwerk, saubere Abzeichen. Naturscharf guter Kampftrieb

2. a) Geschlechtsgepräge: ausgeprägt, vorhanden.   b) Konstitution: kräftig, trocken, etwas derb, etwas fein.

3. Wesen einschl. Nervenverfassung: lebhaft, ruhig; aufmerksam; etwas zurückhaltend, gutartig; dreist, furchtlos, nervenfest und-frisch; leicht übererregt.

4. Ausdruck: rottweilermäßig, lebensvoll, geweckt, edel, etwas unfreundlich.

II. Gebäudebeurteilung im Stand:

1. Gebäudeverhältnisse: gestreckt, etwas lang, etwas kurz. Kräftig, reichlich schwer, schwer, mittelschwer, etwas leicht, gehaltvoll, ausreichend gehaltvoll; untersetzt (gedrungen), fest, etwas breit, etwas schmal, leicht flachrippig; guter Stand.

2. a) Widerristhöhe: 64 cm;   b) Brusttiefe: 30 cm;   c) Brustumfang: 86 cm;
d) Körperlänge: 78 cm.

3. a) Knochen: kräftig, mittelkräftig, etwas grob, etwas fein.
b) Bemuskelung: kräftig, genügend kräftig, trocken.
c) Stand- und Bänderfestigkeit vorne: sehr gut, gut, genügend.
d) Stand- und Bänderfestigkeit hinten: sehr gut, gut, genügend.

4. a) Haarverfassung:
gesund, glanzlos, in Haarung;
b) Art der Behaarung:
stockhaarig; etwas lang, derb, kräftig, Unterwolle vorhanden, kurz.

5. a) Farbe und Abzeichen: schwarz mit braunen Abzeichen
b) Pigmentierung: viel, genügend.

6. a) Kopf: sehr kräftig, kräftig, etwas leicht, etwas schmal, leicht verkürzt, leicht übastreckt.
Augenfarbe: dunkel, hell, dunkelbraun, hellbraun, gelb.
Ohrenhaltung: hoch / seitwärts angesetzt, klein, schwer.
b) Fangtiefe: gut, noch ausreichend, voll, lang, zu schmal.
c) Kieferbildung: Scherengebiß.
d) Gebiß: gesund, kräftig, etwas schwach, teilweise angebrannt.
7. Hoden: kräftig entwickelt, klein.

III. Gangbeurteilung im Schritt und Trabe (an der Leine und frei laufend):
Gesamturteil:
Treber: federnd, raumgreifend, geräumig, aus dem Rücken flach über den Boden gehend;
gute, genügende Festigkeit der Vorderfußwurzelgelenke;
gute, genügende Festigkeit der Sprunggelenke;
Nachschub: wirksam, genügend wirksam, etwas gebunden;
Vortritt: sehr gut, gut, ausreichend;
Neigung zu Paßgang.

IV. Besondere Gebäudevorzüge oder Gebäudemängel (als Ergänzung zum Gesamturteil unter I. 1.):

V. Beurteilung der Wesensveranlagung (nicht von Leistungen): Der Befund ist nicht durch Bewertungsangaben wie "vorzüglich", "gut" usw. anzugeben, sondern Zutreffendes zu unterstreichen.

1. Wesen und Nervenverfassung:
a) Wesen: fest, natürlich, temperamentvoll, ruhig.
b) Aufmerksamkeit: vorhanden, rege, stetig.
c) Nervenverfassung: fest, leicht übererregt.
d) Unbefangenheit: vorhanden, genügt.
e) Verkehrssicherheit: vorhanden, genügt.
f) Schußgleichgültigkeit: vorhanden, genügt.

2. Mut und Schärfe:
a) Kampftrieb: ausgeprägt, vorhanden.
b) Mut: ausgeprägt, vorhanden.
c) Schärfe: ausgeprägt, vorhanden.

3. Bewertung auf Leistungsprüfungen:
SchH I – 257 Pkt./gt.

Beratung für Auswahl des Zuchtpartners (Empfehlungen oder Warnungen):

(Körort): Kaiserslautern , (Körtag): 23. Mai 1965

Der Körmeister: Hermann Diehl

Stuttgart, den 9.Juni 1965

Für die Richtigkeit: Zuchtbuchamt des ADRK

recorded, as are the results of the hip X-ray, the venue of the test, the date and the name of the person administering the test, the dog's sire and dam with registration numbers, the breeder and the owner with his address. In the character analysis section, the shaded boxes denote what the Germans consider to be the ideal for a Rottweiler in each category. Beneath the shaded boxes can be seen the terms, "Breedable" and "Eligible for the Körung."

On the test sheet we show, the box below "HD Nr." is not checked because the bitch is ineligible to go to the *Körung* (test for highest breeding suitability). Her hips disqualify her. Only dogs that are HD free (–), or with minor irregularities (+/ –) are eligible. Where "Breedable" is checked, it denotes she has passed the *Zuchttauglichkeitsprüfung*.

We have referred to the *Körung* as the test for highest breeding suitability. Dogs presented for this test must have a working degree (minimum Schutzhund I for females and Schutzhund III for males). They must have a record of having been shown in the conformation ring under different judges and with the rating of "Very Good" [*Sehr Gut* (S.G.)], or "Excellent" [*Vorzüglich* (V)]. In addition, they must have demonstrated through a prescribed number of litters that their progeny do not exhibit any serious genetic faults, such as too many puppies afflicted with HD, long hair, white markings, etc. Dogs presented are measured and then tested for character and sound temperament in a much more rigorous manner, but similar to the *Zuchttauglichkeitsprüfung*. You may note I have not been specific regarding all the qualifications a dog must have to be "Eligible for the *Körung*," as the criteria change from time to time.

When and if a dog passes the *Körung,* the results are entered on its pedigree in the space provided for same under the *Zuchttauglichkeitsprüf-ung* data. The dog is then properly referred to as having been "endorsed" (*gekört*) for two years from the date of the test. In order to retain this status after two years have elapsed, the dog must be presented a second time to repeat the test. If it again fulfills the physical and temperament test and the progeny are still clear of genetic faults, the dog is endorsed for highest breeding suitability to the end of its breeding days. The German designation for this is *gekört bis* EzA. These are the dogs most sought after and, naturally, their progeny are in the greatest demand. As a result of the requirements being so stringent, No. 1 and No. 2 *Körung* sections on the pedigree are relatively seldom completed.

We referred to the breed ring when it was stated a dog must be rated either "V" or "SG" to qualify for the *Körung*. It now seems appropriate to examine the dog show scene as it is conducted in Germany.

The Breed Ring

There are exceptions but at most shows a class is provided for dogs 12-18 months, 18-24 months, 2 years and over without a Working Degree and 2 years and over with a Working Degree in both sexes. From this latter

Rottweiler type!

Europasieger, Klubsieger, Bundessieger NERO vom SCHLOSS RIETHEIM, Sch H III, FH, HD-53782-wh. 6/5/78 (Ives Eulenspiegel, 48232 ex Kira vom Schloss Rietheim, 50120) Breeder: Karl Storz. Owner: Christian Stark.

class, if they are awarded, emanate the dogs qualified for the Sieger and Siegerin titles.

Routinely, dogs enter the ring in catalogue order, taking a position on the perimeter. The handler wears the number pinned to his chest. At one end of the ring is placed a table and several chairs. Seated at the table with a typewriter is the person responsible for typing the judge's critiques as he dictates them.

The judge proceeds around the ring making the mouth and, in the case of males, testicle examination. In Germany one missing tooth is disqualification. From this point on, procedure usually consists of the class circling the ring for the judge to observe the side gait. Then the dogs are individually stood, critiqued, and gaited coming and going. Whereas double handling is not permitted by AKC, in Germany this is the approved method. The line is drawn when the double handler is brazen enough to enter the ring. Eviction is fast and furious.

When the judge has completed the individual critiques, he then asks that the dogs be gaited around the ring. For the older dog classes, 20-25 minutes is not unusual. As few people are able to maintain the pace for that length of time, a change of handlers is permitted, but the dogs must barely break their stride.

As the gaiting progresses the judge will move his choices up to the front, so when he calls a halt to the gaiting they are in the order of placement. In the older classes quality can be expected to merit V1 (Excellent 1) for the first dog, perhaps V2 for the second and even V3 for the third. There could be any number of V's awarded, or none. It depends solely upon the merit of each dog. The next category is S.G. (Very Good) and that rating is also dependent upon the individuals. "G" (good) is the next, then Fair, Disqualification and also the judge is permitted to refuse a rating. This rarely occurs, and when it does it is as a result of a suspicion on the judge's part that he cannot substantiate in the ring.

The classes for the younger dogs are judged in a similar manner except that the rating of "V" is rarely given. Thus S.G.1, S.G.2, etc., are usually top placements in these classes.

As opposed to our method where placements are awarded with no explanation, by day's end the German exhibitor is armed with a detailed critique of the dog's phenotype and movement and with the rating it has earned.

The motto of the ADRK is the "Breeding of Rottweilers for Conformation and Working Ability." The Presidium elected to carry out this dictum consists of a President, Vice President, Head Breed Warden, Head Training Warden and Head Judge. In a meeting of this quintette, one can only surmise the entire "Rottweiler scene" is discussed. Rules and regulations are revised to update the program. Recommendations are adopted. Obviously the Head Breed Warden is likely to have the biggest input. He has the broadest exposure. Every Rottweiler is his domain. Whereas the Head Training Warden is concerned with those dogs being

Tilla and Friedrich Berger with their beloved Wirehaired Dachshund. Friedrich was Head Breed Warden of the ADRK for 17 years. He is sorely missed.

B/S 1968/1969—Igor v. Hause Henseler, SchH3, wh. 3/23/66. Great type.

B/S '63, Blitz vom Schloss-Westerwinkel, Sch H3, to be found in many German and American pedigrees. Owner, Richard Schmidgall.

trained and the personnel required to carry out the program, the Head Judge's responsibility is confined to the relatively small percentage of Rottweilers exhibited at conformation shows and those Judges under him.

In our discussion of the *Körung,* we noted that changes in requirements are to be seen from time to time. One such change concerns the mouth pigment requirement. This change affects not only the eligibility to go to the *Körung,* but also the rating which may be given a dog at a conformation show. Today, no dog with "pink" pigment in its mouth, no matter how excellent he may otherwise be, can be given a "V" rating. Undoubtedly, this dictum was agreed upon by the five Directors of the ADRK and passed down the chain of command to every Breed Warden and every judge. That is how the Germans get the job done. It is also why we in America suddenly have such an influx of German dogs with pink mouths.

The Judge's Credentials

A German conformation judge rises through the ranks of exhibitor-handler (almost all dogs are owner-handled) to breeder to breed warden, to apprentice judge and finally emerges as a full-fledged Specialist. This evolution does not take place overnight. Long experience, with at least a modicum of success in a breeding program must be attained before a person is even considered.

Quite contrary to our posture, the German judge is acquainted with most of the dogs and exhibitors showing under him. There is no pretense to disguise this. Thus if exhibitor A enters the ring with his bitch that whelped eight uniform puppies of quality four months ago, the judge knows it and takes it into consideration. This is where the difference occurs. In our country, placements are made solely on the merits of the phenotype, whereas in Germany, the merits of the genotype weigh very heavily. Those are two different aspects of the dog and it can readily be understood that to evaluate the latter a person must have an in-depth knowledge of the breeding program. This is the tie-in between the breed wardens and the judges. The breed wardens are the eyes and ears of the breeding programs. The judges can be said to be the computers of the program. Their decisions, just as in our country, are vital to the success of the breeding program, as it is human nature to flock to the winners.

The Training

This important aspect of the Rottweiler has suffered the most "in translation." In Germany, Schutzhund training is a sport. It is enjoyed in much the same way as tennis, golf, bowling, etc. Interspersed throughout the country are people who meet in their free time at the training *"Platz"* and work with their dogs. It is social, it is exercise and it is fun. Some of these training clubs are fortunate enough to have experts, people who have successfully trained many dogs, in their midst. These experts logically

Ferro v.d. Lowenau, SchH2, 43819, wh. 5/5/68. A much used stud dog. Breeder: Karl Reinecke. Owner: Artur Gallas.

— *Photo, courtesy Ida and Meyer Marcus*

B/S '70, '71, Int. Ch. Falko von Grunsfeld, SchH3, FH, wh. 3/1/68. A fantastic phenotype! But not a producer. Breeder: Andreas Dorr. Owner: Ewald Hagele.

1951 Sieger, Dieter vom Kohlwald, ScH1. Breeder, Eugen Schertel. Worthy phenotype and genotype.

Not all German winners are without faults. This photo is of the 1961 Bundessiegerin, Andra vom Ruhrstrom, SchH1. Andra's ears, foreface, coat, croup and feet are not ideal. But appreciate the rest—it is.

244

Ch. Asta v. Forstwald, CD, BOS at the 1975 Medallion Rottweiler Club Specialty, Best Brood Bitch at the 1979 MRC Specialty. This lovely bitch was imported from Germany by Joan Klem and subsequently owned by Dr. Yvonne Fine. Below is a copy of a critique Asta received at a German show in 1974—every exhibitor receives a critique at an FCI show.

Nr. 54 Asta vom Forstwald 46 203

sehr schöne, kompakte, edle, gedrungene Hündin in
richtiger Größe und in sehr guter Verfassung.
Sehr schöner, gedrungener Hündinnenkopf mit dunklem Auge
und kleinem, gutgetragenem Ohr. Kräftiger Nacken,
tiefgestellte, breite Brust. Schulter gut angelegt.
Der Rücken stramm, gerade, volle Keulen. Sehr gute
Winkelungen. Froies, ausgreifendes Gangwerk ,
schöner, satter Brand, Scherengebiss.

surface as the teachers. When their pupils go off to trials and return with the highest scores, their prowess is enhanced and as a result they become working trial judges. One among them becomes the *"Hauptausbildungswart."* This is the position in the training area which corresponds to the *Hauptzuchtwart* in the breeding area. He is a member of the afore-mentioned five-man Directorate of the Club. His duties include the scheduling of the working trials, the monitoring of the results, the training of assistants and every facet of the working aspect of the Rottweiler.

Years ago the most highly regarded Rottweilers could get by with a Sch H1 degree. Today that is not the case. The top conformation winners are also Sch H3 dogs with FH (Advanced Tracking) degrees. (Refer to Chapter 9 on Schutzhund Training.)

The following is a list of reading matter which may be of help:

DER ROTTWEILER by Hans Korn, New Edition (translated from the German and available through the Colonial Rottweiler Club)

STUDIES IN THE BREED, HISTORY OF THE ROTTWEILER by Manfred Schlanzle (translated from the German and available through the Colonial Rottweiler Club)

ROTTWEILER by Adolph Pienkoss (available through Allgemeiner Deutscher Rottweiler Klub e.V - not translated to date)

DIE BESTIMMUNGEN über das Zuchtwesen fur den Rottweiler-Hund (available through Allgemeiner Deutscher Rottweiler Klub e.V. - not translated to date)

A drill team in Germany.

16

The Rottweiler in England

by Mary Macphail

Just about 15 years ago, sitting ringside at the Bundessieger Show in Frankfurt, I made the acquaintance of Mary Macphail. This chance meeting has resulted in a lasting friendship. In the ensuing years, I have learned to know her as a true devotee of the Rottweiler. There is no facet of the dog game which does not concern her, be it the breeding of proper phenotypes, training, health, or proper care. Her efforts to educate newcomers are tireless and her willingness to assume a role of leadership to promote the welfare of the breed is common knowledge.

Mrs. Macphail's judging credentials permit her to officiate at Championship Shows in Britain. She is also one of very few foreigners to have officiated as a Rottweiler Specialty judge in Germany and has on several occasions judged in the United States and Canada.

Her ability to express herself on paper is just one more of her many talents. It should be noted that this article was submitted to me in 1981.

THE NAME of Mrs. Thelma Gray of the internationally famous Rozavel Kennels is most often associated with the Welsh Corgi (Pembrokeshire), for it was she who supplied HM Queen Elizabeth II with her first specimen of that breed. But for her, yet another distinction can also be claimed; she introduced the Rottweiler to England in 1936.

Although the breed had been featured in English dog books and encyclopedias from the beginning of the century, 30 years were to elapse before any were to come into the country. Mrs. Gray went to the Sieger Show held at Cologne in May, 1936 especially to select foundation stock. As a result of her visit, four Rottweilers were chosen: three bitches, Enne v. Pfalzgau, who whelped a litter in quarantine to Grand Ch. Ido v. Kohlerwald; Asta v. Norden, who also whelped a litter in quarantine, to Sieger Hackel v. Kohlerwald; Diana v. Amalienburg; and a dog, Rozavel Arnolf v.d. Eutinger Ruine. All were to make their appearance at Crufts in

A 1937 photo of Mrs. Thelma Gray with three of her early winning Rottweilers—Rozavel Arnolf v.d. Eichener Ruine, Anna from Rozavel and Rozavel Asta von Norden. At left, Int. Ch. Rozavel Vefa von Kohlerwald.

Ch. Chesara Dark Destiny, first English-bred champion Rottweiler. Owner, Mrs. Elsden.

Ch. Gamegards Bulli v.d. Waldachquelle, son of the very important producer B/S Bulli von Hungerbuhl, SchH2, and himself of outstanding value to the program in England and Australia. Owner, Joan Woodgate.

1937. Later that year, Mrs. Gray brought in a very well known bitch, International Champion Vefa v. Kohlerwald, considered by German specialist judges to be an outstanding representative of the breed. Another young dog was imported in 1938, Arbo v. Gaisburg, this time by Mrs. Simmons, Diana's owner.

These early Rottweiler pioneers attempted not only to bring in the best German bloodlines, but also to foster the image of the Rottweiler as a first-class all-round dog, pleasing to the eye, an excellent and intelligent companion as well as a working dog. Diana v. Amalienburg qualified for Companion Dog (CD) and Utility Dog (UD) and was placed in working trials over here, as was Anna from Rozavel CDex, who had many prizes to her credit.

One more dog came in before the outbreak of World War II: Miss Homan acquired Benno v. Kohlerwald from Germany. Soon after hostilities started, Miss Homan joined the Women's Royal Air Force; she lent Benno to the Royal Air Force, in which he served as a police dog for the remainder of the war. Dog activities and especially breeding were very greatly curtailed by the war and consequent food shortages. Rottweiler breeding stopped, and Mrs. Gray sent her Rottweilers over to Ireland for the duration of the war, intending to resume breeding and showing when peace came. However, this was not to be, for she was unable to trace her dogs in Ireland and she never again owned a Rottweiler, although she retained, and still does retain, her interest in the breed. At the end of the war, the stock remaining in this country which could be traced was too old for breeding, and so the first chapter of the Rottweiler in England came to an end.

Reintroduction After World War II

It was not until 1953 that the breed was reintroduced to England. Captain Frederick Roy-Smith MRCVS, then serving with the Royal Army Veterinary Corps in Germany at an Army Dog School, seeing one for the first time, had been greatly impressed by the dog's looks, intelligence and working ability. So much so, that when he left the Army to return to private practice in England, he brought a dog and a bitch with him, Ajax v. Fuhrenkamp and Berny v. Weyher. Although a sterling character, Berny was not a really high class specimen, and she only produced one puppy which was not used for breeding. Captain Roy-Smith imported another bitch, again from Germany, Rintelna Lotte v. Oesterberg. She possessed a strong character and conformed closely to the standard. Ajax and Lotte were not prolific producers; one litter was born in 1958, consisting of five dog puppies, four of which were exported to India and Pakistan. The one remaining was Rintelna The Bombardier CDex UDex, my own first Rottweiler, who was to sire three champions. Another litter was born to Ajax and Lotte two years later, but only one bitch, Rintelna The Chatelaine, survived.

Ch. Chesara Dark Jasmin, winner of 12 challenge certificates—a record in her day for a bitch of the breed. Bred by Mrs. Elsden, and owned by Mrs. Pat Lanz.

In 1954 Rudi and Quinta Eulenspiegel of Mallion were imported, the foundation stock of the Mallion kennels of Mrs. Joanna Chadwick. Rudi and Quinta were extremely good producers and, before she had to restrict her activities due to the growing demands of a young family, Mrs. Chadwick campaigned Rudi and Quinta in variety classes at shows, thus introducing the breed to a wider public. The best known dogs from this combination were Abelard of Mallion, the first Rottweiler to become a Police Dog—he joined the Metropolitan Police in the summer of 1957; the litter brother and sister, Working Trials Champion Bruin of Mallion CD, UDex, TDex, owned and trained by Mrs. Wait of the Lenlee prefix, and Brunnhilde of Mallion, owned by Mr. and Mrs. Garland of the Pilgrimsway Kennels. Both Bruin and Brunnhilde were the first Rottweilers to achieve Best in Show awards, and the bitch also had many awards in Obedience competitions. Other Mallions which won well in Obedience/working trials were Miss Cole's Alberich of Mallion CDex, UDex, the first post-war Rottweiler to qualify in trials, and Mrs. Gawthrop's Adda of Mallion. Another staunch exhibitor was Mrs. Joan Wheatcroft who owned the very nice dog, Caspar of Mallion. He was out of Quinta Eulenspiegel of Mallion by Ajax v. Fuhrenkamp, the only time that Quinta had a litter other than to Rudi. Finally, Miss Cook's Erich of Mallion became a champion at the age of 7 years.

In 1958 another Rottweiler bitch was imported by Mrs. Chadwick in partnership with Mr. Newton, Bim Eulenspiegel (by BS '57 Arros v.d. Kappenbergerheide SchH 1) which, shortly after leaving quarantine, changed hands and went into the ownership of Mrs. Wait and Miss Cole. Bim was quite different in type and character from the other two Eulenspiegels, being smaller and exceedingly lively. Had she been trained to competition standards, I am sure she would have done extremely well. Her daughter, Lenlee Neeraum Brigitte CDex, UDex, produced a Working Trials Champion, Mrs. Osborne's Lenlee Gladiator CDex, UDex, TDex, PDex, the sire being WT Ch. Bruin of Mallion CD, UDex, TDex.

The 1950's was a period of very slow growth as far as the Rottweiler was concerned; one litter consisting of one puppy was born in 1955 and four litters (total 21 puppies) in 1959. But by the end of the decade the breed was gradually becoming better known to the public through breed classes being scheduled at shows, articles in books and magazines, and personal recommendations for its sterling character. The steadiness and intelligence of this "new" breed attracted many who had been disappointed with the lack of these qualities in other breeds. Much credit must go to Mrs. Wait who devoted much time and energy in competing in conformation, Obedience and working trials to help put the Rottweiler "on the map."

The Influence of Imports

England is one of the few countries which has a mandatory quarantine period, six months, for any dog or cat, as well as many other animals, coming into the country. Each animal has to come in by a designated port or airport of entry, and there are only a few of these. It does not put a paw on English soil until it is in the quarantine kennel. Here, each animal is housed separately, with a run attached, that is unless two dogs belonging to one owner come in together and the owner wants them to remain together. The best type of kennels are those which allow maximum visibility to the dog to see the other inmates and general goings-on, but not all kennels are designed to permit this, being constructed entirely of breezeblock. The kennel staff in quarantine establishments are usually most caring and do everything possible to give each dog as much individual attention as possible.

Of course, quarantine makes the cost of importing much higher and the arrival of an import in any breed is quite an advent. When a breed is introduced (or re-introduced), it is hardly possible to overestimate the importance of the imported dogs in the formative early years of that breed, and so there is a considerable element of chance in the selection of a young puppy, which most imports are. With not every duckling growing into a swan, it always is something of a lottery.

During the 1960's there was an acceleration in the growth of the breed; there were a number of imports, about 12, the first of which was Vera v. Filstalstrand, in whelp to Droll v.d. Brötzingergasse SchH 2, a most influential sire in Germany, imported by myself and Captain Roy-Smith in 1960. Vera had her puppies in quarantine but the change of scene proved too much for her and she killed five of the eight puppies. This was a great blow. Of the three remaining, one went to the police—he was aptly named Rintelna The Detective; the bitch, Anouk from Blackforest, came to me, and Captain Roy-Smith kept the dog Rintelna the Dragoon, which he took with him, along with Rintelna The Chatelaine, when he emigrated to Australia with his family in 1964. Anouk, although not a first-class show specimen, proved of value to the breed in that she produced very typical, sound stock to the three different dogs to which she was mated. She was to be probably the longest-lived Rottweiler here—almost 14 when she died. The best known of these were my own Champion Horst from Blackforest, CDex (the first champion to gain a working qualification), Miss Harrap's Ch. Hildegard from Blackforest, and Mrs. Woodgate's Emil from Blackforest, CDex, star of films and television.

Four dogs came in from Holland: Mr. Britton's Ajax v.d. Lonneker Bult (Herold v. Kaltenbrunnen ex Casta), Mrs. Elsden's Chesara Luther (Dutch Ch. Baldur v.d. Habenichts ex Astrida) later to become the first dog champion; Mrs. Wait's Lenlee Cabiria v.h. Brabantpark (Ajax v.d. Brantsberg ex Ch. Rona v.d. Brantsberg), and one other, a family pet whose owners settled in England and which was not shown or used for breeding.

Ajax, a sturdy, typey dog, unfortunately sired only two litters, eight puppies in all—a pity, in that his contribution to the breed was small.

252

Three generations of the dual-purpose line at Mary Macphail's Blackforest Kennels:

Father, Rintelna The Bombardier, CDex, UDex, sire of three champions.

Son, Ch. Horst from Blackforest, CDex, first English champion to gain a Working Certificate.

Grandson, Blackforest Meister Mark, CDex, UD.

Luther, on the other hand, had, for those early dogs, many progeny. Mated to bitches carrying predominantly Mallion lines, the offspring were large. He sired four champions. Cabiria was a small bitch, very active and an extrovert, who lived to the ripe old age of 12. Unfortunately, she too, only had one litter (by Luther) of five puppies, one of which, a dog, was exported to the States.

In 1964 came the first arrival from the United States, Blackforest Rodsdens Jett v. Sofienbusch (Int. Ch. Harras v. Sofienbusch SchH 1 ex Am. Ch. Afra v. Hasenacker SchH 1). Jett was a big dog who, due to some bad experiences after leaving quarantine, never really took to showing. He, like Ajax, only sired two litters.

The following year a dog puppy was sent over from Sweden who was to exert a very considerable and beneficial influence on the breed; Mrs. Elsden's Chesara Akilles (by the very well-known Int. Ch. Fandangos Fair Boy ex Dackes Ina). Akilles went Best in Show at an Open Show just days after leaving quarantine, and became a champion within a very short time. He was a small to medium sized dog, very typical and compact, with great presence. He had a most appealing head, with deep broad muzzle, and his type came through most strongly. He sired nine champions and many other prizewinners, and today his good qualities are being passed on in good measure by his son Poirot Brigadier.

At about the same time, Mr. and Mrs. McLean brought back with them from Germany their young bitch, Blanka v. Ostertal (Bodo v.d. Heiden SchH 1 ex Cara v. Leopoldsthal) who, mated to Ch. Horst from Blackforest, CDex, produced Mrs. Boyd's Ch. Retsacnal Gamegards Gallant Attempt, a dual purpose dog who did very well in Open Obedience competitions. Two puppies sired by Bundessiger 1966/67 Emir v. Freienhagen SchH 3 FH were imported in 1967: Mrs. Woodgate's Gamegards Basula v. Sachsenherz (out of Asta v. Bollerbach) and Mr. Baldwin's Ero v. Bucheneck (out of Indra v. Schloss Westerwinkel), who was later to become a champion. Both of these when adult exhibited the outstandingly good temperament of their sire, and the bitch became quite a seasoned performer in films. Ch. Ero sired many litters which included two champions, one of which—Ch. Bhaluk Princess Birgitta (Mrs. Joseph)— was awarded a challenge certificate by Mrs. Freeman when she judged at the Southern Counties Championship Show in the summer of 1972.

Mrs. Woodgate imported a dog puppy in 1968, Gamegards Lars v.d. Hobertsburg (Caro v. Kupferdach SchH 3 ex Adda v. Dahl SchH 3 FH). He died from distention at the age of two, but his influence was far reaching—he was most dominant for good hips and for this we must be very thankful. He sired one champion.

By 1970 the Rottweiler had become quite well known, and the demand for puppies grew steadily after the breed had been given a separate register in 1965, when challenge certificates were first granted. After that, registrations increased significantly each year.

Vera v. Filstalstrand, imported in w
to Droll v.d. Brotzingergasse, SchH
Mrs. Macphail and Capt. Roy-Smit
1960.

Ch. Ausscot Hasso v. Marchenw
German import, sire of three En
champions to date. Owner, G. Mc

Ch. Castor of Intisari, Danish import
of four English champions. Owne
Peter and Joyce Radley.

During the next ten years, new arrivals into the country included: 6 from Germany; 3, Holland; 1, Denmark; 1, Norway; 1, Sweden; 1, South Africa; 1, Canada; 2, USA. Two of these have been widely used at stud: the late Ch. Gamegards Bulli v.d. Waldachquelle (Bulli v. Hungerbuhl SchH 2 ex Anka v. Reichenbachle), whose influence has been far reaching. He belonged to Mrs. Woodgate, and was a dog of strong character with a very powerful head and sturdy build, qualities he passed on to his many progeny. He sired many litters, which included six champions. The best known of these are Mr. Gedge's Ch. Prince Gelert of Bhaluk, Mrs. Bloom's Ch. Janbicca The Superman, and Mr. Martin's Ch. Princess Malka of Bhaluk, CDex, UDex (the first champion Rottweiler bitch to gain a working trials qualification). Bulli died at the age of five from a heart attack.

The other stud dog is from Denmark, Mr. and Mrs. Radley's Ch. Castor of Intisari (Int. Ch. Farro v.h. Brabantpark SchH 2 ex Danish Ch. Ursula PH AK), who to date has sired four champions. He again is a substantially built dog of medium size, compact and with a particularly good character. Two other dogs, both from Germany, are making their mark: Mr. McNeil's Ch. Ausscot Hasso v. Marchenwald (Int. Ch. Elko v. Kastanienbaum SchH 1 ex Cora v. Reichenbachle), sire of three champions to date, and Mrs. Bowring's Lord v.d. Grurmannsheide of Herburger (Carlo v.d. Simonskaul SchH 1 ex Asta v.d. Bolt), sire of one champion.

Two dogs who were in this country, albeit briefly, were Joris, who came over with his Dutch owners, and Mrs. Elsden's Torro Triomfator from Chesara, whose dam was the outstanding bitch, Int. Ch. Fascha Triomfator; he sired two champions.

The latest arrivals are three dogs: Mrs. Woodgate's Dolf v. Rebenhang from Germany, Mrs. Bowring's Herburger Arno v. Ross from the States, and Mr. and Mrs. Hammond's Breesegata's Dago from Belgium. It is too early to forecast what their contribution is likely to be. I have dwelt at some length on the dogs which have shaped the Rottweiler as it is today in England.

The Rottweiler as a Working Dog

There is little doubt that the early stalwarts of the breed showed much more interest in the Rottweiler as a working dog, and by working dog, I mean they emphasized the importance of working ability and a higher proportion trained their dogs and competed in Obedience competitions and Working Trials.

Working events licensed by the Kennel Club are of two types (and, of course, I exclude gundog trials): Obedience and Working Trials. The former consist of exercises such as heel on and off lead, retrieve, sit-stay, down-stay and, in the more advanced classes, scent discrimination. The dog must work with extreme precision and these events are extremely competitive, attracting large entries. Working Trials, on the other hand, besides Obedience exercises which do not have to be executed with such precision, include agility with three types of jumps, which for a dog the size of a Rottweiler (i.e., any dog over 18 inches at the shoulder) would be: scale jump of 6 feet, long jump of 9 feet, and clear jump of 3 feet; and nosework. The most elementary stake is that of Companion Dog (CD) where there is no requirement for tracking, but after that all the stakes include a track as well as a search. For the remaining stakes the dog must qualify at Open Trials before being allowed to proceed to Championship Trials. These stakes are: Utility Dog (UD), Working Dog (WD), Tracker Dog (TDO) and Police Dog (PD), and they are taken in invariant order, as one qualifies in one, so one becomes eligible for the next. The two top stakes, TD and PD, are of equivalent standard, but with different emphasis.

The total number of Rottweilers which have qualified in Working Trials in the post-war period is about 40. Rottweilers seem to be much better suited to working trials than to Obedience competitions where the ubiquitous Border Collie sweeps all, or almost all, before it. Although interest has been shown by various police forces in the Rottweiler, only a few forces have actually tried them out. Some of the reasons for this are resistance by the die-hard German Shepherd Dog faction (who seem to find it difficult to concede ability to any other breed), the higher purchase price of Rottweiler puppies, and the higher cost of feeding them. Furthermore, Rottweilers are not, as we say, every handler's "cup of tea." To train a Rottweiler successfully demands a rather different approach from that adopted for, say, the German Shepherd.

To date, there have been about 12 dogs serving with the civilian police and other security organizations, including the railway police who have also had Rottweilers on their strength, where they have acquitted themselves creditably. Unfortunately, too, the Rottweiler has come to the notice of what I will describe as the "strong arm faction," who use dogs to guard scrap yards and the like, and as weapons of fear.

There is yet another type of working Rottweiler—the one featured in TV, films and advertisements, and in this area the dogs trained by Mrs. Woodgate are on their own, which calls for no mean skill by the trainer. It is a fact that the role the Rottweiler is most often called upon to play in film sequences is that of the "tough guy" dog, which is a great pity, as they are so much more than that.

The Show Scene

To those accustomed to a one-dog, one-class system, English shows may seem very puzzling affairs. First of all, we have different types of shows, Exemption, Sanction, Limited, Open and Championship, and it is only at the last named that challenge certificates are on offer. Three certificates, obtained under different judges, are required for a dog to gain the coveted title of champion. Not every championship show is allocated

Rudi Eulenspiegel of Mallion, foundation stock of the Mallion Kennels of Mrs. Joanna Chadwick.

Working Trials Ch. Bruin of Mallion, CD, UDex, TDex, owned and trained by Mrs. Wait (Lenlee).

Ch. Bhaluk Princess Birgitta, awarded a Challenge Certificate in 1972 by Mrs. Freeman. Owned by Mrs. Joseph.

258

Ch. GBOS Gaytimes, winner of 16 challenge certificates. Breeder: Miss Ogilvy-Shepherd.

certificates for every breed; the number each year is decided upon the overall entries at shows for that breed. There is no separate class for champions and up and coming fliers have to compete against champions to gain their titles. So in England it is not easy to make up a champion!

Sadly, the very early kennels are no longer active. Captain Roy-Smith (*Rintelna*) died in Australia in April, 1980; Mrs. Chadwick (*Mallion*) no longer has Rottweilers; and Mrs. Wait (*Lenlee*) lives in retirement in South Africa.

The two longest established kennels in the breed still active today are my own, *Blackforest,* established in 1958, and that of Mrs. Elsden, *Chesara,* established in 1960. The Chesara have had a continued record of success since 1960, producing champion after champion, and it is unlikely that their record will be beaten in the foreseeable future. Mrs. Elsden awards certificates in the breed and has frequently visited shows and kennels overseas. She had the distinction of breeding the first Champion Rottweiler here: Ch. Chesara Dark Destiny. Apart from her, probably

Ch. Panevors Proud Kinsman, bred and owned by Mr. and Mrs. Hammond.

Owner Violet Slade's pride in her Rottweiler is its own evidence of the fast rising popularity of the Rottweiler in England.

the best known dogs bearing this prefix have been Chesara Dark Inquisitor, who lived to the age of 12, Ch. Chesara Dark Kruger, Ch. Chesara Dark Warlord and Mrs. Lanz's Ch. Chesara Dark Jasmin, who holds the record for the number of challenge certificates held by a bitch— 12. Chesara stock has been exported all over the world and its influence on the breed here and overseas is considerable.

My own operations are on a much smaller canvas and I like to think my contribution has been to foster the dual purpose image of the breed by producing dogs of show quality and working them, and I have qualified 5 so far. There are now three generations of dogs with Blackforest working qualifications in their pedigrees. I served as an apprentice judge in Germany and qualified under their system, as did Mrs. Freeman. It was a very worthwhile experience.

The upsurge of interest in the breed has brought many new fanciers, some of whom stay, more of whom are birds of passage (as in any breed). Some of the best known kennels and up-and-coming kennels are: *Bhaluk,* Mrs. Joseph; *Borgvaale,* Mrs. Lanz; *Gbos,* Miss Ogilvy-Shepherd; *Upend,* Mrs. Butler; *Attila,* Mr. and Mrs. Bryant; *Panevors,* Mr. and Mrs. Hammond; *Herburger,* Mr. and Mrs. Bowring; *Cuidado,* Mrs. Wood; *Poirot,* Mrs. Wallet; *Nygra,* Mrs. Summers; *Ritonshay,* Mrs. Parratt; *Panelma,* Mrs. M. Bryant; *Ronpaula,* Mr. and Mrs. Young; *Graefin,* Mrs. Burton; *Adoram,* Mr. Quinney; *Intisari,* Mr. and Mrs. Radley; to name but a few.

Fostering the image of decency. Bettina from Blackforest, bred by Mary Macphail and owned by Mrs. Egerton-Williams.

The entries at championship shows are now very large. With the exception of breed shows where the entry is over 200, general championship shows usually attract 100 or more Rottweilers, the exceptions being when the show is up in Scotland where there are fewer exhibitors. Many people who exhibit have never done so before and quite often, the Rottweiler is their first dog—something I view with some concern, as I do not believe that a member of the so-called guard breeds is the best one with which to gain experience of dogs.

The Future

The Rottweiler in England is the fastest growing breed as far as registrations are concerned. Popularity never did any breed good, so it is to be hoped that the fickle public gaze becomes attracted to something else. Popularity brings along the band-waggoners, anxious to get in on the act to make a "fast buck" and then leave the ship when the going gets rough, with a consequent mess for the dedicated few to clear up. Having seen what can happen to a breed, it is good to be able to say that we have a nucleus of dedicated breeders who try to maintain standards in the stock they produce and in the service they offer to buyers of their puppies. They show and/or work their dogs, they keep abreast of veterinary developments; and they represent what is best in breeders. They are the backbone and the salvation of any breed; we can never have enough of them.

17

The Rottweiler
in Australia

by N. J. Pettengell

Mr. Pettengell and his wife have been associated with Rottweilers in Australia since 1966. Their kennel name, *Auslese,* is widely known and much respected and justifiably so as the names of many outstanding Rottweilers past and present bear the Auslese prefix.

Mr. Pettengell is an ardent student of pedigrees—not only those of Australian dogs but of German, English and American stock also. He is a copious correspondent in touch with Rottweiler people all over the world. One can hardly mention a name but Jim responds with "he or she owes me a letter." His interests extend to all facets of breeding, care and training. Jim is indeed fortunate to have a wife just as devoted to the dogs and more than willing to contribute her share.

I am extremely grateful for his willingness to prepare this section on Australia. From the correspondence, I gather that collecting photographs of some of he outstanding dogs ranged somewhere from difficult to impossible. How unfortunate.

As the article was presented to me, at the start of 1981, I have taken the liberty of adding some few facts and figures passed on to me at a later date.

ROTTWEILERS were introduced into Australia in 1962. An abortive attempt had been made earlier when Mr. Mummery, of Victoria, purchased a grown dog, Balthasar of Mallion, but the dog died on the ship while coming out to Australia. Captain F. Roy-Smith emigrating from England where he had successfully bred dogs using the Rintelna prefix, arrived in Freemantle, West Australia, in August of 1962. (*Author's note:* Reference is made to Captain Smith and the dog, Ajax, in the chapter on England.) With him came a dog and a bitch. The man, himself, deserves special mention. As a young man serving with the British Veterinary Service in Germany after the war, he made the acquaintance of the breed and was so impressed that he took a dog and bitch back with him to England. The bitch, unfortunately, was not purchased through the ADRK

Pilgrimsway Loki being greeted upon his arrival in Melbourne by Mr. Douglas Mummery.

Mr. N. J. Pettengell and Ch. Auslese Bold Galileo, CD.

Galileo demonstrating Rottweiler herding instincs.
Breeder-owner: N. J. Pettengell (Australia).

and was not registered; she had no influence on the breed. The dog, Ajax von Fuhrenkamp, had a considerable influence as a sire in England and through his descendants, in Australia.

The dog that Roy-Smith brought to Australia was Rintelna the Dragoon. The bitch was Rintelna the Chatelaine. The pair had been mated prior to their departure from England, and the Chatelaine whelped the first litter to be born in Australia in the Perth quarantine station on September 2, 1962. The litter—Rintelna "E"—produced six pups but, unfortunately, all but one were destroyed because suitable homes could not be found for them. The surviving bitch, the Empress, was sold to Mr. de Jonge, a Dutch policeman, who had migrated to South Australia.

The pair was mated again, producing three pups. One bitch was given to the Guide Dogs' Association. The dog, Rintelna the Field Marshall, and his sister, Rintelna the Fatale, were sold to Douglas Mummery, being registered with the K.C.C. of Victoria on June 22, 1964. Mr. Mummery adopted the kennel name, Heatherglen. Roy-Smith moved to Queensland in April 1964. He campaigned the Dragoon, who became the first Australian champion on January 19, 1967. The "G" litter was born in 1966; one of the dogs, Rintelna the General, came to me. The General, known as "Brandy," was a fine character and a great ambassador for the breed. Unfortunately, the Dragoon developed a tumor and had to be put down in March 1967. The Chatelaine followed in July of the same year.

Victoria was invaded by another Rottweiler personality when Pilgrimsway Loki arrived from England. He was bred by Mrs. Garland and sold to Mrs. G. Bailey. He then went to Mrs. W. Holland before being purchased by Mr. Mummery.

Mr. Mummery mated Loki to the Fatale on many occasions, the first litter being whelped on June 23, 1964. My first Rottweiler, Heatherglen Chablis Khan, was whelped from this combination on December 5, 1965.

Chab was one of the most remarkable dogs that I have come across and it was my good fortune to have him as my constant companion for eight years. He worked sheep and cattle, retrieved from land and water and, although presenting a terrifying front to the iniquitous, he never drew blood. The criminal always finished on the ground with Chab's massive paw on his chest. We went to the obedience school, but he was held in such awe, by both dogs and trainers, that we discontinued the practice. He is best described by the adjective, "dominating."

Mr. de Jonge mated Rintelna the Empress to Loki and the resulting litter produced a dog, Marthleen Balthazar, who was retained by Mr. De Jonge's son. Balthazar became a champion in South Australia, coming over on two occasions to win the Melbourne Royal Rottweiler dog challenge. He became the first Rottweiler in Australia to qualify for a CD and later CDex. He was whelped May 2, 1966, became a champion in 1968, qualified for his CD in 1969 and CDex in 1970.

Mr. Mummery then imported a bitch, Lenlee Gail, bred by Mrs. Maud Wait, registering her with the Victorian K.C.C. in March 1965. She was mated to Loki on many occasions. The first litter was stillborn. The second produced three pups; the third litter, born November 10, 1966, left a lasting influence on the breed. One of the dogs, Heatherglen Rudi, although never shown, produced some fine progeny

The 1979 Rottweiler Specialty was judged by Mrs. Muriel Freeman, who is acknowledged as one of the top authorities in the world. Her Best of Breed was Heatherglen Franz; in addition to the conformation title he acquired, Franz also qualified for CD and CDex. His sire was Rudi. Rudi's litter sister, Cliquot, came to me at the age of six weeks. She gained her title February 15, 1969, being the first Rottweiler to do so in Victoria and the first champion bitch in Australia. She was an excellent brood bitch, her last litter producing Auslese Contessa, the challenge winning bitch at the first Specialty and the challenge winner at the first big Rottweiler entry, the 1972 Melbourne Royal. Her sister was an even better show and breeding prospect. Auslese Pinot won the challenge in the 1973 Royal and was unbeaten for Best of Breed; she was chosen as the Rottweiler model in the official standard produced by the K.C.C. of Victoria. Her granddaughter, Auslese Bold Kristy, was chosen by Mrs. Freeman for the bitch challenge at the age of 14 months.

All the Rottweilers in Australia, at this time, were bred from Roy-Smith's imports or from the two imported by Mr. Mummery. There was considerable in-breeding. When we heard that Mrs. Elsden, famous for her Chesara kennel in England, had imported a Dutch dog we immediately booked a bitch pup. (*Author's note:* Quarantine regulations from England are of shorter duration.) Chesara Dark Impression was born on Christmas Day 1966 and came out by sea as soon as she could travel. She had an enormous influence on the breed for many years thereafter. Her daughters and granddaughters became the foundation bitches for such outstanding kennels as: Allerhöchst, Anverdons, Brabantsia, Din Perry, Escort, Grunwalds, Kerusgal, and Ormslee.

The year 1971 is remembered for the rabies scare. An embargo was placed on all imports into Australia. It was lifted the following year and there was a flood of imports. Mr. Mummery imported Attila Ajax (Lars v.d. Hobertsburg ex Gamegards Border Rising), Chesara Dark Nobleman (Eng. Ch. Chesara Akilles, imp. Sweden, ex Chesara Dark Memory), Chesara Dark Wishful (Eng. Ch. Ero v. Bucheneck, imp. Germany, ex Chesara Dark Katrin), Baroness Delviento (Eng. Ch. Chesara Dark Inquisitor ex Chesara Dark Gamble). Mrs. Terry of Kerusgal Kennels imported a bitch bred by Mr. R. Johnson, Black Shiva (Eng. Ch. Chesara Dark Kruger ex Bathsheba Black Velvet). Mrs. Mary Macphail, one of the top authorities on the breed, assisted us in the purchase of Jentris Gloriosa (Lars v.d. Hobertsburg ex Chesara Dark Revelry). Gloriosa was the dam of two champions. Her son, Auslese Beaujolais, was best exhibit in an all-

Author Mrs. Bernard Freeman judging at the 1979 Rottweiler Club of Victoria Specialty. BOB was Aust. Ch. Heatherglen Franz, CDX (owner: Miss B. Rawson) and BOS was Auslese Bold Kristy (owner: I. R. Young).

Aust. Ch. Auslese Bold Gammon, the only Australian champion Rottweiler who has qualified for the CDex, TD titles. Bold Gammon was Best Intermediate Bitch at the 1979 International Show under Mrs. Bernard Freeman (USA) and Best Exhibit at the 1981 International under Mrs. Margareta McIntyre (USA). Owned and trained by Helen Read.

breeds championship show, the first Rottweiler to score such a win in Australia.

The mid-'70's saw a dozen imports into the country, the most significant being a granddaughter of Bulli vom Hungerbuhl. Mrs. Biltris purchased a bitch, Attila Bathsheba, bred by Mrs. Bryant. Sheba (Eng. Ch. Bulli v.d. Waldachquelle ex Attila Astrid) was mated to Upend Gallant Elf and flown out to New Zealand where she whelped a litter. She was shown in that country and became a champion before coming to Australia with a son, Korobeit Hud, and a daughter, Korobeit Helga, both retained by Mrs. Biltris. Another son and daughter were imported, one staying in Victoria and the other going to Queensland.

Another Bulli v.d. Waldachquelle son, Jentris Kyrie, was imported into New South Wales by Mr. Seymour-Johnson. His dam, Jentris Gypsophilia, was a litter sister to Gloriosa. Kyrie moved to West Australia, but not before he sired a daughter, Finforest Emmanuelle. She was bred by Mrs. Larha and owned and trained by Mrs. Bull. Emmanuelle was the first Rottweiler in Australia to qualify for U.D. She qualified for T.D. and was a champion.

The third Bulli v. Hungerbuhl grandson, Gamegards Mayhap (Bulli v.d. Waldachquelle ex Brooklow Cool Angel of Manisis) was imported by Mrs. Anver of Anverdon Kennels. Mayhap probably had more influence on the breed than other Bulli stock, but the effect of this bloodline in Australia is somewhat disappointing. However, Mayhap, himself, won Best of Breed at the 1979 Melbourne Royal, beating his daughter for that honor.

The only other state to import Rottweilers is West Australia. The first import—she did transfer from New South Wales—was Borgvaale Sunday Morning (Arkle of Cenlea ex Chesara Dark Jasmin), bred by the irrepressible Mrs. Pat Lanz. Gamegards Zodiac (Bulli v.d. Waldachquelle ex Gamegards Double Dare)—imported into New South Wales in the same year 1976, also moved to West Australia. Mr. Goedemonte imported two dogs, Chesara Dark Rustler (Torro Triomfator ex Borgvaale Venus) in 1977 and two years later, Gilda Debruse (Eng. Ch. Ausscott Hasso von Marchenwald ex Owlcroft Anita). Mr. Goedemonte with the kennel name Brabantsia is the most prolific breeder in the West. In 1975 he purchased Auslese Givry and Auslese Lambray, followed by Auslese Mercury. Givry and Lambray finished their titles in 1975 and Mercury gained his in 1976. They were the first champions in the West. Others are Auslese Bold Guido (later sold to Malaya), Auslese Bold Ballad, Kemmelberg Lady Leah, Brabantsia Tanja and Brabantsia Faru, the latter made up in 1979.

All dogs imported into Australia come from or through the United Kingdom with the exception of one bitch that did her quarantine in New Zealand. Such dogs are quarantined for only two months if they travel by sea and three if they travel by air. There is no restriction between Australia and New Zealand. A dog coming in from any other country must spend six

Mr. Pettengell's first Rottweiler, Heatherglen Chablis Khan. (By Pilgrimsway Loki ex Rintelna the Fatale.) Breeder: Douglas Mummery. Owner: N. J. Pettengell.

Chesara Dark Impression, imported from England by N. J. Pettengell.

Gamegards Mayhap, Bulli v. Hungerbuhl grandson, imported by Mrs. Anver (Anverdon Kennels).

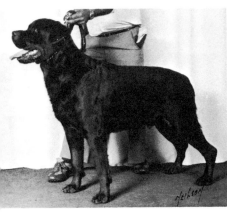

Aust. Ch. Tayvelka Noble Marcus, son of import Chelsea Dark Nobleman. Breeder: Mrs. Taylor. Owners: Mr. and Mrs. V. Borg.

Mother and son. At left, Catja vd Flugschneise, imported in April 1978 with four of her puppies sired by Eng. Ch. Castor of Intisari (a Danish import). At right, one of the pups—Auslese Iago Rabe, Best Junior Dog at the 1979 Specialty under Mrs. Freeman, and Best Dog in Group at the Queensborough All-Breeds Championship Show, 1980, under W. Crowley.

Mother and son. At left, Aust. Ch. Anverdon's Olympia, CD, bred by Mr. and Mrs. Anver and owned by Mr. and Mrs. G. Hall. At right, Aust. Ch. Stromhall Torrey, UD, sired by Chesara Dark Nobleman (U.K. import) out of Olympia. Torrey, bred and owned by Mr. and Mrs. Hall, was Best Exhibit at the 1980 Melbourne Royal show, thereby gaining his championship and a CD before the age of two. At the same show, he and his dam won Best Brace.

months quarantined in England and an additional six months out of quarantine in England before leaving for Australia. Allowing for the time taken for travel arrangements after the dogs have been cleared for leptospirosis, etc., one year is minimum and it could be longer. A dog imported from Hawaii or the islands bordering the north must be quarantined in Brisbane for a period of nine months.

Our next import was Catja von der Flugschneise who arrived in our kennel in July 1978. She had been mated in England to Eng. Ch. Castor of Intisari and there produced six dogs and four bitches on 12/12/77. Catja and four of her puppies left by air for Australia in April, 1978. One of the dogs, Auslese Iago Rabe, made a promising debut in the show ring. Mrs. Freeman made him best Junior Dog at the '79 Specialty and one of our most senior judges, Mr. W. Crowley, picked him from a strong field as best dog in Group Six at the Queensborough All-Breeds Championship show in April of the following year.

The question generally asked by people in one country, with regard to the quality and standard of the breed in another is, "How do the dogs compare with ours?" The answer to the question should be based on depth and general standard rather than on just a few of the top dogs. These could have been imported or the result of "lucky accidents" that can be expected when large numbers of pups are produced.

The general standard in Australia cannot compare with Germany, for example, because Australia is quite disadvantaged. Apart from the distance factor, quarantine restrictions are most stringent. The time factor and the costs involved with imports from England are high. The additional cost of imports from Europe or the States is almost prohibitive. There are some breeders who have the future of the breed at heart, but "breeding discipline" and "breeder's integrity" are terms not generally appreciated.

Notwithstanding these difficulties Australian breeders have done well and there are some excellent dogs in the country. The maintenance of the standard is jeopardized by our remoteness and the complete lack of rapport with current thinking in parts of the world where the breeding of Rottweilers is serious business.

The standard of Rottweiler judging in England is superior to that found here. Some of our senior judges and a few of the younger ones who are prepared to discuss the breed, can recognize type better than some of the overseas all-rounders who have judged here recently. The judging system in Australia is based on the group and not the breed. Aspiring judges attend breed lectures, after which they are required to take practical tests. Only a few breeds are picked at random, but in a large group of say 25 breeds no candidate is tested on all breeds. The system suits Australian conditions and it is the only one that could be used successfully. Some breeds, mostly those introduced lately, may suffer. The Rottweiler comes within this category, unfortunately.

The Rottweiler Club of Victoria was formed in May, 1971. It encouraged and assisted new exhibitors and promoted a great deal of social activity. The club conducts competitions four times a year and it holds a championship show and a parade. In 1979 it brought Mrs. Bernard Freeman from the States to judge the Championship show and conduct a breed symposium. It brought Mrs. Margareta McIntyre out in 1981. The membership approaches 500 and the club goes from strength to strength.

The N.S.W. club was formed at a later date and has an active membership. Like its Victorian counterpart it produces a quarterly magazine; its championship show is well attended with Victorian dogs taking out the major trophies. There is a club in South Australia but the strength of the breed lies very much in Victoria.

From the start of our association with the breed our kennel was conscious of the working ability of the Rottweiler. We used our dogs on the farm; without them the movement of sheep and cattle would have been difficult and a tedious business. We discovered that our dogs, with two exceptions (and we owned some thirty Rottweilers over a period of fifteen years) had a well developed hunting instinct. They retrieved from land and water and followed scent almost as well as a Pointer. On many occasions fifty or more rabbits were bagged, using only one dog. We joined Southern Obedience Dog Club in 1966 and later held classes on the farm with Mr. Michael Tucker, Victoria's top trainer, as instructor. With the exception of Mr. de Jonge's dog, no Rottweiler qualified for a title until the early '70s.

Early on, the Victorian club concentrated on conformation, but during the last two years its members have been encouraged to join Obedience classes and more dogs may be seen competing in the Obedience ring than in conformation classes at the shows. The N.S.W. Club is also keen on training and a number of their dogs have qualified. Ch. Finnforest Emmanuelle, bred by Mrs. Larha and trained by Mrs. Bull, was the top Obedience Rottweiler, but the dog unfortunately died young. A number of the N.S.W. dogs have dual qualifications.

Tarquinian Apache, bred by Mr. Lowther and trained by John Stewart, qualified for CDex, TD and was the first dog in Australia to get his UD. At the present time Mrs. Helen Read owns the only champion Rottweiler, Auslese Bold Gammon, who has qualified for CDex, TD. Another breeder who has done much to promote the working Rottweiler is the ex-Secretary of the Victoria club, Mrs. Pat Hall, whose kennel name Stromhall is very much in evidence also around the breed ring. As of 1980, Victoria has some 20 champions with Obedience qualifications. Many owners are finding Obedience a field that offers a more objective yardstick in measuring the quality of the dogs and is more satisfying than the show ring.

Bazille has been dead for nearly thirty years and Köpf and Hans Korn have passed on, but the seed that they sowed still bears fruit wherever the Rottweiler is cultivated. Their motto is still the guideline for conscientious breeders: "The breeding of Rottweilers is the breeding of working dogs."

Aust. Ch. Tarquinian Ambassador, (8/19/76), with over fifty CC's to his credit. Owners, Mr. and Mrs. John Weir.

Aust. Ch. Tarquinian Adante, litter sister to Ambassador. Adante won first CC at only 10 months, and in limited showing had 40 CC's by the age of 4½ years. Owned by Mr. and Mrs. John Weir.

Aust. Ch. Tarquinian Dejanira, wh. 4/14/79, won her first Challenge at 6 months, and by 21 months had acquired 30 more. First in the Intermediate Bitch Class at the 1981 Championship Show under Mrs. McIntyre (USA). Owners, Mr. and Mrs. John Weir.

Aust. Ch. Lanzeon Vaughn (by Ch. Rotvel Zeon ex Kalatara Allatou). Owners: R. J. Miller and J. A. Hart.

Some additions by the Author

The name of Pat Hall was mentioned in connection with her interest in Obedience. Mr. and Mrs. Hall are also the proud owners of Ch. Anverdon's Olympia, CD.

Olympia is their foundation bitch. Bred to Chesara Dark Nobleman, she produced Stromhall Torrey who went Best Exhibit in 1980 at the Melbourne Royal show, thereby gaining his Australian Championship title and a C.D. before the age of two. At this same show, Olympia and Torrey won Best Brace.

The Halls have recently imported a dog from the United States: Powderhorn's Fetz of Wencrest (Am. Ch. Oscar v.h. Brabantpark ex Ilona v. Haus Schottroy) with every hope of successfully injecting some new bloodlines into Australian stock.

Recent additional successes in the show rings have been reported by Mr. and Mrs. John Weir, owners of Aust. Ch. Tarquinian Ambassador (Aust. Ch. Kerusgal Black Houdini x Kerusgal Black Iolanthe), wh. 8/19/76, and his litter sister, Aust. Ch. Tarquinian Adante. Ambassador took his first Challenge Certificate when only 13 months old and as of 1/81, had 56 CCs to his credit. Adante won her first CC at 10 months, and—in limited showing—amassed 40 certificates by the time she was 4½ years of age.

Aust. Ch. Tarquinian Dejanira (Aust. Ch. Kennelberg Black Watch ex Zambax Lars Amanda), wh. 4/14/79, also owned by Mr. and Mrs. Weir, won her first Challenge at six months and by 21 months had acquired 30 more. Mrs. McIntyre placed her first in the Intermediate Bitch Class at the 1981 Championship show.

This is also quite a record for the breeders of all three dogs, Mr. and Mrs. T. Lowther, to enjoy.

Lorelei vom Heidenmoor. Breeder: Olavi Pasanen. Owner: J.A. U. Yrjola.

18

The Rottweiler
in Finland

by Olavi Pasanen

Mr. Olavi Pasanen's credentials entitle him to a prominent spot in the International "Who's Who" of Rottweiler people. Since 1939 he has been active with working dogs and for 30 years has been President of the Finnish Rottweiler Club. He and Mrs. Pasanen have been breeding Rottweilers, using the vom Heidenmoor suffix, for about 35 years. Their kennel is the oldest in Finland and the vom Heidenmoor dogs have for decades been prominent in the Winner's Circle at dog shows and are much sought after for breeding stock.

Mr. Pasanen has been an approved Rottweiler judge since 1945 and an ADRK Richter (approved German judge) since about 1961, having judged at the Klubsieger Show on more than one occasion. He has also judged Rottweiler Specialties in the Chicago area and in California and Canada, as well as in other Scandinavian countries.

Six years ago Finland played host to a Conference of the "International Friends of the Rottweiler." As Vice President, Mr. Pasanen was responsible for planning and expediting the program. Under his tutelage the participants were treated to an outstanding educational program, beautiful accommodations and a most convivial atmosphere. No stone was left unturned in an effort to please everyone.

I am indeed grateful to him for providing the material used in writing this section.

Suomen KENNELKLUBI, The Kennel Club of Finland, was founded in 1889, but no Rottweilers were registered until 1927. The original dogs came from Sweden as did many subsequent Rottweilers.

Before 1939 there were no organized breeding programs and no contact between Rottweiler breeders; therefore, good imported animals were not used.

Naturally, during the war years breeding was non-existent, and the German stock was severely curtailed. When the war ended there were

274

Best in Show Winner at 1981 Helsinki show—Nero (SF-23514K/77), (by Joukonheimo Caracalla (SF-10847C/75) ex Amalia (SF-11899A/75). Judge, Curt Bokefors (Sweden). Owner: Timo Laaksonen, Helsinki. Handler: Kari Turunen.
— *Photo, J.A.U. Yrjola*

Xantippa vom Heidenmoor (10521/60P). Grandmother of Erna. Breeder-owner: Olavi Pasanen.

Erna vom Heidenmoor (6546/68). Breeder-owner: Olavi Pasanen.

perhaps 10 Rottweilers in Finland. A few Swedish dogs of the Compsand Lindhaga lines remained and traces of Finnish breeding in the Kiikkuniemi kennel became known through Tarmo, owned by the Police Dog Training Center (*Poliisikoirakoulu*).

In 1944-45 dogs of the Finnish kennels Solo, av Majviken and Tharass were registered.

1946 saw the beginning of what might be called a proper breeding program in Finland when the organization *Suomen Rottweileryhdistys-Finlands Rottweilerförening ry* was registered.

Fortunately for the breed those who were active in the formation of the Club and desirous of launching a breeding program were working dog experts. Some had even been so-called "war dog officers" during the war. They were therefore acquainted with the requirements for a working dog of any breed. Their limitation was the meager number of Rottweilers extant in Finland and the lack of documentation concerning the hereditary handicaps of those individuals with which they might have to cope.

As a group they hit upon the plan to effect a swap with Sweden of one trained German Shepherd Dog for one Rottweiler bitch in whelp. The bitch was descended from German lines and was to be the Finnish "Great White Hope," as the Finnish dogs were deemed unsuitable.

It must be borne in mind that though there is free passage of dogs from one Scandinavian country to another, they all impose a quarantine upon the importation of dogs from elsewhere. So in addition to the initial expense of purchase and transportation, a boarding charge must be considered in the eventual cost of importing a dog. Thus importation of Rottweiler breeding stock from Germany was very limited because, as Mr. Pasanen put it, "no money bags" existed among them. Consequently they were forced to do a great deal of inbreeding. As a result, the inherent weaknesses in the line became blatantly apparent. At the same time Jakob Köpf, the much respected German Head Breed Warden, judge and breeder of von Gaisburg dogs, was consulted and confirmed that the same problem with inbreeding existed in Germany.

It was thus apparent new blood was needed to revitalize the Finnish stock. It came in the form of Karo vom Jakobsbrunnen, in Mr. Pasanen's words, ". . . like a gift from heaven. He suited us well although he had a 'pike's head'. He gave the breed an inspiring injection of temperament and restored the vigor of our dogs which so far had been a little too calm (phlegmatic)." I am not at all certain what a "pike's head" looks like, but those among you who are fishermen will better understand.

The next paragraph, a direct quote, serves to illustrate that breeders face common problems internationally.

"Breeding is a fight against appearing faults. It is also a fight against slander, delusion, wrong ideas. So-called fashionable diseases have also become a 'drag anchor' these last years. Among the most dangerous phenomena are those walking encyclopedias who scare people and spoil all the enthusiasm of breeding with their persuasive behavior."

His ensuing statement points up a marked difference in practice from ours in the United States.

"With the characteristics of our race we have proceeded slowly but securely, and we can say that our breeding committee is trusted by our members—we have clear sailing in breeding matters. We have divided the country in breeding districts with a breeding advisor who is responsible and reliable to report to our principal breeding advisor."

He continues with:

"S.R.Y.-F.R.F.ry has 1500 members at present and is thus second in size in Europe after ADRK. This is quite a number, considering that Finland has less than 5 million inhabitants and the Rottweiler is no special favorite. Our principal breeding advisor, J.A.U. Yrjola, has had this position for more than 20 years and our president his position for 30 years."

In retrospect the German imports which most influenced the Finnish bloodlines are Vogt vom Köhlerwald, ADRK 20547, wh. 5/9/34; Tell von der Hackerbrücke, ADRK 23960, wh. 3/3/40; Droll von Wolfsgarten, ADRK 37012, wh. 10/23/58; and the aforementioned Karo vom Jakobsbrunnen.

The most active kennels in this period were Taiston and vom Heidenmoor (the oldest)—vom Heidenmoor dogs have been exported to 12 countries world-wide.

Mr. Pasanen states: "At present the most active kennels are Joukonheimon, von Heidesee, Katajiston, Emmaboda and Löytövuoren, among others."

Finnish Rottweilers have been exported to every continent with the exception of Asia. These transactions were all monitored by the breeding advisory service.

Customarily there are some 50 to 60 Rottweilers entered at the Finnish dog shows. However, at the aforementioned IFR Congress, 240 Rottweilers were exhibited, truly a record.

S.R.Y.-F.R.F., ry has performed character testing for 10 years and breeding control even longer. Their dedicated purpose is to preserve the character, the social usefulness, the hardness and agility and stamina expected of Rottweilers as good representatives of their breed.

Mr. Pasanen offers: "In our opinion we have achieved good results. Our Rottweilers are trained to serve as guide dogs, watch dogs, drug and ruin search dogs, dragger and draft dogs." He ends with the comment that were it not for the hindrance imposed by quarantine, the Finnish breeders believe their Rottweilers would compete with success internationally.

19

The Rottweiler
in Holland

by Mrs. A. J. Brinkhorst

The material on Holland is by courtesy of Mrs. A. J. Brinkhorst, a most charming "Grande dame" of Holland Rottweiler breeders. Her admirable command of the English language reflects just one of her many accomplishments.

I am not certain of the exact date, but Mrs. Brinkhorst bred her first Rottweilers sometime before 1949 using the kennel name of v.d. Brantsberg, and enjoys top respect in Holland and Germany alike for the breeding of quality dogs. In the United States, many Rottweilers can be found having v.d. Brantsberg dogs in their background.

She has served as Club Secretary and Club President over a period of more than 25 years. We are indeed fortunate to have so reliable a source for this information.

MY FIRST knowledge of a Rottweiler dog originates in a book *De Diensthond* (the service dog), edited in 1929. In this book there was a picture of a Rottweiler with its owner, a county constable.

Rottweilers were already in Holland between 1925 and 1935. Most of them were in the possession of farmers who, although they wished to have pure-bred dogs, were not yet interested in pedigrees.

After 1935 the interest in the breed increased and many specimens were imported from Germany; among others, from the kennels von Gaisburg, von der Spielburg, vom Pleikartsforst and Frankofurtia.

Between 1940 and 1948 in my searching for Rottweilers I came across brown specimens (a symptom of degeneration?).

During the war years, 1940-1945, only a few litters were bred from the material on hand.

Dutch Ch. Arnout Benno v. Lijndenstein NHSD 964217 (By K/S B/S Benno vom Allgauer Tor SchH3, FH, ADRK 46586 HD-gkt EzA ex Anatevka v. Canis Frisiae NHSD 648428 HD—back to Triomfater and Brantsberg lines). Owner: L. C. Gruter (Triomfator).　　　　　　　　　　— *Photo, courtesy Murray Ross.*

After the war the breeding was started again by way of various imports. I think the first imported dog then was the bitch Asta vom Kocher, a daughter of Sieger Xerxes vom Jakobsbrunnen and Burga von der Neudenau. For the purpose of improving the breed, bitches were taken to Germany and the litter was brought forth in Holland, as raising was underdeveloped here.

Until about 1946 here the Rottweiler with white breast- and/or belly-spots was still acknowledged. After 1946 the characteristics of the breed were conformed to those of the country of origin (Germany) and acknowledged in Holland.

The interest in the breed was continually increasing and in 1952 the *Nederlandse Rottweiler Club* was established, which obtained Royal approbation and recognition by the *Raad van Beheer op Kynologisch Gebied in Nederland*. The latter has its office: 16 Emmalaan - 1075 AV, Amsterdam.

At the time of the foundation the number of members of the *Nederlandse Rottweiler Club* was 23. In 1980, this number had risen to about 1500.

In endeavoring to improve and keep up the standard of the breed there were many ups and downs in Holland. Faults like light colored eyes, wrongly carried ears, long stretched backs, long muzzles, coats too long, have been pushed back and fortunately the heavier type of dog has regained territory. In Holland we don't see many longbacked, longlegged Rottweilers with a hound-like muzzle anymore.

At present very much attention is also paid to the character of the dog. What is the use of a physically excellent dog when its character is imperfect!

After many years of profound research, in 1965 the *Nederlandse Rottweiler Club* decided voluntarily on looking at HD as a serious objection to breeding.

In 1971 the *Raad van Beheer* passed a resolution that from 1972 on only litters from HD Negative parents would get pedigrees. As a result of the severe (perhaps even too severe) regulations, trustworthy breeders experienced a very hard time. In the first six years there was no TC Class. There was one distinction only: right or wrong. Many dogs had to be excluded from breeding and so otherwise valuable material was lost.

After a period of about six years the HD TC standard was set: the dogs of which both parents are HD negative or HD TC, get a pedigree. This however leaves the danger that many dogs, HD negative, but otherwise below average, will nevertheless be used for breeding. Indeed, many owners of HD negative dogs were inclined to breed.

Even with dogs that did not meet the HD requirements, owners were breeding on a large scale. So there are many Rottweilers at large without a pedigree.

Author's Note: Since this article was written, a new policy became effective April 1, 1983. The Netherlands Kennel Club has dropped its regulation requiring the breeding of only HD free dogs. However, the Rottweiler Club will maintain the policy of breeding only HD free dogs, and those not upholding this standard will be dropped from club membership.

Thanks to the many bonafide breeders, who meticulously stick to the HD regulations and attend to good character and physical properties the Dutch Rottweiler is of an extremely good average.

Some years ago we had a great number of very good bitches and fewer good male dogs. At present the number of good male dogs is increasing.

Since the end of the war in 1945 the interest of the Dutch public in the Rottweiler race has been rising strongly. This is evident from the number of Rottweilers participating in exhibitions and club matches: From 1940 until 1947 an average of 3; in 1955: 45 and in 1979: 174.

Here follows a survey of dogs, registered in the *Nederlandse Honden Stamboek* (Dutch dog-pedigree-book), in the years:

	dogs		bitches
1933 - 1940	35	-	40
1940 - 1947	No information.		
1947 1948	35	-	26

1949 - 1950	16 -	12
1951 - 1952	34 -	25
1953 - 1954	18 -	25
1955 - 1956	40 -	39
1957 - 1958	60 -	60
1959 - 1960	78 -	79
1961 - 1962	147 -	155
1963 - 1964	179 -	132
1965 - 1966	212 -	164
1967 - 1968	270 -	225
1969 - 1970	246 -	273
1971 - 1972	485 -	441
1973 - 1974	375 -	377
1975 - 1976	396 -	434
1977 - 1978	455 -	513
1979 - 1980	807 -	780

New registrations are on the climb. I think that at this moment there are about 17,290 Rottweilers in the Netherlands with an acknowledged pedigree.

The look is Holland, but the dogs are American. Frolic'n Acres own Fire Department—Frolic'n Grand Moff Tarkin and Frolic'n Darth Vader.

APPENDIX

BREEDER'S PLAN FOR BUILDING A WHELPING BOX
SUITABLE FOR A ROTTWEILER BITCH

This plan (there are, of course, many) for building a whelping box suitable for a Rottweiler bitch was designed by Clara Hurley, and was sent to me by Mrs. Richard Wayburn, who has described her use of it.

Here is the list to get at the lumber yard or wherever:
Four 2x2, four feet long
Two Sheets, 4 feet x 8 feet, ½ inch plywood
One 2 feet x 4 feet masonite panel ⅜", (or ¼" plywood)
Four pieces, 5" x 18", ⅜" masonite or ¼" plywood
Four 1x3, 30 inches long

Hardware needed:
Twelve 5" butt hinges with removable pins
Three 4' piano hinges
Four galvanized metal strips, ⅛" thick, 1½" wide, 15-18" long and 8 small
    bolts and nuts
Eight 2½" angle irons with 16 screws and wing nuts

The 2x4 masonite panel is to have a hole cut in it. It is to be used to separate the compartments of the whelping box.

The hole is located 24" on center from the end of the panel. It is oval in shape. The bottom of the oval is 2" from the bottom edge of the panel. The top of the oval is 17" from the bottom edge of the panel, and is 15" from the other end of the oval.

It should be made by cutting a 7½" circle which is within 2" of the bottom edge of the panel, and a 7½" circle which touches the top of the oval, and then by cutting straight sides to connect the two holes.

Here is a diagram of the hole:

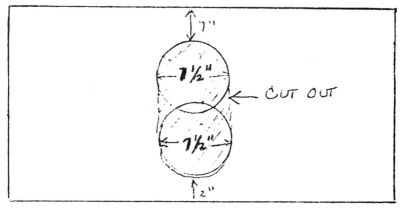

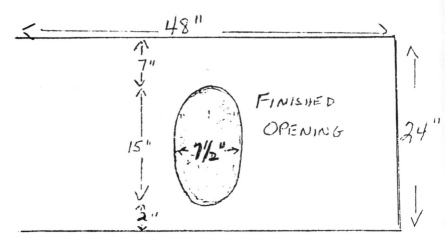

Now, start with the two 4x8 sheets. Cut a 2x4 piece from the end of each 4x8 sheet. This will leave you with: two 4x6 sheets and two 2x4 sheets.

Split one of the 4x6 sheets into two sheets, 3x4. Split the other 4x6 into two sheets, 2x6.

The two 3x4 sheets will become the floor of the box. Join the 4' edges of these two sheets with 2 butt hinges with removable pins. (When pins are removed, the two pieces are again separate.) This breakdown 4x6 sheet is the bottom of your whelping box. The side with the hinges is placed on the floor. The top side (where one does not see the hardware) is the floor of the whelping box. As so:

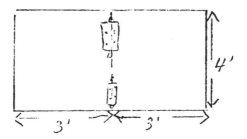

Turn this now 4x6 sheet over so that you do not see the hinges and join one of your 2x4 sheets to each 4' edge with a 4' piano hinge. Position the piano hinge so that 2x4 piece folds into floor of box. Now you have something that looks like this:

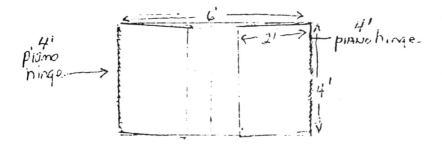

Next, join one 2x6 sheet to each 6′ edge with three spaced butt hinges, on the outside. Then, each side will look like this from the outside:

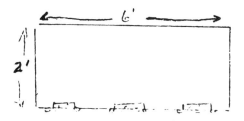

Next, open piano hinges to right angle position, and join each of the four 2′ sides with a butt hinge to the outside, giving a picture like this:

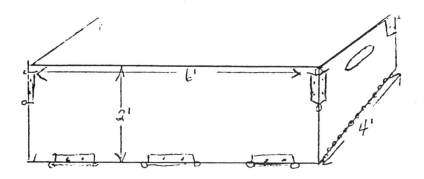

This is now your basic collapsible box.

Now, take the 2x4 masonite panel with the hole in it and attach to the floor of the box two feet from one end with the remaining 4′ piano hinge—making sure to position piano hinge so that masonite panel folds onto floor of the box in the same direction as the end piece nearest to it.

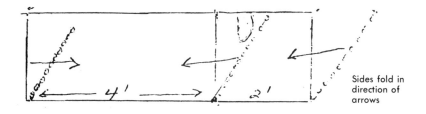

Sides fold in direction of arrows

Now, stand masonite (potty) wall upright (right angle) and fasten to the 6′ side of the box with a screw eye and bolt, one on each side of the potty wall—four screw eyes and bolts in all—to stabilize the potty wall.

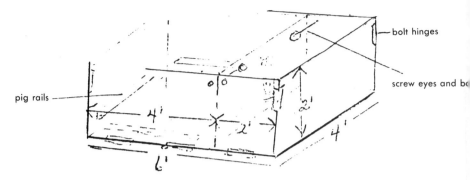

Finally, approximately 3″ up from floor in the whelping area of the box—the 4x4 section—screw a 1x3 on each side as a "pig" rail, using angle irons to do this.

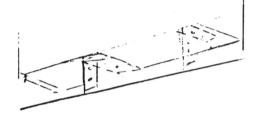

In front of box, per diagram below, cut out a section 20″ across and 15″ deep. Cut the portion removed into three pieces, 5″x20″ each. Screw the four galvanized strips onto the box—two on each side of the opening to form a channel for the 5x20 pieces to slide into—thus making it possible to lower the height of the side at this point.

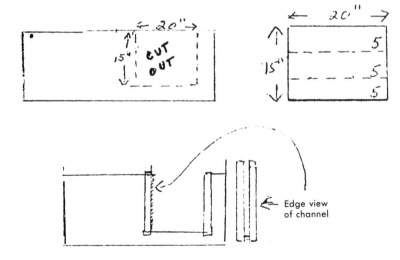

We also cut small ovals on their sides at approximately ¾″ below the center top edge of each of the 2x4 sides, at each end of the box, to form a hand-hold to grip the box if you should wish to move it while put together.

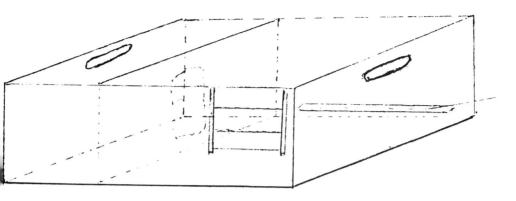

I line the floor of the box with indoor-outdoor carpeting.

Incidentally, the four 2x2's four feet long are to rest the box on should you wish to get it up off the floor and out of any draft. No need to attach them, as the weight of the box will keep them in place.

Adaptation of Whelping Box Plans

by Mrs. Richard Wayburn

We followed Clara Hurley's whelping box plans, with some few changes.

We felt that a 4' x 4' whelping box would be better in case the bitch should need assistance during whelping. When our puppies reach the age of three weeks we remove the pig rails, unhinge one side and use that side for the "floor" of the potty box. Then we attach (with hinges) a 2' x 4' potty box to the whelping box. We cover a piece of lightweight (paneling) board with rubberized flannel and place it in the bottom of the whelping box. The flannel need not be a great deal larger than the board and is held in place with masking tape to make it easy to change, as necessary. We chose this material as it washes well, gives the puppies some "footing" and is not as rough on their tummies as indoor-outdoor carpeting.

The potty box is really unbelievable!! With our last litter, there was not one wet spot in the box after six weeks and we used very little shredded paper.

COLONIAL ROTTWEILER CLUB
CODE OF ETHICS

I PURPOSE

In Rottweiler breeding, the emphasis shall be placed upon working ability and other outstanding qualities of character of this breed, as well as upon appearance. It is mandatory that a Code of Ethics be subscribed to by those who are concerned with the propagation of physically, mentally and temperamentally sound Rottweilers of proper breed type. Measures should be taken to acquaint the general public with the contents of this Code so that they may not become innocent partners in improper breeding practices.

Consistent with the above, I will agree to breed discriminatingly and only upon strong evidence of the possibility of finding suitable homes for the resulting puppies. I understand and agree that to breed inadvisedly may lead to over-population and contribute to the deterioration of the Rottweiler breed.

II RECORDS

If I breed my bitch or use my stud dog in service, I agree to keep accurate records of stock, matings and pedigrees and to register my breeding stock with the American Kennel Club.

III BREEDING

I agree to use for breeding only those Rottweilers which have OFA Normal hip X-rays with certification number, no disqualifying faults and no radical departures from the official AKC Rottweiler standard (A Rottweiler dog or bitch, X-rayed HD Free by Utrecht, Giessen or Gottingen at two years of age or older, may be used for breeding for the first six months that they are in this country. After that time, they must be OFA certified). I also agree not to use for breeding monorchid or cryptorchid dogs or Rottweilers with any of the following: undershot or overshot bites; more than one non-eruptive or missing adult tooth; ectropion or entropion; long or curly coats; unsound temperaments such as extreme shyness, nervousness or viciousness; excessive white markings as described in the Standard; incorrect or very pale markings.

Further, if, to the best of my knowledge, I should breed from lines in which any of the above occur, I will disclose this to my buyers.

As owner of a bitch, I will breed only normal, healthy, mature bitches which are OFA certified. I will not permit my bitch to produce litters in three consecutive seasons. I will cull deformed puppies and those which deviate substantially from the Rottweiler Standard.

As the owner of a stud dog, I will breed only normal, healthy, mature dogs which are OFA certified. I will refuse stud service to any bitch which does not have OFA certification, which has disqualifying faults, or which I consider to be in poor health. When a bitch has failed to conceive after being bred to one of my stud dogs, I will allow one repeat service, at such time and place as are mutually agreed to by the owner of the bitch and myself, provided that the stud dog is still in good health and available.

IV HEALTH

I agree to maintain good standards of health and care for my dogs, including proper veterinary care. I further agree that proper health includes regular contact with people and exposure to the outside world.

V SALES

I will refuse to recommend or sell to breeders who do not conform to this Code, or to dog wholesalers and retailers. I will not donate a Rottweiler for raffle purposes or sell to any home if I have reason to believe that the puppy or dog will not be properly cared for.

I will use a sales contract or written agreement with any sale or purchase involving a dog. To the best of my ability, I will state clearly to a buyer whether the puppy or dog being sold is potentially a show or pet type.

I will not release puppies before they are seven weeks of age, and only with full knowledge that they are healthy and have had the required medical innoculations and care.

I will give buyers of puppies or adult dogs accurate health, breeding and registration records and at least a four generation pedigree. Registration papers may be withheld on a dog which is suspected of carrying a serious fault that would make it detrimental for breeding purposes, until the dog has been proven otherwise or rendered incapable of reproducing (proof required per veterinarian's letter).

I will adhere to the terms of my sales agreement or written contract with the buyer, following the general practice of breeders that any puppy sold as a show prospect, which subsequently develops hip dysplasia or a disqualifying defect shall be: (1) replaced by the breeder with another show prospect puppy or (2) returned to the breeder who will then refund the sales price or (3) retained by the buyer, with the buyer's money being refunded by the breeder to the extent of the difference between the price paid and the price of pet puppies sold from the same or similar litters, after the breeder has received veterinarian's certification that the dog has been rendered incapable of reproducing or (4) any other mutually agreeable alternative made between the buyer and breeder.

I will urge my puppy purchasers to provide obedience training at the proper age.

I will recommend to my puppy purchasers that they render incapable of reproducing any dog which has developed disqualifying or serious faults.

As a breeder, I will make a serious effort to see that every dog will have an adequate home and will be properly cared for.

VI ADVERTISING

I agree that my advertising, oral and written, shall be factual and not worded so as to attract undesirable buyers, or to encourage the raising of purebred Rottweilers as an easy money scheme. No price should be given in public advertising of Rottweilers.

VII GENERAL CONDUCT AND SPORTSMANSHIP

I shall conduct myself at all times in a manner which will reflect credit upon me and the breed, regardless of the location or circumstances, but especially when attending dog shows or trials, whether as an exhibitor or spectator.

I agree that I will not co-own a dog and participate in the breeding of said dog with a person who does not subscribe to and support this code.

I agree that I will not have members of my household or immediate family participating in activities that are contradictory to the principles set forth in this Code.

If I should become aware of the maltreatment, misuse or need for relocation of any Rottweiler, I will notify any or all of the following for resolution of the problem: a member of the Board of Directors, the correct authorities in my area, the breeder, the CRC Rescue League.

VIII VIOLATIONS AND RECOURSE COMMITTEE

The incoming Board of Directors shall appoint at its first Board meeting a three member Violations and Recourse Committee and one alternate member, for a two year term. Written charges of violations of this Code by a member may be sent to any member of the Board of Directors. The Board member will send the allegations to the Committee within two weeks of receipt. The Committee will investigate and report its findings to the Board of Directors within two months of receipt of the charges and may recommend any or all of the following levels of discipline:

1. Warning (a member may not receive more than one warning in a year's period without incurring further disciplinary action).

2. A monetary fine, which shall be awarded to the CRC Rescue League.

3. Action as described in the CRC By-Laws, Article VII.

Following receipt of the Committee's report and recommendation, the Board of Directors will proceed as described in the CRC By-Laws.

A twenty-five dollar fee will be required from any person bringing charges. If the charges are upheld, the fee will be refunded. If the charges are dismissed, the money will be retained by the CRC.

If a member has special problems or circumstances, or if through no fault of his own is in violation of any of the provisions of this Code, he may have the Committee review the matter and make recommendations.

Revised 1/1/83

BIBLIOGRAPHY

ALL OWNERS of pure-bred dogs will benefit themselves and their dogs by enriching their knowledge of bree
and of canine care, training, breeding, psychology and other important aspects of dog management. The follo
ing list of books covers further reading recommended by judges, veterinarians, breeders, trainers and other authoriti
Books may be obtained at the finer book stores and pet shops, or through Howell Book House Inc., publishe
New York.

BREED BOOKS

AFGHAN HOUND, Complete	Miller & Gilbert
AIREDALE, New Complete	Edwards
AKITA, Complete	Linderman & Funk
ALASKAN MALAMUTE, Complete	Riddle & Seeley
BASSET HOUND, New Complete	Braun
BLOODHOUND, Complete	Brey & Reed
BOXER, Complete	Denlinger
BRITTANY SPANIEL, Complete	Riddle
BULLDOG, New Complete	Hanes
BULL TERRIER, New Complete	Eberhard
CAIRN TERRIER, New Complete	Marvin
CHESAPEAKE BAY RETRIEVER, Complete	Cherry
CHIHUAHUA, Complete	Noted Authorities
COCKER SPANIEL, New	Kraeuchi
COLLIE, New	Official Publication of the Collie Club of America
DACHSHUND, The New	Meistrell
DALMATIAN, The	Treen
DOBERMAN PINSCHER, New	Walker
ENGLISH SETTER, New Complete	Tuck, Howell & Graef
ENGLISH SPRINGER SPANIEL, New	Goodall & Gasow
FOX TERRIER, New	Nedell
GERMAN SHEPHERD DOG, New Complete	Bennett
GERMAN SHORTHAIRED POINTER, New	Maxwell
GOLDEN RETRIEVER, New Complete	Fischer
GORDON SETTER, Complete	Look
GREAT DANE, New Complete	Noted Authorities
GREAT DANE, The—Dogdom's Apollo	Draper
GREAT PYRENEES, Complete	Strang & Giffin
IRISH SETTER, New Complete	Eldredge & Vanacore
IRISH WOLFHOUND, Complete	Starbuck
JACK RUSSELL TERRIER, Complete	Plummer
KEESHOND, New Complete	Cash
LABRADOR RETRIEVER, New Complete	Warwick
LHASA APSO, Complete	Herbel
MALTESE, Complete	Cutillo
MASTIFF, History and Management of the	Baxter & Hoffman
MINIATURE SCHNAUZER, New	Kiedrowski
NEWFOUNDLAND, New Complete	Chern
NORWEGIAN ELKHOUND, New Complete	Wallo
OLD ENGLISH SHEEPDOG, Complete	Mandeville
PEKINGESE, Quigley Book of	Quigley
PEMBROKE WELSH CORGI, Complete	Sargent & Harper
POODLE, New	Irick
POODLE CLIPPING AND GROOMING BOOK, Complete	Kalstone
PORTUGUESE WATER DOG, Complete	Braund & Miller
ROTTWEILER, Complete	Freeman
SAMOYED, New Complete	Ward
SCOTTISH TERRIER, New Complete	Marvin
SHETLAND SHEEPDOG, The New	Riddle
SHIH TZU, Joy of Owning	Seranne
SHIH TZU, The (English)	Dadds
SIBERIAN HUSKY, Complete	Demidoff
TERRIERS, The Book of All	Marvin
WEIMARANER, Guide to the	Burgoin
WEST HIGHLAND WHITE TERRIER, Complete	Marvin
WHIPPET, Complete	Pegram
YORKSHIRE TERRIER, Complete	Gordon & Bennett

BREEDING

ART OF BREEDING BETTER DOGS, New	Onstott
BREEDING YOUR OWN SHOW DOG	Seranne
HOW TO BREED DOGS	Whitney
HOW PUPPIES ARE BORN	Prine
INHERITANCE OF COAT COLOR IN DOGS	Little

CARE AND TRAINING

BEYOND BASIC DOG TRAINING	Baum
COUNSELING DOG OWNERS, Evans Guide for	Eva
DOG OBEDIENCE, Complete Book of	Sauno
NOVICE, OPEN AND UTILITY COURSES	Sauno
DOG CARE AND TRAINING FOR BOYS AND GIRLS	Sauno
DOG NUTRITION, Collins Guide to	Col
DOG TRAINING FOR KIDS	Benja
DOG TRAINING, Koehler Method of	Koel
DOG TRAINING Made Easy	Tuc
GO FIND! Training Your Dog to Track	Da
GROOMING DOGS FOR PROFIT	G
GUARD DOG TRAINING, Koehler Method of	Koel
MOTHER KNOWS BEST—The Natural Way to Train Your Dog	Benja
OPEN OBEDIENCE FOR RING, HOME AND FIELD, Koehler Method of	Koe
STONE GUIDE TO DOG GROOMING FOR ALL BREEDS	St
SUCCESSFUL DOG TRAINING, The Pearsall Guide to	Pear
TEACHING DOG OBEDIENCE CLASSES—Manual for Instructors	Volhard & Fis
TOY DOGS, Kalstone Guide to Grooming All	Kalst
TRAINING THE RETRIEVER	Ker
TRAINING TRACKING DOGS, Koehler Method of	Koe
TRAINING YOUR DOG—Step by Step Manual	Volhard & Fis
TRAINING YOUR DOG TO WIN OBEDIENCE TITLES	Mor
TRAIN YOUR OWN GUN DOG, How to	Goo
UTILITY DOG TRAINING, Koehler Method of	Koe
VETERINARY HANDBOOK, Dog Owner's Home	Carlson & G

GENERAL

A DOG'S LIFE	Burton & Al
AMERICAN KENNEL CLUB 1884-1984—A Source Book	American Kennel (
CANINE TERMINOLOGY	S
COMPLETE DOG BOOK, The	Official Publicatio American Kennel (
DOG IN ACTION, The	L
DOG BEHAVIOR, New Knowledge of	Pfaffenbe
DOG JUDGE'S HANDBOOK	Tie
DOG PSYCHOLOGY	Whi
DOGSTEPS, The New	E
DOG TRICKS	Haggerty & Benja
EYES THAT LEAD—Story of Guide Dogs for the Blind	Tu
FRIEND TO FRIEND—Dogs That Help Mankind	Schw
FROM RICHES TO BITCHES	Shai
HAPPY DOG/HAPPY OWNER	Si
IN STITCHES OVER BITCHES	Shai
JUNIOR SHOWMANSHIP HANDBOOK	Brown & Ma
OUR PUPPY'S BABY BOOK (blue or pink)	
SUCCESSFUL DOG SHOWING, Forsyth Guide to	Fo
WHY DOES YOUR DOG DO THAT?	Berg
WILD DOGS in Life and Legend	Ri
WORLD OF SLED DOGS, From Siberia to Sport Rac	Coppi